Not Straight, Not White

The John Hope Franklin Series in
African American History and Culture

WALDO E. MARTIN JR. and PATRICIA SULLIVAN, editors

Not Straight, Not White

Black Gay Men from the March
on Washington to the AIDS Crisis

KEVIN J. MUMFORD

The University of North Carolina Press
Chapel Hill

Set in Utopia by codeMantra

Manufactured in the United States of America

The paper in this book meets the guidelines for permanence and durability of the Committee on Production Guidelines for Book Longevity of the Council on Library Resources.

The University of North Carolina Press has been a member of the Green Press Initiative since 2003.

Cover illustration: © iStockphoto.com/curtoicurto

Library of Congress Cataloging-in-Publication Data
Mumford, Kevin J., author.
Not straight, not white : black gay men from the march on Washington to the AIDS crisis / Kevin J. Mumford.
    pages cm — (The John Hope Franklin Series in African American History and Culture)
Includes bibliographical references and index.
ISBN 978-1-4696-2684-0 (cloth : alk. paper) —
ISBN 978-1-4696-2685-7 (ebook)
1. African American gay men. 2. Gay men, Black—United States.
I. Title. II. Series: John Hope Franklin series in African American history and culture.
HQ76.27.A37M86 2016
306.76'6208996073—dc23
2015031954

In memory of a lost generation, and in hope for the next

Contents

Illustrations

Not Straight, Not White

Corrections

In 1982, toward the end of his career, James Baldwin addressed a packed audience of the recently formed interracial gay organization Black and White Men Together (BWMT). As reported in the group's monthly newsletter, the "famous black author[,] who lives in Paris, gave a lecture for BWMT-New York and its guests. This was a first for Mr. Baldwin, who had never addressed an entirely gay group before." The membership applauded Baldwin's appearance as historic, reporting, "The black gay religious leader, James Tinney, observed that 'for the first time in his career . . . he openly identified with the gay community by addressing more than 200 persons at a forum.'"[1] This understanding of Baldwin was both erroneous and correct. Since the late 1950s journalists had questioned Baldwin about his sexual identity, and typically he confirmed his homosexuality, making him one of the most out and visible gay men of the twentieth century. Yet his appearance before a gay interracial audience was unprecedented, something unimaginable only two decades before, when local homophile organizations advocated for acceptance by demonstrating their respectability and most chapters remained invisible, often anonymous, and overwhelmingly white. Several years later, in 1986, Bayard Rustin, the veteran civil rights activist and lead organizer of the March on Washington, appeared before the BWMT to help celebrate the Philadelphia chapter's fifth anniversary. In his address, Rustin observed that "one chief obstacle to the freedom of gay people is . . . gays in the closet because if one does not stand up for himself, other people will never be moved to stand up for one."[2]

This book examines the interplay between dominant, usually stigmatizing representations of black gay men and resistance against defamation in order to understand how the pervasive repression that Baldwin and Rustin once confronted—and often lost to—was transformed into a more visible, collective voice for the next generation of black gay men. It traces a winding historical path from misrecognition and marginalization to a place of shared identification while continuously subjecting to critical scrutiny the politics of representation, claims for individual sovereignty, and the promise of liberal equality.

Not Straight, Not White seeks to open conversations about black gay issues and identities with students of race and ethnic studies, civil rights and black power, and sexual and gender history, as well as to contribute to the historiography on postwar culture and social movements. LGBT historiography has largely proceeded in directions first mapped in the 1980s and early 1990s by John D'Emilio, Allan Bérubé, George Chauncey, and Marc Stein, who practiced social and urban history to advance theoretically sophisticated investigations into the evolution of gay male organizations, neighborhoods, and identity constructions. Recent works that take up a queer methodology, such as Matt Houlbrook's *Queer London*, map a wide variety of male sexual encounters to challenge a certain teleology that celebrates the arrival of the once isolated homosexual in the promised land of gay liberation. Rather than a decisive historiographical break, in my view, this queer turn in the scholarship has stimulated a subtle shift in interpretive emphasis: where the first wave presented a range of same-sex encounters in homosocial settings that eventually formed a gay identification, Houlbrook discovers an urban landscape of sexual variety and argues for a disordering of identification. For some queers, class position determined their sexual options, for others renunciation of same-sex contacts and eventual entrance into straight marriage was expected, and for yet others the inversion of gender roles (usually seen as an identity mode in decline by the 1930s) proved eternally compelling as a way to make sense of and signify their sexual desires.[3]

As more researchers engage the queer turn, wholly new sexual landscapes promise to emerge, and yet one methodological flaw that limits both the older and recent scholarship has been inattention to questions of diversity and prejudice. Many of the best and most important studies have avoided further investigation into the meanings of race for the gay past. There are a handful of exceptions—Cathy Cohen's *Boundaries of Blackness: AIDS and the Breakdown of Black Politics*, John D'Emilio's *Lost Prophet: The Life and Times of Bayard Rustin*, E. Patrick Johnson's oral history, *Sweet Tea: Black Gay Men of the South*, and Joshua Gamson's *The Fabulous Sylvester: The Legend, the Music, the Seventies in San Francisco*—but the generalization accurately characterizes the direction of a new academic enterprise of queer studies developing along a neoliberal path toward color blindness.

The depth and reach of the new queer scholarship on sexuality in general and LGBT identity in particular has advanced our understanding of the ways in which institutions (the state, courts, prisons) and political activities (of homophiles, New Left activists, right-wing conservatives) have influenced the contours of gay life, and yet the orientation of such work has avoided important racial questions: about the role of racial representations, such as gay pornography; about the changing construction of masculinity; and about struggles to reconcile gay desire with religious faith.[4] These issues and problems turn out to be crucial to understanding the formation of individual and collective black gay identities and to remaking black gay history.

At the same time, the field of African American history has flourished over the past twenty-five years, and yet here again much of the scholarship seems to have overlooked the contributions of black gay men. The one major exception has been the reevaluation of the Harlem Renaissance as a thoroughly gay or bisexual moment, and now general textbooks in African American history recognize the queerness of the leading writers and poets of the era.[5] Beyond this, despite the proliferation of works in African American urban and cultural politics—surely areas where gay men resided—very little has been said about homosexuality, perhaps because of the fraught nature of black eroticism. As historians have documented, African American sexuality was a site of domination and terrorism, from the era of slave importation to Reconstruction to the civil rights movement, when black demonstrators sought to present an image of respectability as a form of moral suasion to attain full citizenship. White supremacists of the South demanded of black men a kind of impotence (bowed, crouching, deferential), while at other times they cast black men as dangerously hypersexual (uncontrolled rapists, insatiable studs). The performance of what one historian has termed "dissemblance" to characterize black female deflection of harassment and what others have described as a kind of ultra-civility were key strategies in the black struggle against defamation and toward racial justice. All of this has contributed to a legacy of sexual reticence. But *Not Straight, Not White* explores how and why the politics of respectability, particularly the elite's strategy of prescribing chaste comportment and asserting the normalcy of the black family, resulted in the erasure of black homosexuality, even for researchers and readers of the African American past. According to recent survey data, an estimated 1,018,700 LGBT African American adults reside in the United States, with 84,000 individuals joined in same-sex couples, 33 percent of which report raising children. This book argues that they have a genealogy of black gayness and a collective past that deserve serious study and full recognition.[6]

In other words, black gay lives matter. At the height of the civil rights movement, when Baldwin wrote novels that pushed the boundaries of public discourse on sexuality, he was attacked in the press and sidelined by the leadership. Bayard Rustin's story has become more widely known but not entirely understood, given the role homophobia played in his marginalization not only by the respectable leadership but also by a new generation of radical activists. Even as sexual authorities, such as black physicians and social scientists, advocated for the loosening of constraints that bound black sexual expression, liberalization or further acceptance of homosexuality slowed to a halt. With the rise of black power cultural politics in the 1960s, in my reading of the archive, black men were expected to claim the same sort of sexual aggressiveness and erotic entitlement that white men had always enjoyed with relative impunity. This black power rhetoric cast adherence to the dictates of respectability and sexual restraint as the purview of the integrationist or the racial sellout, and this redefinition of black masculinity in the 1960s and 1970s reconstructed the meaning of being a black gay man in negative ways.

Questions of femininity, feminism, and lesbian identity are addressed in my narrative, but not for a sustained period or through a major focus, in part because of the need to understand better how the politics of black manhood continually restructured black gay identity. At a historic moment, James Baldwin recruited the prize-winning dramatist Lorraine Hansberry to stage a civil rights demonstration for the Freedom Riders, and studying their relationship serves to cast light on the tensions between protest for social justice and the sacrifice of sexual silence; but the preponderance of evidence about black homosexuality in media and culture before and after this singular moment overwhelmingly concerns black men, masculinity, and male homosexual etiologies. By the 1980s the emergence of black lesbian feminism clearly affected black gay identity politics, illustrated in chapter 6, which examines the influence on Joseph Beam of such towering figures in queer letters as Audre Lorde. Studies of black lesbian identity and activism are surely forthcoming, but my understanding of the extent to which constructions of masculinity structured black gay identity has determined the scope and design of my research.

Drawing from un-mined archives, personal papers, and black and gay print cultures, this study develops a multifaceted interpretation of a particularly visible identity formation that shifted dramatically over the years from the March on Washington to the devastation of the AIDS crisis, buffeted about by the tumult of social movements and cultural change that both inspired and marginalized black gay men. It is a story of gay desire and racial objectification, of searching for community and sharp separatist withdrawal, of protest for inclusion in the mainstream and an abiding recognition of the unbridgeable divergence between straight and gay, white and black life paths.

One cause of the marginalization of black gay men was what scholars refer to as homophobia, or the fear and loathing of subjects identified as gay or lesbian. Early theorists of homophobia linked antipathy to sexual minorities with the ideology of misogyny in a way that tended to obscure additional factors of race and color, while other attempts to connect the two forms of discrimination resulted in an explanation that stressed psychological impulses "rooted in moral attitudes." Because most historical interpretations of homophobia center on the punishment of the sodomite or, later, the public behavior of the homosexual, they overlook the multiple prejudices converging on subjects living at the intersection of racial and sexual marginalization. Whether they were partnered or celibate, masculine or effeminate, active or passive, black gay men fought not only for civil rights and the end to homophobic discrimination but also against more subtle forms of prejudice that resulted in silencing and disrespect by those who labeled them immoral and inauthentic, from within and outside their social groups.[7]

The point is that the status of being black and gay involved not only sexual prejudice and defamation but also racialization and misrecognition. To understand this interaction of forms of stigma, I explore the historical operation of what I have come to term *objectification*. In my usage, objectification was a marginalization process akin to the designation of social pathology. In his classic text *Difference and Pathology: Stereotypes of Sexuality, Race, and Madness*, Sander L. Gilman conceives of socially ascribed difference in terms of stereotypes that individuals use to perceive and organize deviation, and this registers most potently in the body and in perceptions of the other's sexuality. Designating the other as "pathological" also serves to protect one's precarious sense of the normal self. According to Gilman, "Physiognomy or skin color that is perceived as different is immediately associated with 'pathology' and 'sexuality.'" What would it mean, then, to study the pathological black body that was associated with homosexual pathology? The philosopher of racial encounters Frantz Fanon first begins with what he terms the fact of blackness: an inferiority complex structured into the black psyche as a result of domination, a symptom of which was always desiring to be white. Fanon also theorizes the association between blackness and pathology, arguing that the black man's absence and negation in European culture resulted in his extreme dependence on whites. An adaptation of Fanon that illuminates the archive that I have collected might be to observe that black gay men begin more as objects than as subjects and, after some period of time, become not only an object of ridicule but also caught up in a process of sexual objectification. "The Negro is the genital," writes Fanon. Secretly and neurotically desired by the white woman, "the black man is the symbol of Evil Ugliness." He continues, "I subjected myself to an objective examination, I discovered my blackness. . . . I took myself far off from my own presence, far indeed, and made myself an object." Then, in a footnote on racism and pathology in the Caribbean, Fanon mentions, "Let me observe at once that I had no opportunity to establish the overt presence of homosexuality in Martinique. This must be viewed as the result of the absence of the Oedipus complex in the Antilles."[8]

If key theorists of racial difference have not conceived of sexuality in ways that provided for an effective analysis of gayness, the same may be said of the major theorists of sexuality with respect to race. As the cultural critic Marlon Ross has argued, "in absenting and bracketing race, [Michel] Foucault and [Eve] Sedgwick respectively are able to erect a coherent epistemology of the closet as a ground for modern identity," and therefore Ross proposes that scholars construct an alternative to the standard gay narrative of migrating to the city, discovering sexual community, and coming out for liberation. This book takes up that project. More recently, several writers have published attention-grabbing books on the subject of the so-called down low in which black men may engage in same-sex relations without publicly acknowledging the label of gay or bisexual. In 2004, J. L. King released his study, *On the Down Low: A Journey into the Lives of "Straight" Black Men Who Sleep with Men*, presenting a series of homosexual encounters in the context of marriage, church life, and incarceration and cataloging various "down low" types. In 2005, the black gay journalist Keith Boykin penned an important corrective that presented a range of actors and rejoinders to media misrepresentations of black gay men, and other writers have sought to defend black bisexuals (an effort that is explored later). Yet the politics of visibility have preoccupied black queer studies—to what extent, as Ross asks, are the strategies and politics of white gay liberation, specifically public advocacy and activism as the path to justice and happiness, relevant to black gay identities and communities? In highlighting what they see as the empowering possibilities of discretion, black queer scholars question the liberationist injunction to "come out" and remind us, as Jeffrey Q. McCune Jr. elegantly observes, that the concept of the down low or the DL is "not only a contemporary metaphor for discreet acts, but also a signifier of a people's being in the world—a location that conceals private desires for the sake of pleasure, protection, and politics." The broad thrust of *Not Straight, Not White* takes issue with McCune's contention that discretion signifies political efficacy by illustrating how black gay men chose to speak up against injustice and why they needed to come out to remake black gay history.[9]

That is not to suggest that *Not Straight, Not White* is the first and only study of the historical construction of identity, for I have relied conceptually and empirically on the work of many other scholars, as a glance at the endnotes will immediately reveal. In 1996, *One of the Children: Gay Black Men in Harlem* was published posthumously, several years after the death of Columbia University graduate student William Hawkeswood. An anthropologist by training, Hawkeswood conducted extensive research among black gay men in Harlem to understand sexual and gender performances, the construction of an alternative family structure that relied on a fictive kin system, and leisure practices and social rituals. Researching both southern-born and native informants, Hawkeswood mapped alternative geographies of belonging "at the intersection of gay and black cultures," where inhabitants "had constructed a culture of their own." Some were more black-identified than gay, while others felt the reverse, but for the first time a published social science study recognized the complexity and subtlety of an urban phenomenon of black gay men that even the best-intentioned academic writers had routinely overlooked, dismissed, or pathologized.[10]

Around the same time that Hawkeswood was conducting his research, filmmaker Jennie Livingston directed the indie sensation *Paris Is Burning* (1990), which featured black and Puerto Rican gay men in Harlem and Queens. In a study of what was known among insiders as ballroom culture, the camera dove into the dance halls, dressing rooms, and "houses" of a network of queer men of color to look at their styles of survival. Again, not surprisingly, a main theme of the film turned on the creation of an alternate kinship system that mirrored parents and siblings within an urban world of disadvantage. Individual and collective performances appropriated dominant imagery or norms and refashioned disownment and invisibility by remaking and recognizing as "real" their everyday lives. Black gay fantasy about another world and desire for another narrative also inspired the black British filmmaker Isaac Julien to direct a kind of docudrama about the gay meanings of the Harlem Renaissance. In 1989, his *Looking for Langston* quickly became a gay classic, redefining the parameters of historical memory. In this case, Julien's direction mixed archival footage, voiceovers, photographs, poetry, and performance to recast the Harlem Renaissance as a period of explicit gay desire, entangled bodies dancing along a spectrum of colors and poses, evidencing their lyrical longing for sexual recognition. *Looking for Langston* satisfied a collective desire for a history that had been repressed and erased.

Now, after untold numbers of potential black gay scholars have been lost to the AIDS crisis before their work could be published, a new wave of scholarship is finally emerging. Freshly minted Ph.D.s and assistant professors are reclaiming the gay past, new journals and book series signal the arrival of the field, and Long Civil Rights Movement and LGBT panels at academic conferences increasingly address queer people of color. In 2014, the distinguished historian Martin Duberman released a dual biography of Michael Callen, the a cappella singer, and Essex Hemphill, the black gay poet (and close friend of Joseph Beam), publishing the first study to cover a black gay man after Baldwin and Rustin's generation, in the age of gay liberation and the AIDS crisis. In drawing on representations and biography, as well as on urban history and culture, my book joins this next wave of research and scholarship—this effort toward remaking black gay history.[11]

The study of black gay life in the second half of the twentieth century brings together the histories of race relations and sexuality, the expansion of media and activist organizing to control visibility, and mobilizations for social justice. First, my study engages historiographical debates over the politics of respectability. Chapter 1 reconstructs a historic moment in the summer of 1963 when black queer activists—Lorraine Hansberry, James Baldwin, and Bayard Rustin—each advanced the cause of civil rights while in some ways repressing and being repressed by their sexuality. The next chapter looks at this politics of respectability from another angle by assessing representations that associated black gayness with vice, crime, and deviance in a range of sources. By the 1960s, when white experts espoused liberal views of homosexuality as a naturally occurring drive in a percentage of the population, or as a social role deserving of acceptance, the deviance attributed to black gay men escalated, specifically because of the public controversy sparked by reports of a "tangle of pathology" in black families. At the same time, the increasingly visible imagery or discourse of black pathology became a site of reversal through which black gay men might resist and begin to refashion both a public representation and a personal sense of themselves. Such was the case in the almost forgotten avant-garde film *Portrait of Jason*, directed by Shirley Clarke in 1967. Conceived as cinema verité, it featured an interview-like performance by black gay actor and hustler Aaron Payne/Jason Holliday that attracted extensive publicity. Chapter 3 contrasts this highbrow vision of pathological black gayness with representations of race in gay pornography to understand how a variety of texts that depicted black gay bodies, sex acts, and poses interacted with early-1970s representations of black straight sexuality and masculinity in the media. The next chapter questions the real and imagined connections between black power and gay liberation by analyzing not only moments of radical black and gay activist cooperation and contention, but also the fledgling attempts by scattered writers to advocate for black gay liberation.

Caught between the politics of black power and the rise of gay liberation, a unique voice emerged to speak for radical social justice in the form of an important but little-known 1970s activist, Brother Grant-Michael Fitzgerald. My biographical portrait of Brother Fitzgerald in chapter 5 focuses on how activism and the new politics of "coming out" affected a single life while exploring his contradictory relationships to black nationalism, gay rights, and the church. By the late 1970s, the emergence of black lesbian feminist networks as well as black electoral politics in cities seeded a new black gay identity politics. Set in Philadelphia, chapter 6 presents the life of Joseph Beam and his efforts to build a black gay cultural community and social network.

The final biographical portrait, in chapter 7, examines the life of James Tinney, a Howard University professor and founder of the first black gay church. Traveling in the same circles as Fitzgerald and Beam, Tinney pioneered a black gay theology while he conflicted with his academic colleagues who disagreed with his writings on sexuality and other subjects, and he later found himself battling for his place in the church. And like the other figures in this book, Tinney lived outside the boundaries of a traditional community—gay or black—while seeking to defend a shared identity and locate a safe space.

As the political losses due to rightward backlash and the death toll from AIDS mounted in the 1980s, surviving black gay men founded and staffed community institutions to care for and bury their friends and lovers. Chapter 8 examines memorials and the meaning of black gay death but also centers on continuing local activism. The efforts of the Philadelphia-BWMT to address the problem of racism in the gay community highlight the persistence of black gay mobilization around questions of inclusion and recognition.[12]

My approach or methodology developed in this book is both recuperative and critical, not only bringing the invisible to light and giving voice to the silenced, though I have a strong investment in this reconstruction project insofar as it advances black gay recognition, but also critiquing the operation of the margins from which I am excavating these men and women.[13] In thinking through the politics of recognition, the philosopher Seyla Benhabib links political discrimination with intersubjective distortion: "Collective practices can result in individual injuries: through the denigration of one's collective identity in the public sphere, individuals in a group may lose self-confidence and internalize hateful images of themselves."[14] In a society that produces and tolerates negative images about nonwhite groups and relies on defamatory nomenclature to designate same-sex desires, social recognition for black gay men remains a difficult challenge. Without an acknowledged heritage, at any moment one's voice may be drowned out, one's social standing is disabled, and one's chances for civic belonging plummet. Certainly, this was the case for the subjects in this book. Among their many uses, historical narratives serve both to represent and to redefine social groups, and they may be shared among groups and across boundaries of difference. It is my hope that readers will feel welcome to grapple with my interpretation of black gay men, that all will find meaning, and that all will discover something to take away, even if not precisely a sense of corrected identification.

Chapter One

Losing the March

Lorraine Hansberry, James Baldwin, and Bayard Rustin—each belongs to African American gay history while contributing to a turning point in the civil rights movement in the summer of 1963. Their queer intervention concerned, first, the federal government's role in protecting southern demonstrators, during an important meeting between Baldwin, Hansberry, and an assortment of other celebrities with Attorney General Robert Kennedy in his Manhattan home, and, second, Rustin's disputed role in the iconic mass demonstration the March on Washington for Jobs and Freedom. By this time Baldwin had published *The Fire Next Time*, the best-selling "disturbing examination of the consequences of racial injustice," and Hansberry had distinguished herself as the youngest and first black woman to win the New York Drama Desk award for the Broadway sensation *A Raisin in the Sun*. The two writers were introduced during the workshop production of Baldwin's *Giovanni's Room*, based on his controversial 1956 gay novel, and met again at the premiere of Hansberry's play in Philadelphia. Though a box-office success, a few had criticized the drama for its apparent celebration of the American dream of upward mobility, but in a brief 1961 review Baldwin instead compared Hansberry to the radical novelist and essayist Richard Wright, emphasizing their shared critical vision of an American dystopia.[1]

Their meeting with Kennedy on May 24, 1963 was prompted in part by Baldwin's essay "Letter from a Region in My Mind," which appeared during the increasingly violent spring of police-demonstrator confrontations in Birmingham and other southern cities.[2] Published in the *New Yorker*, the long piece meditated on American racism, seeing white prejudice as arising from the reality that the "white man's masculinity depends on a denial of the masculinity of the blacks" and that therefore the nation subjected the "Negro" to many "horrors." After reading the essay, Kennedy had reportedly contacted Baldwin and sought the meeting because he wished to hear "fresh" ideas on "coping with civil rights problems." If he had invited only the older and more moderate celebrities, such as Lena Horne or Harry Belafonte, it seems unlikely that the meeting would have ended as it did, in frank disagreement and an acrimonious exit. But the presence of Jerome Smith, a participant in the southern Freedom Rides that continued to press for the desegregation of buses and stations, had raised the stakes. Baldwin referred to Smith as a "tremendous man," recalling his police beating with brass knuckles in demonstrations in New Orleans. Smith's presence attested to the need for stronger federal protection of demonstrators. Along with Smith, Baldwin and Hansberry became the most notable participants in the secret meeting, with photographs of the two published the day after, dubbed by the *New York Times* as the "'angry young Negroes,'" which presented the public with a compelling combination of rebellion, celebrity, and creative genius.[3]

Disagreement over the government's approach escalated when Baldwin asked Smith if he would fight for his country and Smith replied that he would not, quite to the astonishment of the attorney general. Baldwin reported, "Kennedy's face turned purple but he remained silent. The meeting could not be put back on the track of amicable discourse." Next, Lorraine Hansberry entered the stage, according to several accounts, and said, "Look, if you can't understand what this young man is saying, then we are without any hope at all, because you and your brother are representatives of the best that a white America can offer; and if you are insensitive to this, then there's no alternative except going out in the streets . . . and chaos."[4] Then Kennedy heard Jerome Smith say that being in the same room with him was nauseating and, to paraphrase, made him want to throw up. Baldwin recalled that "Bobby took it personally," "turned away from him," and apparently looked to the others in the room in search of support from a "representative Negro," which Baldwin felt was a mistake. They were "the reasonable, responsible, mature representatives of the black community," summoned by Kennedy not only to advise but also to lend public support to the president's moderate approach to civil rights that was coming under attack. The famed social scientist Kenneth Clark recalled that "Bobby got redder and redder and redder, and in a sense accused Jerome of treason." In turn, Hansberry directly challenged him: "You've got a great many very, very accomplished people in this room, Mr. Attorney General. But the only man who should be listened to is that man over there," indicating Smith. Baldwin exclaimed that because of the government's failure to protect southern demonstrators, he was contemplating violence. It was to become the meeting that "shattered them all," in the words of the presidential historian Arthur Schlesinger, a turning point that Clark described as the "'most intense, traumatic interchange among adults, head-to-head, no holds barred . . . the most dramatic experience I have ever had.'"[5]

Bobby Kennedy was surprised by the vehemence of the young members of the contingent, and in turn the press portrayed the scene as a crisis that raised questions about his capacity to deal with race issues, at one point reporting that he was in for the fight of his life. Baldwin became a formidable combatant of the government—"the bitter and brilliantly articulate spokesman for the Negro who says, 'integration now,'" wrote the *New York Times*. Likewise, Hansberry, usually assigned only a few paragraphs if any in the standard textbooks, was making civil rights history. Upbraiding the attorney general, she in effect took on Smith's burden and reportedly "exploded," charging that the government was "worrying about 'specimens of white manhood'—recently immortalized in photographs showing their knees on the breasts of Negro women who had been dragged to the ground." According to Baldwin's 1979 recollection, "the meeting ended with Lorraine standing up" and saying "Goodbye, Mr. Attorney General," followed by the others. For Baldwin, the atmosphere became "caustic," and Kennedy later reported that "it was all emotion, hysteria—they stood up and orated—they cursed—some of them wept and left the room." Baldwin attributed the insurgency to the irrepressible anger of Hansberry: "We passed Lorraine, who did not see us. She was walking toward Fifth Avenue— her face twisted, her hands clasped before her belly, eyes darker than eyes I had ever seen before—walking in an absolutely private place." This memorable moment of emotionality, radical refusal, and principled resolve ought to be seen as a signal beginning of modern black gay activism.[6]

The following day, President John F. Kennedy took a fourteen-minute phone call from his brother on the meeting, alternating curt affirmations with silence. At one point the president asked about Baldwin, and then about "Lena," and then about Birmingham: "They don't have any appreciation for our situation in the south." In response to the confrontation, he said, "I think a lot of this thing is to have a shock value—they compete with themselves." "I guess this Birmingham just really did it," he added, and asked his brother, "They're that mad?" At this point, the attorney general reported, "They say that they'll get guns and fight violence with violence," but he believed that "the Negroes depend on some white support. I don't blame them for being frustrated, but if they are going to extremes." In this context, Baldwin and Hansberry were characterized in the press as "militant Negro integrationists," even though so-called moderates also objected to the Kennedys' political characterizations. For example, King's attorney, Clarence Jones, wrote to an editor at the *New York Times* to reject a depiction of him as a moderate, largely inferred from his relationship to King, and added that the "Attorney General would be compounding errors already made if he regarded . . . Baldwin" as an "extremist."[7]

Sweet Lorraine

Who was Lorraine Hansberry, and where did this queer anger originate? What is remembered about Hansberry depends to a great extent on what records and documents have been preserved and made accessible for researchers. The Hansberry archive consists of her writings, newspaper accounts, and several short biographies, as well as more problematic sources, such as the Lorraine Hansberry Papers and the Federal Bureau of Investigation files. (J. Edgar Hoover, the notorious director of the FBI, sent unsolicited dossiers on all of those who attended the May 1963 meeting to the White House and then increased the surveillance of the assembled group.) Although several scholars have studied connections between Hansberry's literary output and her radicalism, none of the scholarship addresses crucial dimensions of her bisexual, if not essentially lesbian, desire or how hidden parts of her personal life unfolded in relation to her political activism.[8]

In 1948 Hansberry matriculated at the University of Wisconsin but dropped out of classes after two years with an erratic academic record, apparently the result of distraction or perhaps of marginalization as a black woman and a lesbian in a small midwestern city. Ironically, her lowest course grade at the university—a D—was given for her work in a history of theater course. At the age of twenty-three, Hansberry had acknowledged her attraction to women, composing a list of favorite things, entitled "Myself in Notes," that included "to look at well dressed women" and "deeply intelligent women," and her dislikes included "masculinity in women." In Madison, she protested against segregation, joined and then headed a progressive political organization, and campaigned for the leftist presidential candidate Henry Wallace. After Hansberry arrived in New York, she joined the Communist Party and assisted the black radical entertainer Paul Robeson with the production of a Left-leaning journal, *Freedom*, contributing reviews and essays on the intersection of race and gender but not yet publicly writing on issues of sexuality. Perhaps she was seeking to rebel against the respectability she had inherited from her privileged background as the daughter of a prominent Chicago family with extensive real estate holdings. Hansberry's desire for women, evident in the personal recesses of her life, not only mobilized but also isolated her, and her involvement with the Communist Left led her to marriage rather than to a lesbian relationship or a gay community at a time when homosexual men and women, even involved those involved in homophile organizations, were often still hidden and furtive.[9]

Dramatist Lorraine Hansberry at the time of her play *A Raisin in the Sun* opening in New Haven, Connecticut, prior to its run on Broadway, 1959. Hansberry authored the prize-winning drama to international acclaim, but few were aware of her passionate relationships with other women. She was a supporter of the homophile movement and wrote a number of unpublished stories with gay and lesbian themes. (Photographs and Prints Division, Schomburg Center for Research in Black Culture, New York Public Library, Astor, Lenox and Tilden Foundations).

After the extraordinary success of *A Raisin in the Sun*, Hansberry's personal life became more complicated and her opportunity to speak openly as a lesbian less feasible. The FBI had continued to monitor her activities and then increased their surveillance after the drama's premiere, assigning an agent "to determine whether the play in any way follows the Communist line." The agency concluded that it did not.[10] Hansberry had drawn the characters in racial-gendered stereotypes—the failing black son, the strong black matriarch, and the dilettante bohemian (with her describing Beneatha as "just me at that age, during my two years at the University of Wisconsin"), while the FBI described a play "about a Chicago Negro family's struggle to attain middle income standards." At the same time, Hansberry found herself embroiled in controversy when the press reported that her family's business, Hansberry Enterprises, run by her two brothers and a sister, owned at least thirteen properties that were in violation of building codes. The city of Chicago had fined the company more than $40,000. Depressed, embarrassed, and isolated, Hansberry engaged an attorney to advise her and, in the hopes of clearing her reputation, declared in a signed affidavit that she had no personal or remunerative ties to the family business.[11]

The legal maneuver addressed the immediate controversy, but she remained an easy target for a variety of detractors. Her unconventional lifestyle—from an open interracial marriage to Greenwich Village environs—enabled a queer desire but also strained her relationship with straight black intellectual traditions. In his classic account *Crisis of the Black Intellectual*, Harold Cruse attacked both Hansberry and *Raisin in the Sun*, beginning with the entirely incorrect observation that the inhabitants of the ghetto—with its "perverts"—was in fact "abhorrent" to Hansberry. He then went on to portray her as inauthentic, not only because of her upper-middle-class background but also because of the "quasi-white orientation through which she visualizes the Negro world."[12] The subsequent generation of black power writers criticized the drama as assimilationist and bourgeois, but more recent scholarship has recuperated Hansberry as the vanguard of an anti-imperialist Left. Erik S. McDuffie, Dayo F. Gore, and Carole Boyce Davies have demonstrated that throughout the 1940s and 1950s, a number of radical black women—not unlike Hansberry—joined the Communist Party and forged a new political analysis of the interconnections between race, class, and gender. Although Hansberry aligned with Left political causes, her literary productions appealed to a mainstream audience, and based on my reading of her diaries it would seem that her Communist connections (including her marriage to Robert Nemiroff) were becoming less significant than other political and personal commitments, especially to other women. Though not yet entirely visible to audiences and friends, her desire for women often occupied her imagination. *A Raisin in the Sun* had not centered on a gay or lesbian character but did feature a narrative in which women proved more ambitious, aggressive, resilient, and independent—characteristics sometimes associated with lesbian identity. In her two subsequent dramas, *Les Blancs* and *The Sign in Sidney Brustein's Window*, Hansberry chose to write of gay themes, and she also left behind an unfinished roman à clef that featured several gay characters, including a thinly veiled James Baldwin.[13] If a still-pervasive anti-Communist paranoia triggered the FBI surveillance of Hansberry, her impulse to cover evidence of her lesbian desires sprang from other anxieties of respectability and conventions of marriage, even though it would seem that Hansberry was well on her way to coming out.[14]

In 1957, around the time she separated from Nemiroff, Hansberry sent the first of two letters to the editors of the national lesbian journal the *Ladder*, along with a money order for two dollars to purchase as many back issues as the amount covered. In the first published note, Hansberry offered several observations about social difference—what she described as "off-the-top-of-the-head reactions"—and developed what may be identified as a founding theory of black feminist intersections. In her reading of the "homosexual" literature, which was not apparently her first, Hansberry negotiated the problem of difference, juxtaposing the progress of the civil rights movement against the question of lesbianism. After addressing the merits of group separatism—the idea of "wishing to foster any strict separatist notions, homo or hetero"—Hansberry compared the dictates of black respectability to the homophile's pursuit of a kind of respectable integration, maintaining that the "most splendid argument is simple and to the point: Ralph Bunche, with all his clean fingernails, degrees, and, of course, undeniable service to the human race, could still be insulted, denied a hotel room or meal in many parts of our country."

On the one hand, Hansberry addressed the *Ladder* and its audience as "you people," as if to notice but not clearly identify with lesbians. On the other, she offered a number of observations about the homophile movement that seemed to reflect a sustained reading of their journals and more than a passing interest in lesbian issues (a full run of both the *Ladder* and *One*, another homophile publication, were preserved in her personal papers). She readily compared the case of African Americans to that of homosexuals, and did so from an insider's perspective: "What ought to be clear is that one is oppressed or discriminated against because one is different, not 'wrong,' or 'bad' somehow." She mentioned the "personal discomfort at the sight of an ill-dressed or illiterate Negro" and then predicted that "someday, I expect, the 'discrete' Lesbian will not turn her head on the streets [at] the sight of the 'butch' strolling hand in hand with her friends in their trousers and definitive haircuts." On the subject of these prejudices within the group, Hansberry wondered if the West Coast was more tolerant than the East Coast, and therefore had spawned more homophile groups, or if they were "Pioneers still?" As for New York, she observed "a vigorous and active set almost bump one another off the streets."[15]

Hansberry's venture into the homophile movement reflected her abiding concern with ethics and "moral conclusions" based on an "acceptance of a social moral superstructure which has never admitted to the equality of women and is therefore immoral itself." For her, this immorality intersected with "homosexual persecution" and what she presciently referred to as "anti-feminist dogma." In considering the direction of homophile political strategy, she sided with the integration position: "What the homosexual wants and needs is not autonomy from the human race but utter integration. I feel, however, I could be wrong about this." Just on the cusp of international fame, perhaps only a black female intellectual pioneering a new role in the arts could have written these letters, applying so much pressure on the connections between race, gender, and sexuality.[16]

If recast through black gay history, in the orbit of James Baldwin's provocations, Hansberry's activism becomes an enactment of the intersection at the margin, inspired by her sense of herself as a queer outsider. Baldwin sometimes referred to Hansberry as his baby sister, observing years later that she died not of cancer but of the racial violence in the South, especially Birmingham: "It was the incomprehension of her country and the disaster overtaking the nation" that ruined her health. Later that year, Hansberry reflected on the assassination of President Kennedy but, not too surprisingly given her alienation from the attorney general, refused the national scene of mourning, calling the president and his brother "a playboy and a rather driven young politician and very little else as far as I can make out."[17] Meanwhile, her reputation as a rebellious artist brought her to the attention of the grassroots activists in the Student Nonviolent Coordinating Committee (SNCC), storming the South for citizenship rights and social change. Around 1963, SNCC invited Hansberry to compose the text for a photographic volume, *The Movement: Documentary of a Struggle for Equality*, and Nemiroff later stressed her commitment to SNCC in his biographical rendering: "For Lorraine Hansberry, insurgency was a necessity, an essence of the artist. A necessity inseparable from her blackness, her womanhood, her humanism." But this statement misrepresented the iconic figure by eliding what was clearly a driving force—her lesbian desire.[18]

Every archive presents its own entries and barriers, traces and lacunae, but the anxieties over disclosure in African American history and the tension between respectability and personal sexuality peaked at the height of the civil rights movement and has since then closed off access to Hansberry's complicated identity. In donating Hansberry's personal and professional effects to the New York Public Library, Nemiroff separated out the lesbian-themed correspondence, diaries, unpublished manuscripts, and full runs of the homophile magazines and restricted them from access to researchers. Recently the new executor, Nemiroff's daughter, agreed to release the boxes with written permission to me in the summer of 2013. To my knowledge, none of the presidential or civil rights scholarship or African American historiography has seriously considered Hansberry's lesbian desire. At work on Hansberry's biography in the 1980s, Margaret Wilkerson mentioned the 1957 letters to the *Ladder*, observing that they "raised the problem of a lesbian in a heterosexual marriage" without taking into account the couple's subsequent divorce. Recent scholarship stresses her ties to political radicals, but Hansberry's separation from Nemiroff and her pursuit of passionate relations with women highlighted a personal break from the Left. Whether her lovers were black or white—she did not say in the materials that I found and read—her passionate female relationships appear to have freed her imagination across and through differences while the traditional Left continued to restrict such a vision.[19]

What was restricted from view may not have seemed flattering to the conventional or official image of Hansberry. In her diaries, she often felt isolated at the same time she was being catapulted into the limelight. Caught up in the hectic schedule of a downtown bohemian, dashing to coffee dates and star-studded cultural events, lunching with friends in the Village, Hansberry still complained of the dullness of her engagements. Then, one morning, Hansberry awakened in a different mood: "As for this homosexuality thing (how long since I have thought or written of it in that way—as some kind of entity!) am committed to it. But its childhood is over. From now on—I actively look for women of accomplishment—no matter what they looked like. How free I feel today. I will create my life—not just accept it." In subsequent pages, Hansberry described lunches and dates with other women in terms of their beauty—"a grand smile and grand eyes"—and of their intelligence. Considered as a whole, the recently released documents reveal a woman who valued female intimacy and embraces but also an activist-artist grappling with the politics of identity. "I am back and it is lovely and it reminds of every other thing which has passed through my mind in connection with you. . . . You are remarkably cool on a hot day, did I tell you that?" And then some lines later: "It occurs to me that you and I have never ever allowed the words 'homosexual' to enter our conversation and I wonder about it. According to a little publication which came in this morning's mail there appears to be something of a controversy raging among the sophisticated damned about the superiority of 'homophile' over 'homosexual' or some such nonsense. The closest I have heard you come to articulation in terms of label was some charming mumbled phrase about 'queer beer' [Hansberry wrote an unpublished story with this title] and 'gathering of the clan' as per Provincetown." Then: "I doubt you can stomach the sort of publication that I am referring to. I think that is a pity. They are a little strange and confused, but I consider them necessary and apparently in the hands of remarkably intelligent and healthy people and even a little coragious [*sic*]."[20]

Almost up until her death, Hansberry appeared unaware that she had cancer, the pain in her shoulders diagnosed as "calcium deposits" and the pain in her stomach as "ulcers." When she finally underwent treatment, her diary noted, "Great day but a queer day. Much pain last night. Took a Darvon; vomited was instantly relieved. Went on [D]arvon. . . . Thus a day free from physical discomfort." She continued to travel from her upstate New York home and for two weeks stayed in Cape Cod. "Provincetown naturally," wrote Hansberry. On July 29, 1964, her diary entry began: "Health: not good. Continue to lose weight. Down to 107. . . . Frankly, things look rather poor. But the truth is that I am so tired of hurting at this point that I wouldn't mind something rather drastic. I don't mean operations. I do mean death. I feel as if I am being sucked away."[21]

Hansberry's death touched off a wave of publicity and outpouring of grief, while her ex-husband, Nemiroff, received numerous condolences from close friends, distant acquaintances, and the black elite, from Langston Hughes to Leo William Hansberry (the black scholar of Africa and her uncle), as well as songs and poems dedicated to and written for her. The leaders and the grass roots mourned. The director of the New York office of SNCC reported that the group had received a contribution in "memory of our beloved Lorraine," and Jerome Smith, the Freedom Rider with whom she had stood up to the Kennedys, sent a card to express his "heartfelt sympathy for your terrible loss." Whitney Young (National Urban League), Roy Wilkins (NAACP), John Lewis (SNCC), and Martin Luther King Jr. sent telegrams, with King writing,

"Her creative literary ability and her profound grasp of the deep social issues confronting the world today will remain an inspiration to generations yet unborn."[22] More than six hundred attended Hansberry's funeral, including Malcolm X; Paul Robeson delivered the eulogy and Nina Simone performed several of Hansberry's favorite songs.[23]

The title of the posthumous volume edited by Nemiroff, *To Be Young, Gifted and Black: Lorraine Hansberry in Her Own Words*, came from her last speech, delivered at a ceremony for the winners of a writing contest sponsored by the United Negro College Fund. Along with the play, this collection, and the photographs in the volume, have become foundational in the memory and understanding of Hansberry—beautiful, feminine, imaginative, genius. But Nemiroff's presumptuousness in manufacturing a collection of essays—"in her own words"—is matched only by the presumption of her straightness that was deployed.[24]

The only exceptions to the subsequent fifty years of her official closeting were the result of the work of a few lesbian archivists and writers. In Del Martin and Phyllis Lyon's 1972 volume, *Lesbian/Woman*, they referred indirectly to Hansberry when observing that "many black women who had been involved in the homophile movement found themselves forced to make a choice between two 'Causes' that touched their lives so intimately" and that "one of them wrote a play that was a hit on Broadway." Such a claim may seem to attribute to Hansberry more commitment to the cause than she really held. But Martin and Lyon sought not only to acknowledge her as a pioneer but also to reconstruct a more diverse genealogy of lesbian identity. Responding to the rhetorical question of why she mattered to them, they gave a "simple answer . . . Lorraine Hansberry was an early N.Y. DOB [Daughters of Bilitis] member, and she contributed to this magazine in its very earliest years." While she subscribed to both the *Ladder* and *One*, no evidence has surfaced of her participation in meetings, conferences, or other activities. Yet lesbian archivists understandably have wanted to include the evidence of her desire in the record. Barbara Grier responded to what she described as a "capsule ad" posted by Hansberry's husband, Nemiroff, and "offered the *Ladder* material" but claimed that she did not receive a reply from him, which seems entirely plausible given his other choices as executor of Hansberry's estate. Some years later, apparently Nemiroff, or perhaps another archivist, clipped several pages of Jonathan Katz's *Gay American History* that reference her letters to the *Ladder* and deposited them in her personal papers, but this was the apparent extent of Nemiroff's intentions to recognize in a public way Hansberry's enthusiasm for the homophiles and passions for other women.[25]

Another queer genealogy—that is, attempting to document and claim the presumed straight figure as and for a gay and lesbian memory or tradition—appeared in a special 1979 issue of *Freedomways*, the black radical journal for which Hansberry had once worked. Here the lesbian feminist poet Adrienne Rich figured Hansberry as a "problem," insofar as she presented several complicated characteristics—"black, female, and dead"—and then Rich wrote of her frustration that "the Hansberry papers are not simply accessible in an archive open to the public." Yet as a lesbian feminist immersed in the essentialism of the times, Rich felt constrained as a white woman looking at a black woman and awaited the eyes of a black feminist to examine these documents, calling on the black lesbian scholar Barbara Smith for an authentic reading. She then reminded readers of Hansberry's correspondence with the *Ladder* and her mention in Martin and Lyon's work *Lesbian/Woman* in order to consider the terms of the closet, or what she termed Hansberry's "internal and external censors." Drawing on the letters and some of the unpublished "Xerox copies of letters, interview transcripts, essays," Rich retrieved a black lesbian genealogy that aligned Hansberry with June Jordan, Alice Walker, and Linda Tillery, among others, and in a sense Rich's shards of evidence collapsed inquiry into identity, relying primarily on Hansberry's passing observations in the published letters rather than on harder evidence of desire that would surface later (perhaps Rich had heard rumors?). In her 1988 lesbian classic, *A Restricted Country*, Joan Nestle utilized Hansberry's *Ladder* letters to defend the butch-femme relations from criticism of artificiality, highlighting their critique of choosing to present a facade of respectability. The lesbian impulse to claim the Hansberry archive slightly misrepresented the writer's own relationships, to the extent that a gay man, James Baldwin, was one of her oldest and closest friends, forming a queer bohemian couple that comforted each other under the pressures of the limelight. In his introduction to *To Be Young, Gifted and Black*, after noting that there was only "one person Lorraine couldn't get through to, and that was the late Bobby Kennedy," Baldwin recalled his last visit with her at the hospital when she could not speak. In this moving tribute he wrote with tenderness and a sense of love for Hansberry but chose not to mention her relationships with women, perhaps because he knew all too well the price of such a disclosure.[26]

Who Is Jimmy Baldwin?

As for James Baldwin, around the time of the meeting with Robert Kennedy, his prominence as the next great black writer and potential political leader too had skyrocketed. This meant not only greater awareness of his views on race but also more scrutiny of his sexuality, with, again, gay issues pushed through the back door of the civil rights movement. Born to a single mother in Harlem, Baldwin felt the influence of his sometimes cruel and domineering stepfather leading him to the church, and from there to the gay bar scene in the Village. Although Baldwin had briefly married, he was sexually ambivalent from the beginning. Like Hansberry, he longed for a freer space in which to reinvent himself, and so he left for Paris, where he found literary success, romantic connections with other men, and a lively bohemian nightlife. In exile, he found a black gay identity. In a 1963 interview in *Mademoiselle*, Baldwin amplified his critique of the United States—his continual charge was that the nation was founded on and sustained by racism—by blaming whites for failing to be honest and restated his view that the civil rights movement involved complex psychological issues and fear of recognizing oneself in the other. But among his most important observations about the American race problem was the notion that the nation's puritanical hypocrisy prevented a more open and honest reckoning with human sexuality. A turning point came when the interviewer repeated the assertion that Baldwin had two obsessions—as the interlocutor put it, "color and homosexuality." Characteristically evading inquiry into his sexual identity, Baldwin turned to a discussion of masculinity and other topics. Demurring yet irreverent, he concluded with the confession, "I don't know what homosexual means any more, and Americans don't either." *Mademoiselle* asked again, "You don't think it's a disease?," to which Baldwin sharply responded, "The fact that Americans consider it a disease says more about them than it says about homosexuality."[27]

Over the years, interviewers continued to press Baldwin on his sexual desire, and Baldwin routinely declined to clearly identify himself as gay even as he already had admitted it. Appealing to a kind of humanist universalism, he cast homosexuality and heterosexuality as symbolic problems of love rather than as sources of personal identification and argued that "sexual minorities . . . were really the most vivid victims of our system of mortification of the flesh." Into the 1970s, he remained skeptical about the new gay liberation: "I'm very glad that it seems to be easier for a boy to admit that he's in love with a boy . . . instead of what happened in my generation, [where] you had kids going on to the needle because they were afraid that they might want to go to bed with someone of the same sex." Yet his endorsement here seems weak, and in another interview he dismissed both the women's liberation and gay liberation movements as "essentially a white–middle class phenomenon." Part of this evasion had to do with negotiating the politics

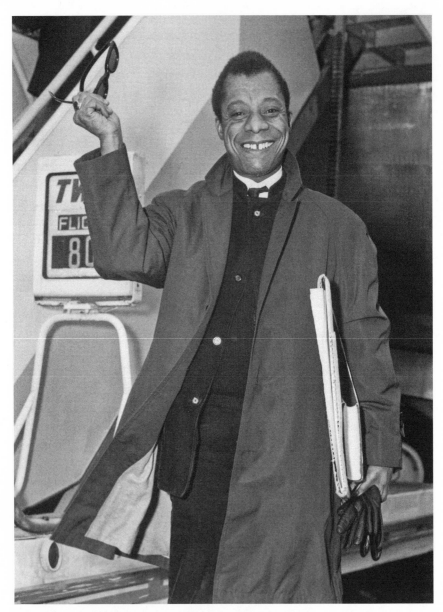

James Baldwin returning from Paris, August 7, 1963, to attend the March on Washington. James Baldwin published novels that consistently pushed the boundaries of popular norms and black respectability, but his openness also pushed him to the sidelines of the civil rights movement. His first gay novel, *Giovanni's Room* (1956), satisfied a longing for gay characters by generations of black and white men alike. (Photo by Orlando Fernandez/New York World Telegram and Sun Newspapers; © Corbis).

of race and passing as straight rather than confronting homophobes with whom he mobilized against racism. When noted black nationalist and openly homophobic Amiri Baraka wrote an essay on Baldwin, he recalled taking him on a tour of Scudder Homes, the public housing complex in Newark, and encountering a "young brother" who had just read Baldwin's last and most openly gay novel, *Just Above My Head*. In that construction of memory, however, it would have been impossible for Baraka to speak the words "gay" or "homosexual" or explain to his readers the themes of the novel. When Baraka delivered a eulogy at Baldwin's memorial service, he again could not or would not identify him as a gay man.[28]

Public appearances like these spotlighted Baldwin as a powerful leader at the same time that increasing publicity resulted in more attention from the FBI. Baldwin's participation in *Freedomways* had already triggered FBI surveillance, and numerous reports classified him as a "sex pervert," as they did Bayard Rustin; in contrast, Hansberry's lesbian desires largely escaped government scrutiny, perhaps because they were less legible and not as threatening to FBI investigators.[29] Undoubtedly aware of his monitoring, Baldwin in turn fought back, not only in public speeches denouncing the failure of the FBI to protect southern demonstrators but also in his published essays.[30]

A series of FBI reports recirculated references to him as a gay man, and some of this was encouraged by bureau director J. Edgar Hoover, who at one point issued a memorandum asking, "Isn't Baldwin a well known pervert?," to which an investigator responded, "It is not a matter of official record that he is a pervert; however, the theme of homosexuality has figured prominently in two of his three published novels." Baldwin himself had referenced homosexuality as a theme not only in his second novel, *Giovanni's Room*, but also his first, *Go Tell It on the Mountain*, which he described as autobiographical. Whether the FBI gathered this information to use against Baldwin or to monitor homosexuals, the agency's profile of Baldwin archived his antiracist activities and gayness as interconnected threats to national security.[31]

Baldwin's capacity to wield power in the civil rights movement remained limited by its culturally conservative profile and particular ideals of civility and morality that rendered homosexuality as anathema to the cause. Although Baldwin tirelessly spoke out for justice and against racism throughout the sixties, had enormous visibility, continually made important contributions, and represented extraordinary untapped potential, he never found acceptance from the civil rights establishment. The internationally renowned Baldwin might have expected to speak at the March on Washington in the summer of 1963, but the platform was limited to the heads of the major civil rights organizations, union presidents, and clergy from the major denominations (except the Black Muslims). His associate and biographer, David Leeming, observed that "Baldwin knew . . . that people were wary of his own reputation as a homosexual, and he was disappointed that he had not been asked to participate in any meaningful way." Instead, he organized a delegation in Paris to convene at the U.S. Embassy and present a scroll bearing some three hundred signatures in support of the march. He then flew to Washington, D.C., to join a contingency of celebrities arriving from Hollywood. It was all he could do.[32]

Around the time of the march, Martin Luther King Jr. was asked by his advisers if he would "appear on a television program" with Baldwin, but he was not "enthusiastic" because he "felt that Baldwin was not informed regarding the movement," according to FBI surveillance records of King. Noting Baldwin's increasing visibility and articulateness, King observed that the writer, "although considered a spokesperson of the Negro people by the Press, was not a civil rights leader," while his key adviser, Stanley Levison, questioned his qualifications and capacity to lead because "this group of Baldwin's was not 'too deep intellectually,'" a contentious claim about a major novelist and essayist, to say the least. At one point, in the same conversation, when asked to characterize how "Rustin's position was with Baldwin," Levison replied that "the two were better qualified to lead a homo-sexual movement than a civil rights movement." Although black leadership figures publicly dissembled on questions of sexuality, particularly given King's reputation for engaging in extramarital sexual relations, their homophobia clearly influenced strategic deliberations about the face and direction of the movement.[33]

If Baldwin fell short of the status of recognized leader, his supposed unsuitability was always already exacerbated by his classification as gay, while his voice was also pitched as too gay for the literary establishment, delimiting his role in the movement as well. Although Baldwin had claimed that his first novel involved homosexual themes, none of the reviewers apparently noticed this and instead lauded *Go Tell It on the Mountain* for its authenticity, boldness, and honesty; the *New York Times* referred to its "naked truthfulness," "exactness," and racial pathos. A story of a young boy in Harlem called to serve God as a Pentecostal minister, the novel elevated Baldwin to the status of Richard Wright's heir apparent. The portrait of spirit and passion had moved beyond the protest novel, proclaimed one reviewer, attributing a certain lack of literary merit to that genre (probably much to Baldwin's delight).[34] Most reviews of *Go Tell It on the Mountain* celebrated the discovery of an essential Negro and assumed that his words were autobiographical. In some ways, it is not surprising that for his next novel, *Giovanni's Room*, published in 1956, Baldwin chose to write of homosexual love between two white characters and thereby to identify himself with anything and everything but the authentic experience of the Negro.[35]

Giovanni's Room explores the tortured homosexual relationship between an American and an Italian man and the incapacity to cope with their gay love that ends in tragic loss. Unlike the positive French critical response to the gay novel (where Baldwin set the story), U.S. reviewers resorted to ad hominem attacks and homophobic insults cloaked as serious literary criticism. Although eventually becoming a modern gay classic, its early reception reveals the depth of resistance to discussion of the subject. Strewn throughout the reviews of *Giovanni's Room* were terms of stigma associated with midcentury conceptions of homosexuality—"sordid," "unpalatable," and "deviant"— even as a number of reviewers admired Baldwin for overcoming so distasteful a subject matter and handling it with "candor" and "dignity."[36]

Perhaps no single reviewer better illustrated the overall shift in critical reception between the first and second novel than J. Saunders Redding. A well-respected professor of literature at Howard University, Redding had heaped high praise on *Go Tell It on the Mountain*, commended Baldwin's talent, and lauded the "impact of honesty, sincerity, and truth." "James Baldwin will be a name to remember," he stated, declaring him the true successor to Richard Wright. Three years later, however, Redding opined that Baldwin ought to find a "subject worthy of his talents" and stop writing "tripe." He contended that *Giovanni's Room* was as "stale as a pornographic cartoon," and in the second, more visible review for the *New York Herald Tribune*, he described the book as "a nightmare of degeneracy and lust," concluding that "in the score of books on homosexuality there is nothing so unlovely and repulsive as the protracted anguish" of Baldwin's characters.[37]

Judging from his book reviews, Baldwin never quite regained the literary status he attained from *Go Tell It on the Mountain*. From its publication until quite recently, *Giovanni's Room* remained understudied or ignored; of his novels, it has garnered "the least attention," according to one literary history of Baldwin's writings. Despite the negative reviews, Baldwin weighed the market appeal of controversy and decided to write again of homosexuality in *Another Country*, bringing together race and desire in an explosive story of interracial love and tragedy. Set in contemporary New York, the sultry writing and drama of desire challenged readers to question the fixity of polarized dichotomies of race, class, gender, and sexuality. In what turned out to be a winning gamble, the best-selling 1962 novel delivered to its readers a black bisexual entertainer, Rufus, who engages in sexual relations with a young white man and white southern women while he pines for the attention of another white man. In reflecting on the character, Baldwin felt that Rufus was distinguished not by his bisexuality but rather by the agency with which he is endowed. As Baldwin put it, "There are no antecedents for him. Rufus was partly responsible for his own doom, and in presenting him as partly responsible, I was attempting to break out of the whole sentimental image of the afflicted nigger driven that way [to suicide] by white people."[38]

From both the black and white press flowed a stream of dismissal and condescension. A *New York Amsterdam News* review noted Baldwin's talents and then criticized him for writing on an "appalling subject," explaining that he wasted "433 pages glorifying rhapsodic joys of homosexual love" and pronouncing the novel to be "pure pornography" that fed a prurient interest worthy of censorship. His gay characters inevitably were seen as shallow and unbelievable, what one review called "cardboard lovers" without depth and believability; they supposedly existed in a vacuum and lacked authenticity. What the reviewers implied was what the civil rights establishment had already decided: that Baldwin himself lacked character. From the black nationalist Left, Lawrence Neal (also critical of Hansberry on similar grounds) questioned Baldwin's understanding or absorption of black culture; claimed that he was preoccupied with the "uncertainty of his identity" and suffered from a "failure to utilize traditional aspects of Afro-American culture"; and, speaking for the race, concluded that "we are still awaiting a writer totally committed to the destiny of Black people." If the doubting of Baldwin's racial commitment mobilized the politics of authenticity—the move of questioning the racial loyalty of those with whom one disagrees on matters of ideology— his professed homosexuality always already contradicted his standing as a black man.[39]

For many white straight Americans, the sexual and racial possibilities opened up by Baldwin were disturbing and threatening, and both individuals and groups registered their anxious objections. One concerned citizen wrote to J. Edgar Hoover to complain that *Another Country* had "every filthy word, compound word and phrasing" having to do with "drug addiction . . . [and] sex perversion at its vilest." In 1965, a self-identified Christian from Mississippi sent two of Baldwin's latest books—*Another Country* and *The Blues for Mr. Charlie*—to the government for inspection. "I don't know how far the FBI can go in church organization investigation but I see this as a matter of Obscene literature and poor church organization," complained the reader. In New Orleans, two booksellers were charged with violations of local obscenity ordinances for selling *Another Country*, described in a complaint as the "most filthy and pornographic book I have ever read," but the retailers were not prosecuted. In reflecting on the stormy reception of *Another Country*, Baldwin recalled how the "reception of it was a scandal. That was something to get through." The reviews apparently astonished him—they left him "simply and completely bewildered"—and even eighteen years later he declared, "O Lord, I would not like to go through that again!"[40]

From speech to speech and interview to interview, Baldwin maneuvered through the homophobic prejudice that awaited him. Sometimes Baldwin admitted that his novels were about homosexuality and at other times asserted that the sexual scenarios merely served as vehicles through which to portray larger symbolic themes. In 1989 Baldwin gave an interview to the *Village Voice* in which he was asked if he felt "a special feeling of responsibility toward gay people," and he spoke of a "special responsibility because I would have to be a kind of witness to it." If Hansberry had fashioned an identity of intersectionality, Baldwin discovered the interconnectedness of racial and sexual injustice. "The terrors homosexuals go through in this society would not be so great if the society itself did not go through so many terrors it doesn't want to admit. The discovery of one's sexual preference doesn't have to be trauma," Baldwin declared. "It's a trauma because it's such a traumatized society."[41]

In the continuing cycle of denigration and pronouncement of decline, reviews of his subsequent novels again reiterated the nostalgia for Baldwin's supposed original authentic innocence exemplified in a straight reading of *Go Tell It on the Mountain*—a longing for a time before the author's protest writing had supposedly compromised his oeuvre and homosexuality had perverted his characters. Yet even as Baldwin lost literary status, the respectable homophile movement began to claim his work for its cause. In 1964 an essay in *One* referenced *Another Country* and suggested, "Perhaps sexual pleasure from such pain is always the result of the addition of other emotions such as the highly charged situation of race?" The author went on to observe that among homosexuals, the "racial guilt feeling may lead to a wish to be beaten and among heterosexual males racial guilt feelings may lead one to submit sexually to a member of another race."[42]

Into the 1970s, as gay men searched for portrayals of themselves in the pages of gay fiction, they encountered the imaginary world of Baldwin. One white activist, for example, recalled Baldwin's influence on his youth, noting that "when I was in high school (during the late 50s) and struggling to come to terms with my homosexuality, I turned . . . to homosexual writers to offer me some guidance." And like any number of gay men, he recounted that gay-themed fiction provided a crucial source for recognition of his identity: "I felt a need to integrate these 'secret desires' into my everyday life—How could I live without recognition from the world that I could love or be loved? James Baldwin's novel, 'Giovanni's Room,' was one of the ambivalent discoveries of my library searches." From the African American literary canon to gay bookstores, from the authentic black boy called to faith to the tragic story of white gay romance, black gay identities oscillated back and forth across the color line that Baldwin had so profoundly meditated upon at the height of the civil rights movement.[43]

Bayard's Trouble

The March on Washington is often remembered as a monumental mass demonstration that forever changed the course of history, but at the time it was not a very popular event, with one opinion poll showing respondents disapproving of the protest at a rate of three to one. A number of recent studies powerfully document how the black gay activist Bayard Rustin oversaw the organizing of the march—coordinating the speakers, collecting and distributing funds, and responding to logistical questions.[44] Rustin was at the height of his political powers and tactical skill and would have been poised to lead the final drive for federal civil rights legislation. But a decade before, in 1953, he had been arrested in Pasadena, California, on what were often referred to as "morals charges" involving him and two men in a parked vehicle. Rustin had offered to perform oral sex, and the three were caught and charged by the local police, found guilty, and sentenced to sixty days in prison. The incident had terrible repercussions for Rustin, who lost the support of many of his mentors and friends. Like Baldwin, the exposure of his homosexuality would continue to marginalize him and circumscribe his social impact.[45]

Despite the indiscretion and loss, by the late 1950s Rustin gained considerable influence with Martin Luther King, and historians now credit him (and several other activists) with bringing nonviolent, direct action protest theory and tactics to the larger civil rights movement, a major contribution by any measure. Despite Rustin's important work in the boycotts and other demonstrations, however, King appeared to distance himself. In 1958 King planned a trip to the Gold Coast for a celebration of independence but excluded Rustin, a move that Ella Baker, a highly influential civil rights organizer, questioned him about: "How can Bayard not be included in the leadership of discussions of nonviolence?"[46]

Then in a 1960 struggle over political clout, Adam Clayton Powell Jr., the black congressman from New York, demanded that either King remove Rustin from his contingent at the Democratic National Convention or he would leak a rumor to the effect that Rustin was engaged in a sexual relationship with King—a charge that, though false, probably worried King. The biographers of Powell disagree on the precise turn of events, with at least one author suggesting that Rustin, not King, became nervous, while Powell's popular autobiography, *Adam by Adam*, completely omitted the incident. But in the face of this pressure from the congressman and its possible repercussions for the movement, Rustin offered his resignation and was apparently surprised and hurt when King accepted it. (Rustin continued to follow Powell during his own controversy over his election to Congress, when a majority in the House refused to permit him to take office, and, choosing not to hold a grudge, he penned a defense of Powell). Years later, a scholar wrote to Rustin for his assistance with a proposed King biography and raised again the question of the morals arrest—what he termed "the delicate matter about which I do not wish to embarrass you"—and sent along two pages on the issue of Rustin's resignation, noting that "Rustin had been involved in a homosexual misdemeanor, and Powell hinted that if Rustin stayed on, that episode would be given a full public airing."[47] Rustin bracketed this section of the manuscript but did not apparently write back to the author. Although largely ignored by the civil rights establishment, Rustin's painful resignation attracted the attention of Baldwin, who wrote a front-page story for *Harper's Magazine*, "The Dangerous Road before Martin Luther King." He observed that King "lost much moral credit when he allowed Powell to force his resignation" and noted that Rustin had a "long and able record as a fighter for civil rights, but King was faced with the choice of defending his organizer, who was also his friend, or agreeing with Powell; and he chose the *latter*." It was a powerful defense of one black gay man by another.[48]

Again, at the last moment on the eve of the 1963 March on Washington, Rustin's past exploded into the public after an attack by Strom Thurmond, the conservative southern senator who vowed to read the morals charges against Rustin into the *Congressional Record*, the official transcript of proceedings in Congress. The head of the NAACP, Roy Wilkins, had also objected to assigning a visible role in the march to Rustin, but A. Philip Randolph stepped in to defend him, even as he agreed to head the event with Rustin working behind the scenes. In a published essay, Rustin attempted to respond to and refute Thurmond's charges. He denied that he was a member of the Communist Party and explained the difference between his brief membership in the

Youth Communist League and true, committed Communist affiliation. He admitted that he was arrested for his pacifism, and then instead of dealing with the morals arrest, he simply refused to address the issue of homosexuality. "An individual involved in a character charge," Rustin unconvincingly explained, "cannot deal with it himself." Even in a strategic memo developed to answer the attacks, Rustin and his partner, Tom Kahn, completely ignored the arrest. At some point they presented Randolph with their prepared statement, and later Randolph made an announcement to the press: "That Mr. Rustin was on one occasion arrested in another connection has long been a matter of public record, and not an object of concealment." In conclusion, Randolph suggested that rather than protect Christian morals, in reality Rustin's critics sought to undermine the movement. But neither man could find within reach a workable defense. There was not yet a discourse of legitimacy or a platform of personal morality—in short, not yet a recognized black gay identity—with which to deflect unwarranted attacks on Rustin's reputation.[49]

Rustin's major biographer, John D'Emilio, has observed that on the eve of the march, "not of his own choosing, Rustin had become perhaps the most visible homosexual in America at a time when few gay men or lesbians aspired to any public attention." The other most visible homosexual in America, James Baldwin, later wrote that what saved Rustin and kept him at the head of the March on Washington "was the insistence of A. Philip Randolph, the influential veteran black labor leader, that Rustin was their most experienced crowd-organizer and must work on putting the march together." But the politics of homophobia precluded a secure position in the movement. The day after the march, the *Chicago Sun-Times* called for rethinking the movement strategies from direct action demonstration and toward more traditional negotiations in conference rooms and then criticized him: "Rustin calls for more 'nonviolence' but his record is hardly one to give him the right of leadership," the editors suggested, observing that he had "been jailed on a morals charge."[50]

If Rustin and Baldwin remained on the sidelines of the march, their paths crossed in a prominent appearance after the September 1963 bombing of the Sixteenth Street Baptist Church in Birmingham, Alabama, at the end of a summer of historic protest. The pair, along with Norman Thomas, the socialist radical, and others, addressed a crowd at the Justice Department in Foley Square. (Rustin saved a copy of Baldwin's speech that day for his personal papers.) For his part, Rustin called upon President Kennedy to "send Federal troops into Alabama" in order to "'break the hold'" of Governor George C. Wallace. More boldly, Baldwin laid blame for the "atrocities" of violence in

Bayard Rustin (*left*) and Cleveland Robinson. Bayard Rustin helped to train a generation of civil rights activists in the tactics of nonviolent direct action. But after his arrest on a morals charge in 1953, his role in the movement remained circumscribed by the constant threat of another public exposure of his past indiscretion. (© Bettmann/CORBIS).

the South at the steps of the governor, Washington, and the "Kennedy admin-istration in general." As usual, he also castigated the FBI, claiming that it was "inconceivable that the F.B.I. could not have found the guilty parties," that their "real sympathies" were with the southern law enforcement officials, and that there were at the time twenty-one unsolved bombings.[51]

Rustin's decreased visibility in the movement sometimes contributes to a misunderstanding of his changing political views. For example, some histori-ans point to Rustin's conservative negotiations with and advice to the grass-roots activists in the Mississippi Freedom Democratic Party (MFDP), one of the shining moments of Freedom Summer, to explain his marginalization. In 1964 black and white activists ran a slate of candidates in parallel state elec-tions and sent their Mississippi contingent to be seated at the Democratic National Convention in place of the lily-white one. When the MFDP pro-tested Mississippi's delegation, the president and other party leaders refused to recognize the party. In a last-minute compromise, in part prompted by the moving testimony of Fannie Lou Hamer about physical injuries suffered at the hands of brutal white police officers, President Lyndon B. Johnson agreed to seat two of the delegates, which was in some sense a significant and unprecedented concession. Most historians probably champion the decision of the MFDP to refuse to compromise. But Rustin urged the delegation to take the offer and engage in political dealing rather than stage another protest. In standard accounts of the negotiation, Rustin becomes the conservative vil-lain who entreated the renegade radicals to accept the paltry two-seat com-promise tendered by the president. The MFDP ultimately rejected the offer, but by that time King and other major leaders also believed in compromise. It is often forgotten that King also urged Rustin to bargain with the activists, largely to forge an alliance with labor, given that United Auto Workers presi-dent Walter Reuther opposed disruption of the convention.[52]

Rustin was caught between a rock and a hard place, and he never quite found his way out. Certainly he felt disappointment, even resentment, at his sidelining. Rustin should have been invited back into the inner circles of the civil rights leadership but was not. He had written a major article, "From Protest to Politics," that foreshadowed a crucial transition in the movement toward elections and government and that drew considerable liberal sup-port, but the next several years would reveal to him that his days of influence were behind him.[53]

The outpouring of biographies of Rustin (five and counting) have docu-mented the significance of his contributions to social activism but continually underestimate the losses he endured from a homophobia that he was never able to elude or speak out against. Three years after the March on Washington and more than a decade since the morals arrest, Rustin's trouble erupted yet again in an episode that historians have overlooked and that highlights how homophobia intertwined with anti-Communism to again undermine the famed leader.

In 1966 the Law Enforcement Institute, a training program for police officers in Maryland, invited Rustin to address its class on the tactics of direct action used by demonstrators. But news of the invitation quickly leaked, and a concerned citizen contacted the governor, who then ordered an investigation into the planned program. At the same time, Rustin became the subject of controversy when he refused to sign the Ober Amendment, a pledge of loyalty promising that he had not engaged in so-called subversive activities or in attempting to "overthrow" the government. He returned the document unsigned. Passed in 1949, the amendment prohibited subversive activities or membership in radical organizations for state employees, but the Supreme Court had overturned the constitutionality of a similar state law. Rustin called having to "swear to an oath" to be an "attack upon my civil liberties" and explained that he long had "opposed all totalitarianism, both Communist and Fascist," though he admitted to belonging to the Young Communist League. He concluded by referring to himself as a longtime "Quaker with three hundred year old convictions of peace and nonviolence," studiously avoiding his well-known conviction for a sexual offense.[54]

The invitation sparked a response from a member of the increasingly marginal anti-Communist organization the John Birch Society, in nearby Towson, who warned that he would announce Rustin's criminal record on a telephone message that had a daily audience of at least two thousand. Meanwhile, two local politicians, one from the House of Delegates and the other from a city council, criticized the use of taxpayer money for the event and vowed to have the event canceled. But the director of the University College Center of Adult Education assured Rustin that he had no intention of rescinding the invitation. Rustin's steadfast refusal to sign quickly became national news, hitting the papers in Baltimore and Washington, D.C., while a student wrote to Rustin to encourage his acceptance of the invitation, reporting on a third attempt to start a chapter of the civil rights group the Congress of Racial Equality, which Rustin had helped to build in the 1940s.[55]

In turn, Hoover announced that the FBI would cancel the appearance of its speaker at the same event, and the agency's standard profile of Rustin now became public news. The local press reported not only that he had once belonged to a Communist organization and had resisted the draft but also that he had served a jail sentence for a morals conviction. Even as an editor came out in favor of his appearance, the paper ran a story, "Convicted Sex Pervert and Civil Rights Leader to Be Police Lecturer." Rustin held his ground, refused to sign the oath, and delivered two lectures that were closed to the press and public.[56]

In response, still reeling from the public appearance by the reputed black Communist homosexual, the House of Delegates voted to adopt a resolution that criticized the university for sponsoring Rustin's appearance. In the original legislation, lawmakers had specifically referenced Rustin, but in what was described as a "watered-down" amendment, they resolved only "that consideration ought to be given to the morality or criminal record of invited lecturers who would be using the facilities of the State supported and funded institutions." Here the taint of criminality and sex offense appear to offer a tactical legal tool with which to contain Left causes, and yet antihomosexual sentiments have also filled in at a time when the harshest of anti-Communist repression was lifting.[57]

Into the 1960s, Rustin carved out a new politics of integration, and as the black power movement became more invested in racial separatism, he spoke less of direct action for equal rights and more of building cross-class alliances and advancing more just economic policies. As the decade wore on, he continued to advocate for unions and for improving Jewish relations with African Americans and protested the rise of black studies departments. He praised the famous Memphis Sanitation Workers Strike of 1968 as a "totally new stage" of the civil rights movement, seeing the formation primarily as a class-based protest for fair wages instead of a larger intervention against racial inequality and dehumanization that was signified by the now classic protest signs "I am a Man." Later, in chapter 4, both Baldwin and Rustin are located in a shifting terrain of black power and gay liberation movements, where their roles in the civil rights movement appear to have exited from center stage.

Remaking the March on Washington

In 1982, almost twenty years after the March on Washington, African American leaders planned a commemorative ceremony. Led by the District of Columbia congressman Walter E. Fauntroy on behalf of Rev. Dr. Joseph Lowery, Coretta Scott King, and Rev. Dr. Benjamin Hooks, the organizers approached Rustin "to help organize, even direct again, the upcoming march." But after careful consideration, constructing a table with two columns to compare the context and strategies of the two demonstrations, he rejected their offer. In 1963, "racism prevented examination of or obscured [the] crisis of [the] black family," while by 1983 family problems had materialized, particularly female-headed households. While the black community had learned to demonstrate on racial issues, the same was not the case for economic inequality. While the original movement required "drama," a commemoration was "not dramatic and cannot be made so by protest." In the past, white intransigence, particularly "southern violence," had unified African Americans, but this was no longer the case. Finally, in classic Rustin reasoning, the memo argued for a clear distinction between race and class—"in 1963 the most glaring forms of racial discrimination were in the South (i.e. Jim Crow)," but now "blacks, like whites, are poor because of structural problems in the economy." He then rehearsed a battery of sociological statistics, bolstered by the report that A. Philip Randolph's view in 1963 was that "civil rights would be supplanted by economic rights as the fundamental issue."[58]

The march went on without him. But now a number of black gay activists, led by the recently formed National Coalition for Black Gays (NCBG), protested for inclusion in the commemoration ceremonies. At an August 22 press conference, Fauntroy "specifically ruled out an openly lesbian or gay speaker," saying that, although the march organizers were "unanimously supportive of the civil rights of all . . . they had agreed that the event would not be an aggregation of single issue groups." Reminiscent of Baldwin and Hansberry's impolite intervention at the meeting with Kennedy, seven gay activists "staged a sit-in demonstration in Fauntroy's office," and after refusing to leave, four were arrested and jailed. One of the demonstrators declared that "probably Martin Luther King" would have supported their cause, and perhaps he would have. In Fauntroy's official papers collected at George Washington University is a flier advertising the first March on Washington, featuring the names of the speakers on the top, the goals of the event in the middle, and the names of the cochairmen and five others. Nowhere on the flier was Bayard Rustin listed, speaking volumes to his marginalization. Nor is there evidence in the collection of gay-black confrontation that emerged with the NCBG demonstrations against the D.C. congressman, only a clipping of a newspaper article characterizing the 1983 march as a success.[59]

With the protesters still in jail, the march organizers and NCBG's executive director, Gil Gerald, and others held a conference call, and five demands were presented, including an openly gay speaker, endorsement of pending federal gay rights legislation, retraction of Fauntroy's statement, and a repositioning of the gay and lesbian contingent toward the front of the march. The NCBG proposed James Baldwin or Audre Lorde, the black lesbian feminist poet, as a keynote speaker to represent its contingent, and Lorde was available to deliver the address.

In her twenties, Audre Lorde had traveled to the 1963 March on Washington and recalled how the event drew her into the civil rights movement, and now the internationally renowned writer and activist would repeat history. But she also encountered the sort of troubles that had long constrained a generation of black gay activists; it was reported that because Lorde did not have the proper credentials, she was constantly delayed in the procession. "Through the whole afternoon I felt not only invisible, but I think it was obvious there were a number of people who'd rather I was not there," she recalled. The commemoration ceremony had started at 8:00 A.M. with an hour of inspirational music and Congressman Fauntroy's remarks an hour later. Mayors and celebrities, veterans of the movement and labor leaders, and a cast of others appeared for five minutes each throughout the day. Finally, scheduled for 5:34, Audre Lorde (whose name was misspelled "Audrey Lord") was given only three minutes.[60] By the time she finally reached the podium to speak her few lines, she addressed a smaller crowd, tiring of the long day:

> Today's march openly joins the black civil rights movement and the gay civil rights movement in those struggles we have always shared, for jobs, for health, for peace and for freedom. We marched in 1963 with Dr. Martin Luther King, and dared to dream that freedom would include us, because not one of us is free to choose the terms of our living until all of us are free to choose the terms of our living. Today the black civil rights movement has pledged its support for gay civil rights legislation. And today we march again, lesbians and gay men and our children, standing in our own name together with all our struggling sisters and brothers here and around the world, in the Middle East, in Central America, in the Caribbean and in South Africa, sharing our commitment to work for a livable future. We know we do not have to become copies of each other in order to be able to work together. We know that when we join hands across the table of our differences, our diversity gives us great power. When we can arm ourselves with the strength and vision from all our diverse communities then we will in truth all be free at last.[61]

Echoing Martin Luther King's prophetic declaration that freedom for one necessitated the emancipation of all, Lorde, upon returning home to New England, felt proud but also saddened by the homophobia she had encountered at the event.[62] Understanding the long struggle from there to here—from the sidelining of homosexuals in the civil rights movement in 1963 to the rise of black gay and lesbian leadership in the 1980s—first necessitates a historical excavation of the cultural world that once marginalized and denigrated black gay identities.

Chapter Two

Untangling Black Pathology

The men that James Baldwin imagined into life—*Go Tell It On the Mountain*'s John Grimes, David of *Giovanni's Room*, and *Another Country*'s Rufus Scott— together presented a recognizable repertoire of traits and affects, relation- ships and fates, with which to assemble a black gay identity: ambivalent and deviant, singular and suicidal, confused and tragic, hustling to survive and lost in a sea of forbidden desire. In this period of definitional transition, new etiologies of black homosexuality issued from the overlap of fiction, social science expertise, and public controversies, evolving along a trajectory of multiple sites of exposure and changing locations of production. Between the 1950s and 1960s, familiar signs of the sexual invert (a man performing the role of a woman to signify to others his homosexual desire) or the hustler (a putatively straight man who traded sexual acts for remuneration) intermin- gled with new theories about the effects of overbearing mothers and absent fathers on the increasing incidence of overt homosexuality.

In the influential 1962 monograph *Asylums: Essays on the Social Situation of Mental Patients and Other Inmates*, the social psychologist Erving Goffman presented an array of deviant subjects who concealed their stigmatized background—the ex-convict, the alcoholic, the divorcée—and in particular compared the situation of a closeted homosexual with that of an inpatient at a mental institution who "comes out" by admitting his or her status to a visiting outsider. In a footnote Goffman explained that "comparable coming out occurs in the homosexual world, when a person finally comes frankly to present himself to a 'gay' gathering," and he pointed to Baldwin's *Giovanni's Room* as a "good fictionalized treatment" of this process (seemingly in error, since the novel ends in tragedy). Baldwin wrote so powerfully, and volumi- nously, on a subject that still remained shrouded in secrecy and shame that his novels served as a reference point even for leading academics.[1] By the mid-1950s, some experts and moral authorities held a more liberal view of men and women who sought sexual pleasure outside of marriage, but even the most liberal voices rarely exonerated same-sex desire or relationships. A major exception to homosexuality's invisibility was the sensational reporting by the black newspaper and magazine editors, but these types of stories again left the impression that gay men were deviant, criminal, or crazy. By the mid-1960s, shocks of the urban crisis—northern segregation, deepening income inequality and unemployment, and recurrent race riots—caused a veritable avalanche of social science on ghettos, race problems, and a so-called culture of poverty. In turn, this scholarship introduced (often inadvertently) new ideas about the causes and consequences of homosexuality among black men.

Brag and Drag

Mobilization for World War II had transformed conceptions of not only masculinity but also sexuality across the nation. In this period, many black men signed on for active duty and presented themselves as a new model minority, expecting the rewards of full citizenship in return for proud service, and yet for some their induction into the armed services involved new classification procedures that scrutinized effeminacy in men, queried homosexual tendencies, and assigned racial meanings to sexual difference. As a result, some percentage of black men recognized previously unnamed desires as a homosexual condition that might be shared with large numbers of other men, whether or not they chose to hide their identities. Meanwhile, as a form of recreation, many troops put on musical shows that required female parts, usually played by men in female attire, including black men who later identified themselves as gay. Stateside after the war, black nightlife featured interracial dancing and spectacular cross-dressing or female impersonation balls, as well as bars and clubs that catered to a variety of homosexual tastes. As Allan Bérubé eloquently characterized the impact of mobilization, "The military, ironically, encouraged gay veterans to assume a stronger gay identity when it began to identify and manage so many people as homosexual persons rather than focus narrowly on the act of sodomy." After the war, historians such as Bérubé, John D'Emilio, and David Johnson documented how gay veterans struggled to make sense of their identity, protested non-honorable, blue discharges for homosexuality, and forged new sexual communities and networks in major U.S. cities.[2]

At the same time, African American protests against wartime discrimination, lobbying to desegregate the armed services, and postwar efforts to overturn legal segregation signaled the beginning of the modern civil rights revolution. In his study of the "unsettled meanings" of black citizenship in postwar black Chicago, Adam Green examines how an emergent middle class engaged in "cultural entrepreneurship" that undergirded its social position while fabricating a "collective racial imagination." Here Green maps shifts in the politics of respectability by examining middle-class navigation of urban pleasures, working-class consumption, and political mobilization, in particular documenting the extraordinary rise and impact of the Johnson Publishing Company empire that produced both *Jet* and *Ebony* magazines. According to Green, "Though *Ebony* did not seek to dispense entirely with respectability as a cornerstone of reputation, it is clear that the magazine was willing to play up controversy or even disrepute for public notice." In this new era of the commercialization of racial identification, the black magazines both addressed and constructed a black readership poised to join the postwar landscape of consumption and personal pleasure.[3]

Historians now locate the beginnings of a sexual revolution in the 1950s, when a new cultural liberalism extolled the pleasures of intercourse for both men and women, permitted more personal autonomy for youth, and promoted a growing sexual marketplace. But the anxieties of the Cold War produced the demonization of homosexual men, often depicted as a threat to national security and a danger to youthful morality; this new image of the homosexual menace was most often cast in whiteness.[4] A number of scholars have observed that African American working-class culture was more open to homosexuality and that the black urban press routinely ran stories with homosexual subject matter. Historians Thaddeus Russell and Greg Conerly track this continuing fascination with "drag balls" and queer happenings after the war, locating a significant archive of gender nonconformity and social tolerance.[5] What came to the surface in the sensational reporting and scandal columns was not necessarily a transparent reflection of actual gay identities and relationships that lay below; rather, they indicated how an individual could interpret same-sex desire, particularly how the shifting exposure of black gayness could reconfigure both public perceptions and personal identity itself.

In 1951 the Chicago-based Johnson Publishing Company converted its *Negro Digest* into *Jet* to meet popular demand for a "convenient-sized magazine that will summarize the week's biggest Negro news in a well-organized, easy-to-read format," debuting with a circulation of 100,000. At the time, an advertising journal noted that the fifteen-cent magazine was the company's fourth entry into black publications and that its premier photographic magazine, *Ebony*, had already achieved a circulation of 500,000. Shedding the old reticence of traditional black respectability, *Jet* routinely published stories on sexual infidelity, stag parties, and recent discoveries in the science of sexual behavior, with quizzes for readers to test their knowledge: "Did Masturbation Cause Insanity?" "Were Negro Women Less Affectionate?" "Are Men More Romantic Than Women?" "Sexiness Is New Trend."[6]

Challenging conventions may have entertained readers, but pushing the boundaries of respectability risked retribution. Into the 1950s, individual expression or even representations of sexual desire across the color line could spark controversy, and both black men and black women remained vulnerable to violent retaliation for miscegenation, not only in the South but all around the nation. A high mark of antimiscegenation sentiment was the tragic lynching of Emmett Till for allegedly whistling at a white woman. In the 1955 murder case, *Jet* not only published full-page photos of Till's corpse but also followed up on the faulty prosecution and ran stories of Till-like incidents, including the murder of an eleven-year-old boy in Mississippi, referred to as the "2nd Child Slain."[7] Despite the acceptance of postwar liberalism on both racial and sexual fronts, the news from the South was that integration was staunchly opposed, both legally and violently, and sexuality remained a highly visible medium through which white supremacists displayed their will and enforced the racial caste system.[8]

Flying in the face of this ever-present threat, *Jet* editors nonetheless ran stories of sex across the color line, covering celebrity weddings, reporting on interracial romance, and featuring photos of glamorous white brides on the arms of debonair black grooms. *Jet* also catered to readers' fascination with marriages gone wrong, controversial divorces, exotic infidelities, and even criminal accusations, all the more titillating when the domestic dispute crossed the color line.[9] Mixing crime and miscegenation, bylines reveled in the sordid: "Harlem Sex Party Raided" involving thousands of dollars and a "five-day long, whiskey-sex party of three escaped white convicts and three Negro women." Another reported that a young black maid and an older white man were charged with a "crime against nature" after "Charlotte, NC police caught them in an unnatural and compromising position in a parked car."[10] Representations of miscegenation often involved not only criminality but also prostitution, such as a Wichita sex lottery racket in which black laborers purchased tickets to win a sensational prize: "a weekend at a mountain resort with a white girl."[11] A "beauteous blonde ex-belly dancer, now a photographer's model, and her Negro lover" had their photos featured in a story about an alleged robbery, while another blurb described five "Negroes jailed for interracial sex orgies."[12]

Black readers' responses to such stories may be interpreted in a variety of ways—moral condemnation, personal shock, or a collective cheer—but there is little doubt that black attitudes toward miscegenation were complicated and in transition.[13] Postwar liberalism and an incipient mobilization for civil rights encouraged discussions about the acceptance of "mixed marriage," which was becoming a new touchstone for social tolerance, as evinced by *Jet*'s close coverage of changes in state marriage laws, stories of war brides and biracial offspring, and even personal testimonies about integration into mixed families.[14] Into the 1950s, prominent black congressman Rev. Adam Clayton Powell Jr. predicted that intermarriage would soon be "commonplace."[15]

Known in some circles as "Mr. Civil Rights," Powell campaigned for the extension of the Fair Employment Practices Committee, antilynching legislation, and the desegregation of public transit, as well as for the main tenets of new postwar sexual liberalism. Penning a 1951 essay, "Sex in the Church," he embraced the popular liberal idea that sexuality was crucial to a happy marriage and healthy personality, and yet in almost the same breath, Powell decried "homosexual tendencies." In contrast to "clean-living, normal individuals," he referred to the "boys with the swish and the girls with the swagger" and to the "biologically or psychologically inclined" homosexual, declaring that only vigilance and education could "decrease" homosexuality.[16]

Yet in the world of *Jet* magazine, stories of miscegenation and photos of scandalous couples represented alternative spaces turned upside down, where acts of transgression were not only possible but laudable. In the pool hall, barbershop, saloon, and other spaces of black masculine homosociability, *Jet* presented readers with revealing photos of light-skinned black women alongside stories of racial passing in which very light-skinned men and women crossed over into white spaces and intimate relationships.[17] Passing novels had proliferated in the 1920s and 1930s, and major films about passing appeared in the 1940s and 1950s, even as *Jet* ran reports that the practice of crossing over was fast becoming passé. Those who continued to cross over did so for economic reasons or to play a joke on unsuspecting whites, but the feeling was that racial pride and community outweighed the allure of this act of total assimilation. A number of scholars of this racial crossing, including Siobhan Somerville, Janet Gaines, and Scott Herring, have shown that the national obsession with miscegenation intersected with crossings of gender and homosexuality. One of the more famous stories to appear in the pages of black periodicals, with major photos, reported on Georgia Black, who was a "man who had passed for a woman for 30 years." *Ebony* recounted that he had decided to pass at the age of fifteen, while living on a farm in South Carolina.

Black ran away and became a house servant in a wealthy household that had a male "homosexual" entertainer; this man invited Black to "become his sweetheart" and dressed him in women's clothes and coached him on how to pass as a female. There was speculation about whether Black had deceived the husbands he had married, with some doubting the possibility of doing so. When *Ebony* interviewed him about a month before his death, he proclaimed, "I never done nuthin wrong in my life."[18]

Miscegenation, racial passing, and female impersonation became interconnected transgressions that mimicked one another. *Jet* frequently reported on the popular pastime of men imitating female celebrities such as Josephine Baker, Mae West, and Lena Horne in clubs and ballrooms, and these affairs were racially mixed as well; indeed, it was noted that "white impersonators equaled the Negro ones."[19] *Jet* utilized the term "gay" to refer to a "gayest" Halloween Ball at a club in a hotel that reportedly involved more than two thousand masqueraders and spectators and some "50 Impersonators"; a later headline reported that "Gay Affair Names 'Queen'" in a drag show at Finnies Club at Chicago's Pershing Hotel. In an annual event in New York City, the performers did "such an excellent job of mimicking women that sometimes even the judges are confused."[20] Several years after the story on the transgender life of Georgia Black, another headline declared that "1 in 1,000 Born without True Sex," referring to a physician's report on examinations of apparently ambiguous genitals, what might be classified today as intersex ("150,000 Americans started life with doubt or error over their true sex"). Alongside stories of female impersonation were actual sex changes, introducing readers to the curiosity, for example, of a male dancer being admitted into the Johns Hopkins Hospital for gender reassignment surgery followed by news of her marriage to a male musician.[21]

Catering to its readership's taste for transgression—for rebelling against the constraints of both white repression and black respectability—*Jet* exposed the queerness of the black underworld to an ever-expanding media-hungry audience. Alongside a scandalous marriage uncovered by a police raid, a *Jet* reader might learn of a Toledo man convicted for appearing in public "dressed as a woman," donning ballet slippers and a "woman's blouse and falsies." Story after story reported on the "impersonator," as in the case of "two female impersonators and their boy friends, one of whom is a prize-fighter, [who] were arrested when the would-be girls attracted attention in the ladies powder room of a Brooklyn, N.Y., theater." Once their wigs "slipped," the two boyfriends "were also arrested on an impersonation, sodomy and vagrancy charge." Another promised a report on "The Truth about Female

Jet magazine, November 8, 1951. Started in the early 1950s, *Jet* appealed to African American readers with celebrity gossip, civil rights news, and titillating anecdotes. For many years, *Jet* published numerous stories having to do with sexual behavior and attitudes, including many pieces on black homosexuals. (Courtesy of *Jet* Archive).

Impersonation" who appeared in clubs or venues in nearly every "U.S. Negro community," where "swishing, clean-shaven men dress in women's clothes and entertain cash customers." "Is society now more tolerant of the deviant male and does this encourage men to wear women's clothes?" asked the magazine. Like similar features, this piece linked cross-dressing with the "obscure causes of homosexuality," and again, these oscillated between being "born" with a perversion and developing it as a result of family problems, and in the pages of *Jet* more and more experts distinguished between "transsexuals" and "transvestites" and the more commonly heard terms "drags" and "gays."[22]

Among the representations of homosexuality increasingly available to readers were the cases of black men who did not primarily signify their gayness through female impersonation and cross-dressing. In one item, readers were exposed to scandalous interracial sex parties that were supposedly "staged by a high official of the Czech Embassy in Washington," where the undercover agent discovered that the men "embraced each other, kissed each other, and helped each other take off their coats," and some were flirting and "becoming tender to each other." In another case, a public school teacher and an "an interracial group of eight men" were found guilty of dancing and kissing each other during a New Year's Eve party. The crime blotter doubly served as an exposure of the culture of homosexuality, in one case, for example, revealing the existence of enduring relationships in which "a white man and a Negro . . . admitted living together as 'intimate friends' for seven years." In another, a twenty-four-year-old Cleveland man told police that he served as the male lover of a homosexual in exchange for food and lodging but was charged with causing his death with his bare fists during a "'male lovers' quarrel."[23]

In the 1950s, two major sexual scandals involving celebrities—Prophet Jones and Gladys Bentley—splashed black queerness across the front pages of black popular culture. Jones had built and led Detroit's Church of the Universal Triumph but came under intense public scrutiny amid allegations of the sexual corruption of several young men in his residence. Born in Birmingham, Alabama, and reared in a Pentecostal sect, Jones migrated to Detroit (with a private male secretary) and began broadcasting over Canadian radio stations. His steady rise to fame was not without skeptics who questioned his flamboyant style and lavish taste, but at his peak he reportedly attracted some six million followers and earned millions of dollars. Stories of his activities often mentioned his luxurious lifestyle, serving as a model of success for aspirants to social mobility as well as for his religious devotees. Readers may have found pleasure as well as awe in the news that Jones had commissioned a "$1000 diamond-studded, 14-carat solid pen and pencil set" that featured clips with "13 blue-white diamonds" and a personal inscription dedicated to "His Holiness." They followed the purchase and construction of homes and a new church, reveling in the details of its two-thousand-seat capacity, $17,000 cooling plant, and $35,000 organ, plus stores as well as office space. Despite his extravagance, the reports on Prophet Jones indicated that he advocated abstention and made the notable claim, "The Prophet remains a celibate."[24]

Jones remained newsworthy into the 1950s, with reports on his views of foreign policy and other issues and updates on his extravagant lifestyle—the "bejeweled cult leader" entertaining in the "Sky Room of his 54-room French castle." At one point he became the target of angry protests for publicly using a racial epithet, which he explained away by claiming that he heard the "voice of a woman" instruct him to utter the word. Prophet Jones frequently spoke from the mantle of respectability, calling for marital fidelity and advising his female followers to rid themselves of common-law husbands and to refuse common-law marriages and instead to obtain an official marriage license.[25]

Then in 1956, Jones's remarkable fame erupted overnight into explosive controversy when police descended on his mansion to investigate "morals charges." As news spread of the arrest and police "exposed" what the *Jet* headline referred to as a "'secret' past," it was disclosed that "all hell had broken loose" after authorities announced charges of gross indecency that carried a penalty and lengthy imprisonment. In lurid detail, describing a "pajama-clad Prophet at the time" and "two teen-age boys" who apparently visited him with "cab fare paid and soft drinks," *Jet* also ran the story that police had infiltrated the mansion using an agent, reportedly a young, attractive officer trained in undercover surveillance. When the erstwhile spy pretended to injure his arm to make a hasty exit, he reported on Jones's odd rituals, such as tying ribbons around him: "But, police said, the Prophet had exercised even stranger methods, like asking the handsome Henry to expose considerably more than his sore arm, embracing him warmly and making certain strongly-suggestive remarks." Suddenly, the hugely successful religious figure became a costumed queer—the "dapper, diamond clad minister who wears a $13,000 white mink coat" had a sordid past that he "wished" had never been "revealed." Once living vicariously off his fortune, *Jet* readers now found him languishing in a cellblock. Long gone were the days when the "prophet made merry in fancy dress."[26]

But after a six-day trial, Jones was acquitted to cheering crowds. As one reads through the dozens of stories and reports in black print and periodicals, what is striking is the sheer number of stories of homosexuality that present it not only as freakish or pathological but also, again, as constituting rebellious transgression. Prophet Jones emerged triumphant from the controversy, bragging that "I have won my fight with the devil. Now I am going to launch a nation-wide crusade to save souls." What was presented as criminal might be read as getting over, and what was presented as immoral might be admired as refusing deference.[27]

The second major scandal involved Gladys Bentley, the popular blues singer and entertainer made famous by the Harlem Renaissance who had established a reputation as a so-called bull dagger (defined as a masculine woman who desired other women). Bentley returned to the headlines in the 1950s when she entered into hormone therapy to correct her lesbian condition. By now, her harrowing story served to attest to the wonders of modern medicine while repudiating her past queerness as immoral and unhealthy. As the reports phrased her condition, she once "inhabited that half-shadow no-man's land which exists between the boundaries of the two sexes," but she now sought medical treatment and submitted to an examination that revealed her to be "bisexual," signified by ambiguous genitalia. Bentley presented herself as a "normal female" who was sexually "deformed."

Bentley's past homosexuality was visible to the public through her performance as a male "impersonator," but in the 1950s advanced medicine promised to cure her of a deviant past of black-white vice and singing the "bull-dagger blues." Stories about Bentley's recovery illustrated the overlap of inversion, transvestitism, and hermaphroditism with lesbianism, as well as the pressures of a normative respectability to straighten up. Bentley was "thrilled at her change from 'third' sex to true female," describing her unhappy past as a "personal hell." Like the passing subject or the tragic mulatto, Bentley had piqued public curiosity because her identity remained both ambiguous and plastic, neither clearly male nor female, neither straight nor gay. But Bentley found resolution of her sexual identity crisis by correcting her hormone imbalance and settling down with a partner of the opposite sex. Bentley's search for a cure served to reaffirm Powell's condemnation of homosexuality in black circles. Yet the larger impact of sexual science was to shift discussion of the homosexual beyond stories of lewdness or pathology and to stimulate public conversations about the normality of sexual desire itself.[28]

For both white and black America, the historic turning point was the publication of the findings of Alfred Kinsey, the controversial sex researcher who, with his colleagues, compiled hundreds of profiles and surveys of sex attitudes and practices and presented them in *Sexual Behavior in the Human Male* (1948) and *Sexual Behavior in the Human Female* (1953). Early on,

Jet magazine pointed out that Kinsey had not included African American women in the first rounds of research, reportedly because "not enough middle class colored women were willing to be interviewed," although studies of Kinsey suggest that he had not planned to study African American subjects until after the first volumes were published.[29] But the black press nonetheless ran many stories on Kinsey and generalized from his survey data to the case of black female sexuality. Not only did the press note that the eight-hundred-page report endowed females with a capacious sexual drive and desire for genital orgasm, but *Jet* also stated that "homosexual contacts are highly effective in bringing the female to orgasm."[30]

Jet articles pointed out that Kinsey's research disputed the notion that most "sexual outlets" were not "so-called normal," reminding readers of the absurdity that a "man who considers oral stimulation a routine part of sexual intercourse with his wife can be jailed for 60 years in North Carolina." In the same vein, one writer questioned the "grave disfavor" of the homosexual. The scientific point was that the vast majority of men and women practiced these supposedly immoral, and illegal, sexual acts—some five million acts of homosexuality and even higher numbers of fornication. An African American psychiatrist invoked the older stereotype of "obviously feminine men who flaunt their lack of masculinity by dressing and conducting themselves as women" but also pointed to other apparently normal-appearing men and women beyond the "obvious" types who "make up a small part of the homosexual population."[31] *Jet* later covered additional, smaller sexology studies that specifically included African American women, reporting that one scientist found minimal differences between the races and noting that "nearly one-fifth of all women (about 19 percent) have homosexual contacts at some time in their lives."[32]

In 1948 the Howard University newspaper, the *Hill Top*, reported that Alfred Kinsey had given a lecture on his male sex research that emphasized the "responsiveness" of men, disclosing that "there are exceedingly few males who live happily or efficiently without a regular sexual outlet," and then appealed to those in the audience to volunteer their case histories. From 1938 to 1963, Kinsey and his research team collected hundreds of sexual interviews through the Institute for Sex Research, and some of their later data (not included in the published volumes) presented comparisons between white and black respondents. On questions of approval or disapproval of homosexuality, somewhat less than half of white and black respondents admitted that they disapproved. Black respondents were more likely to have received "homosexual approaches" (of the respondents who listed "often," 29.5 percent were white versus 56.3 percent black). White and black men reported about the same "amount of homosexual experience," with 60 percent having none and 12 percent reporting rare, 6–7 percent citing incidental, and 9 percent claiming extensive experience, and a majority of the surveys suggested parallel patterns of homosexual behavior. But the racial configuration of relationships varied significantly. Less than 30 percent of black homosexuals reported having no white sexual partners, but more than 60 percent of white men reported having no black partners. Similarly, although one quarter of black homosexuals had only white partners, none of the white homosexuals reported exclusively interracial sexual relations. Finally, while both groups preferred masculine partners, a higher percentage of black homosexuals reported a preference for "feminine only" (25 percent nonwhite compared to 7 percent white). Perhaps this reflects the persistence of the female impersonator tradition in which straight audiences (and straight-acting black gay men) admired gay men who mixed and crossed gender lines. In either case, the data suggest a pattern of mixture in which black men who chose to pursue homosexual contacts routinely found white partners in racially mixed spaces.[33]

In postwar America, the Kinsey studies and the wider reporting on a sexual revolution underway in the 1950s challenged male and female sexual norms. Just as sexology demonstrated to an expanding reading public that sexual activity that many believed to be rare or deviant—from female masturbation to prostitution to homosexuality—was in fact not only prevalent but natural, scholars have also argued that "one of the underappreciated contributions of the Kinsey reports . . . was that it aroused suspicion within the mental health profession . . . [about] the diagnosis of homosexuality as abnormal and pathological." Even as conservative politicians sought to repress the volume, in many cases censorship stimulated defenses not only of academic freedom and research but also of a broad array of sexual practices documented in the studies. Sometimes cautiously and at other times contradicting itself, *Jet* magazine rallied around sexual liberation and along the way allowed readers to have a good long look at black homosexuality in all its guises.[34]

The largest magazine for white readers comparable to *Jet* was the *Coronet*, reaching more than two million households weekly. Billing itself as family-oriented with a combination of travel, health, home, and financial news, it served an aspirational or upwardly mobile white readership. Like *Jet*, the *Coronet* too ran a number of stories on sexology and Kinsey, but the tone of its reporting expressed far more caution and anxiety ("What Have 'Sex Experts' Done to Children?"), seeking to mediate news of sexual normalcy and rechannel female expectations back into the sexual double standard of passivity. Love and marriage, rather than desire and satisfaction, were the recommended objectives. One young woman wrote of searching through sexual advice and confessions magazines, "even medical texts," to decide if she was a nymphomaniac while complaining that she was old enough to learn about "hushed-up subjects such as masturbation, homosexuality, abortion, and sex crimes." "Despite the avalanche of propaganda," one article warned, "physical love is only a part of her life," and so while recognizing sexually liberated females, the proper direction for such desire remained marriage. While women had "great power over men," the *Coronet* asked more for compassion than for passion, advising wives to support their husbands by never "making fun" of their physique or sexual abilities. While *Jet* more or less reported the facts of lesbian desire, the rare *Coronet* item identified lesbianism with the female prisoner, from "murderesses to homosexuals, prostitutes, vagrants, narcotic addicts, alcoholics." Finally, in the sharpest departure from *Jet*, *Coronet* rarely mentioned homosexuality, and when it did so, it was in a purely clinical fashion in one or two sexual advice forums. In one question-and-answer feature, for example, it was observed that homosexuality could appear at an early age, requiring medical treatment. "A happily married mother and father are the best safeguards against homosexuality," for "if the son can emulate a strong, virile father who shows real affection, there is little likelihood that the son will become effeminate."[35]

That is not to suggest that black editors and experts were less concerned about the welfare of families and the causes of their possible dysfunction. A prescient 1954 article in the black newspaper *Our World* reported on a new concern with homosexuality, especially urgent given the finding by sexologists that "six out of ten of the pre-adolescent boys groups have engaged in some form of homosexuality; four percent of all males have been exclusively homosexual their entire lives and one percent of the men examined for the armed services." Here a range of symptoms and signifiers became key to understanding the homosexual (now much more clearly distinguished from "female impersonators" at a "drag ball"), beginning with the boy's relationship to his mother, which, if it became overdependent, might cause sexual deviance. If the father was overpowering or weak and ineffectual, the report warned of an increased potential for homosexual deviation in the son.[36]

Into the next decade, increasing concerns over the state of the black family would become evident in social science research as well as consume the media, and as a result the liberalizing effects of sexology that encouraged social tolerance for the innate homosexual were met with countervailing anxieties about the absence of black fathers and its effects on their sons.

Queering the Moynihan Report

Perhaps no other popular discussion of the modern family caused more controversy than the so-called Moynihan Report. Leaked to the press in 1965, Daniel Patrick Moynihan's "The Negro Family: A Case for National Action" led to a broad public debate on the nature of African American culture and community, the problems of race and racism, and the politics of masculinity. The author, a young Irish, Tufts-educated liberal recruited to the New Frontier of President John F. Kennedy, stayed on under President Lyndon Johnson to serve as an assistant secretary in the Department of Labor. In that capacity, Moynihan studied and researched social policy and planning, and by 1964 he worked on a special project about the condition of blacks in society for a major conference on civil rights at the White House. The literature on poverty and black urban problems had increased significantly in the postwar period, and Moynihan and his research assistants read widely, taking notes, making reports, and meeting to discuss their findings.[37]

Moynihan's sense that black men were routinely emasculated by a racist society was pervasive in the report: "It may be speculated that it was the Negro male who was most humiliated"; additionally, "the male was more likely to use public facilities, which rapidly became segregated once the process began, and just as important, segregation, and the submissiveness it exacts, is surely more destructive to the male personality than the female personality." In a famous phrasing, Moynihan argued that "the very essence of the male animal, from the bantam rooster to the four-star general, is to strut. Indeed in 19th century America, a particular type of exaggerated male boastfulness became almost a national style. Not so for the Negro male. The 'sassy nigger' was lynched."[38]

In discussing the effects of repression and pathology, Moynihan chose not to use the term "homosexual," for any number of reasons, but the implications of his analysis seem quite clear: diminished manhood due to the dominating nature of white supremacy, along with the dominance of black women within the family, damaged the ego of the black man in ways that produced passivity, and sometimes this caused black men to become homosexual. And a number of readers drew the same conclusion. In 1966, *Ebony* magazine ran a story on the rise of the sexual revolution that featured a white psychiatrist (with a Freudian emphasis) practicing in Chicago, Kermit Mehlinger. He argued that the civil rights movement enhanced the self-esteem of women and unlocked their erotic feelings, qualifying this analysis with the caveat that "the civil rights revolution is more of a black revolution, [but] the sexual revolution tends to be more of a white revolution." Despite the revolutions, however, there was still a tangle of pathology: "Both girls and boys brought up in the matriarchal family climate find it difficult to assume a mature masculine or feminine identification. In many instances the son will abandon any attempt to free himself from the tyrannical rule of the mother. He will simply identify with her, give up the battle, and resolve his need to be loved by becoming a homosexual." Mehlinger went on to suggest that the son's anxiety about the matriarch instilled in him a "dread fear of all women so that he has become psychologically castrated and is unable to have genuine sexual feeling towards other women," while the black woman became a "completely independent, competitive, aggressive female."[39]

Moynihan constructed an image of the black male as essentially adolescent rather than adult, as a hustler rather than a laborer or professional, and as delinquent rather than an adjusted youth—the sort of contradistinctions observed in social science and reported on in the pages of *Jet*. In *The Mark of Oppression: A Psychosocial Study of the American Negro*, Abram Kardiner and Lionel Ovesey reported that a common response to the racial system, and to the passivity demanded by the observance of caste, was to injure the "self-esteem system"; in turn, "homosexuality is the major reflection of a failure to achieve status." In a formulation that clearly anticipated, and likely informed, Moynihan, Kardiner and Ovesey suggested that "the economic independence of the female plays havoc with conventional male-female roles, and this in turn influences the potency of the males." Black men repressed or managed their potency and aggressiveness to cope with white domination, resulting in a conflicted passivity. The authors argued that studying this "constellation would be very valuable to follow through in Negro homosexuals."[40] Moynihan also consulted Thomas Pettigrew, a Harvard social scientist, who had argued that prejudice and ghettos were responsible for mental problems, which in turn led to sexual dysfunction. According to Moynihan's notes on Pettigrew's research, "The effects of father absent families are to be seen in homocide [*sic*], schizophrenia, and homosexuality."[41]

After the report leaked, article after article rehearsed Moynihan's formulations, circulating the main concepts of matriarchy, emasculation, and pathology.[42] Into the 1970s, the controversy relocated from the front pages of the press to the sphere of academic debate, but the thesis that black families were matriarchal and therefore dysfunctional became something of a strawman argument. To demolish the pathology thesis, academic feminists combined the criticism that Moynihan imposed the values of the white middle class on the family life of others with the argument, associated with the anthropologist

Daniel Patrick Moynihan, 1969. Daniel Patrick Moynihan served as an assistant secretary in the Department of Labor in the mid-1960s but faced criticism when his report on the state of the African American family was leaked to the press. Describing the family as a "tangle of pathology," Moynihan was forced to resign amidst a storm of controversy. (Courtesy of the Library of Congress, Prints and Photographs Division).

Carol Stack, that single black mothers sustained complex networks of adaptive family structures that compensated for absent husbands. As Stack put it, "The underlying assumptions . . . seem to imply that female-headed households and illegitimacy are symptomatic of broken homes and family disorganization. These studies failed to account for the great variety of domestic strategies in urban black communities." Yet her classic book, *All Our Kin*, has no entries for either homosexuality or masculinity in the index and makes no significant mention of the emasculation thesis. In the 1980s, a new generation of writers had complicated and refined the feminist critique of Moynihan, but often without addressing the constructions of black manhood that were at the center of the report.[43]

Rather, it was black power scholars who focused on the role of black men in the family and on their relation to society at large. The most significant new voice was that of the sociologist Robert Staples, who published voluminously on the black family, sex and gender roles, and sexuality to advance social uplift and mount a public defense against the likes of Moynihan.[44] After earning his doctorate, he served as director of research for the St. Paul Urban League in

1967 and later sought teaching positions to further his research on the black family. Staples was a prolific author and active editor, publishing numerous articles and anthologies. He was also one of a handful of black social scientists to take on the subject of sexuality, publishing pieces in *Sexology*, *Sexual Behavior*, and the *Journal of Sex Research*, including "Sex Life of Middle Class Negroes" and "The Mystique of Black Sexuality."[45]

Staples denied the report's association between fatherless families and sexual deviance. In a 1970 article, "The Myth of Black Matriarchy," he argued that the black woman "is economically exploited because she is both female and black and to label her a matriarch is a classical example of what Malcolm X called making the victim the criminal." But he also sought to refute the implication that black men had ever exhibited homosexual tendencies and addressed the "various sociological and psychological studies which purport to show how black males are de-masculinized, in fact may be latent homosexuals," and immediately threw up his defenses, characterizing such a diagnosis as "something that falsely indicted him for his lack of manhood." At another point, in a 1971 anthology on the black family, he admitted that "many black males lack a consistently present male figure with whom to identify and from whom to learn essential components for a male role" and that therefore "one conclusion that ensues from this analysis is that many black males are latent homosexuals."[46]

By the 1970s, the implications of the matriarchal structure that Moynihan had drawn attention to was fast becoming a recognized cause of homosexuality. In response, much of the anti-Moynihan writing, either of the nationalist or feminist variety, converged into a pro-family discourse that valorized strong black mothers and called for a remedy of traditional male role models. After more than a decade of fending off the implications of Moynihan, Staples had arrived at an explanation of black sexual development: "They [males], as well as females, are very early socialized into heterosexual relations by their culture and extended family system. A sexual orientation is well inculcated long before they become aware of the constraints on their other expressions of masculinity."[47]

In the 1950s, the publication of the Kinsey reports, despite considerable controversy, had served to legitimate heterosexual pleasure and to undermine the sexual double standard in which women were expected to remain chaste and men to seek experience. As sexual drives were located in the physiology of sexed bodies and treated as more or less equally potent in men and women, a gradual normalization gained ground, and black commentary in magazines such as *Jet* tended to welcome this liberalism. But by the mid-1960s, *Jet* ran noticeably fewer stories dealing with queer themes, such as female impersonation and sexology, than it had in its first years. Every so often short pieces would appear, such as a four-line item informing readers that some Illinois officials were "concerned over too much publicity about the state's queer sex laws," given that "homosexuality, in private, is perfectly legal." Another story noted that a Pittsburgh man, and father of two, was granted permission to use a female name while undergoing "'sex reassignment'" through surgery and hormones.[48] *Jet* also continued to report breaking news on the downfall of miscegenation laws, covering state reforms as well as Supreme Court decisions overturning miscegenation statutes. In the span of fifteen years, black readers witnessed a remarkable revolution in racial and sexual attitudes, from the terror of Emmett Till to the glamour of Sidney Poitier, the popular star who played the almost too respectable black suitor of a wealthy white daughter in the breakthrough 1967 film about interracial marriage, *Guess Who's Coming to Dinner?*[49]

Yet this was less the case for homosexual pleasure, and even in *Jet* magazine, the number of articles dealing with homosexuality precipitously declined. Perhaps the most important reason for the fewer stories publicizing the queer mix of miscegenation, scandal, and homosexuality had to do with history itself. By the 1960s, black politics was a pervasive concern, civil rights demonstrations dominated the news, and stories on progress and setbacks in race relations took up more and more space. From the rise of Martin Luther King to his assassination (an entire issue of *Jet* was dedicated to the aftermath), from the unfolding of southern demonstrations and white resistance to the election of black officials and the appointment of blacks to major government positions, the ongoing black political conflicts and racial crises dominated the news, shifting the tenor of *Jet* away from its pulp origins of pinup girls, sex advice, and scandal sheets. It was not therefore that *Jet* necessarily sought to clean up its image so much as it covered closely the momentous politics of the times.[50]

By the 1970s, in tandem with the sweeping changes in sexual mores transforming the mainstream, the influential black psychiatrist Alvin Poussaint championed a healthy black sexuality to be celebrated with pride, ushering in what might be termed a black sexual revolution.[51] A professor in the Medical School at Harvard University, Poussaint published frequently on topics in African American life and became a public intellectual in the 1980s when he served as a script consultant for Bill Cosby's television production *A Different World* (a program that sought to portray respectable, normal, and middle-class family life). As an expert on the family, he authored long features for

By the 1970s, *Ebony* magazine headlined stories on the sexual revolution in marital mores and swinging singles. Dr. Alvin Poussaint, a professor of psychiatry at Harvard, contributed a series of articles that reported on the revolution's impact on black sexual attitudes, but he classified homosexuality as a form of sexual dysfunction or a psychological disorder. (Courtesy *Ebony* Archive).

Ebony magazine, several of which weighed in on the merits of the sexual revolution and the "more permissive attitude toward casual companionship." "Today, the long tradition of repressed sexual fantasy is surfacing and some whites are indulging in sexual overkill, wallowing in an orgy of smut, pornography, and obscenity," wrote Poussaint. Therefore, because the sexual revolution had encouraged the expression of erotic behavior, black culture no longer needed to observe a strict public code of sexual respectability to counter the stereotypes of excess and promiscuity because eroticism was no longer stigmatized.[52]

Poussaint continued in the tradition of examining various sexual pathologies and attributed deviant patterns, including illegitimate births, to the historical tragedy of enslavement and the sexual violence of the Jim Crow South. Yet unlike either Moynihan or Staples, he reclaimed the African diaspora as a near-utopian moment of natural, freer sexuality—"from Africa blacks brought with them an un-perverted attitude toward sex and procreation."[53] Undoubtedly, this "un-perverted" diaspora was always already straight.

Poussaint questioned the validity of books claiming to document a greater incidence of homosexuality among black men, but he did note that female-headed households "castrate black men who, perceiving the more sheltered and favored position of the black woman in our society, identify with her."[54] In the context not only of civil rights respectability but also of attacks on community and masculinity, a new generation of experts rose to defend the integrity of the black family and in the process steadfastly disavowed black homosexuality. From the fascinating underside portrayed by *Jet* magazine to the glare of controversy sparked by white social science, the figure of the black gay man remained in the shadows of stigma and pathology—unrespectable or unmentionable.

Chapter Three

Payne and Pulp

In a 1969 study of black inpatients at a Manhattan mental hospital, *Black Suicide*, the psychiatrist Herbert Hendin set out to examine the causes of increased rates of suicide among African Americans and unexpectedly encountered several homosexuals in his small cohort of human subjects. Apparently unprepared to address the issue from a scientific perspective, Hendin too referenced a discussion of James Baldwin's *Another Country*, observing that Baldwin usefully explored both "the racial significance of suicide and male homosexuality . . . and the importance of the white male to the black homosexual." For his study, Hendin interviewed a range of homosexual patients, some of whom were violent and others who were survivors of physical abuse. He observed that the desire to assimilate to whiteness affected the expression of homosexuality, connecting light-skinned black men with a propensity to enact the role of the homosexual passive. In turn, black desire for white men signified self-hate or a "racial death-wish," a theory that received national exposure after the publication of the controversial 1968 prison memoir *Soul on Ice* (discussed in chapter 4).[1] The key to the black homosexual, Hendin argued, was the damaged family that served to "handicap the male and cause him to hate his race, his sex, and himself." Echoing Daniel Patrick Moynihan, he concluded that fathers abandoned the family, leaving overburdened mothers whose sons reported them to be "cold, severe, and rejecting." They therefore resented their matriarchal families, the "excessive control" of the mother, "making them fear women and turning them into homosexuals."[2]

At the same time that mainstream social science, sexology, and popular cultures normalized a variety of sexual behaviors, many African American writers and academics disavowed or marginalized the subject of homosexuality. Thus, in the 1960s the more positive imagery of black homosexuality issued from highbrow avant-garde film and lowbrow pulp fiction aimed at predominantly white audiences but accessible to black gay men. In both cases, despite the increased visibility and potential for recognition, the sense of objectification persisted in these stigmatized representations.[3]

Hustling the Gaze

The 1967 independent documentary *Portrait of Jason*, directed by the avant-garde filmmaker Shirley Clarke, surprisingly attracted national attention, given that its subject was a gay black hustler. At the time that Clarke had been looking for a new project, NBC television studios had donated two-and-a-half-hour rolls of film stock to her, and suddenly she had to come up with cast and crew before it expired. She conferred with her partner, Carl Lee, an African American actor, and happened to meet the film's protagonist, Jason Holliday, on the street, according to her daughter's recollection. It was Lee who had introduced Clarke to Holliday years before and he was reportedly "madly in love with Carl, and hanging around with Carl," and also looking to launch his career as an entertainer. They staged the film in Shirley Clarke's Chelsea Hotel penthouse, and the shooting lasted just twelve hours, from 9:00 P.M. to 9:00 the following morning. "Just imagine," Clarke told an interviewer, "what might happen if someone was given his head and allowed to let go many consecutive hours. I was curious, and Wow, did I find out."[4]

Filming under bright set lights, the camera crew, Clarke, and Lee surrounded the performer at close range. The opening scene presents a formal setting of respectability, signified by an armchair, table, and lamp, with Holliday, clad in a blazer, holding a newspaper, speaking in a calm rhythm, and chuckling to himself after disclosing to the camera that he changed his name. "Jason Holliday was created in San Francisco," he announces solemnly into the camera. "If the name makes you feel well, then take the name." From another angle, Jason's name change, from Aaron Payne to Jason Holliday, becomes an affirmation of his agency, his intention to enact a life of self-possession and pleasure. *Portrait of Jason* presents the life of a black queer man in the 1960s—his gestures and speech; fashion and styling; dependencies and desires; adventures and mishaps.

The postwar revolution in sexual mores and in northern race relations had brought Aaron Payne from Trenton to the Chelsea neighborhood in Manhattan and from abused boy to cutting-edge performer who dreamed of becoming a star with his own nightclub act. It was the sixties, on the cusp of black and gay liberation, and Aaron Payne/Jason Holliday could be anything he desired to become. So could Shirley Clarke—modern dancer, avant-garde

SHIRLEY CLARKE'S
lecture
and
film presentation

MONDAY, JANUARY 20
8:00 P.M.
UNIVERSITY AUDITORIUM
featuring

JASON HOLLIDAY
in
Portrait of Jason

Jason Holliday, 1967. Jason Holliday was featured in a controversial documentary, *Portrait of Jason*, that attracted considerable attention in the press as well as many colorful reviews. Presenting the hustler, drug addict, and mental patient, Holliday played to popular stereotypes of the black homosexual. (Courtesy of Wisconsin Center for Film and Theater Research).

director, and feminist icon. In the film, Clarke asks Jason, "What do you do for a living?" Jason replies that he hustles—that he is a "stone cold whore"— and bursts into laughter. "I have more than one hustle, anything to keep from punching the clock from nine to five," he explains. In arts films of the time, Andy Warhol's *Hustler* had compared sexual hustling with the production and sale of art, and here Jason's artistic performance extends the black hustle.[5]

In the next scenes, Holliday displays his acting and comedic skills, rehearsing his deviance for the crew and camera. The oversized round black glasses are taken off when he imitates Mae West, and soon he tells his story of an arrest for solicitation as he walked on Sixth Avenue along Fifty-Second Street, spying "one of you Ivy League boys in a blazer," dressed like the psychiatrist who treats him. Jason explains that, well, you never can know, and the next moment the man showed him his badge and arrested him. Jason recollects how, once in jail, he began to scream and then broke his glasses against the bars of the cell and used a shard of glass to cut his wrist. Preferring commitment to incarceration, he thereby managed to get himself transported to Bellevue Hospital Center. Clarke's unconventional editing techniques interchange stark black-and-white scenes with slow fading in and out, with the blurring creating a black/white face long enough to create a kind of Sambo image, with the sparkle of the glasses a whiteness, the mouth and eyes black, the remainder blurred white.

"I'm an experimental queen—something's burning," announces Jason, and then he recalls a moment both gay and tragic: "I was in a club, and thought that something was burning, something was burning, and it was me." Jason not only performs a subcultural repertoire (of gestures, anecdotes, impressions, drag) but also reads as a black queer archive. In evidence are iterations of *Jet*'s transgressive race-mixer and gender-bender gay men, replete with police arrest blotters and drag balls. When Jason proceeds to narrate his story of serving as a houseboy for a wealthy woman in Nob Hill in San Francisco, he recounts a sense of degradation—his "bowing and scraping." Asked to elaborate further, he replies, in one of about a dozen iterations of the phrase, "I'll never tell." From offscreen, Carl asks Jason to tell them his prison story. "I never told you about the time I spent at Rikers Island, with a group of prisoners of drag queens?" Uncontrollably laughing, Jason then asks rhetorically, "Why do you girls always do this? I'll never tell. Why do you snap? Why do you pop your fingers like this?" And Jason enacts the gesture several times, dramatically raising his left hand over his head, snapping his fingers. "Why do you snap? This is Jason's story, entitled 'I'll Never Tell: The Secret of His Deviance.' Me, I guess I'm a male bitch, in addition to being a promiscuous gay man. Would you get me a drink please?"

Jason's performances of the black gay man—the jolting switch from easy-chair respectability to tearful inebriation, his voice scaling from the pathos of self-revelation to screeching drag queen—are likely intended to demonstrate a kind of virtuosity. Yet Clarke's investment in untangling his personality works at cross-purposes with his agency. At one point, she has instructed Holliday to recline on the floor, propped up on a low-slung chair, in front of a fireplace. Following so many Scotches, Jason lights and consumes a marijuana cigarette. Stretched now on the floor, he rehearses a graphic conversation between himself and psychiatrists about the size of his penis. Somewhere in the space between an actor and a stripper, Jason skirts to the edge of profanity. In the final scene, Carl entreats Jason to masturbate and have an orgasm on-screen, eliciting a round of laughter and disbelief from Jason. In a sense, such a scene—after so many coerced revelations of his sexual past and criminal intimacy—would have been anticlimactic.

Even in a production billed as cinema verité in which the spectator is presented with a kind of improvisational performance, the director exerted her influence over every scene, gesture, and affect. Numbers of reels of outtakes are preserved at the Wisconsin Historical Society in the Clarke Papers, representing an archive of repression—editorial evidence of what Jason was not permitted to say to the audience. The prospect for self-expression—for a black gay man giving an account of himself—remained tightly constrained throughout the 1960s, in almost inverse relationship to the growing assertiveness of straight black masculinity and eroticism. If under the regime of black civility, James Baldwin and Bayard Rustin were shunted offstage, despite their masculine public image, the new investment in reconstructing black masculinity triggered by both social science and social movements powerfully aligned homosexuality with something outside of authentic blackness and manhood.

The archive documenting the life of Jason Holliday is contained within Clarke's own personal papers. Even these few extant documents have a highly mediated quality—his autobiography dictated to Clarke and recorded on her Hotel Chelsea stationery, suggesting that he came up to her room to draft it. He claimed to have been born in 1934, but researchers later discovered in archival records it was 1924. He was reared in Trenton, New Jersey, by his mother, who was from Newark, and an apparently abusive father. He then spent some time explaining that his aspirations to be an entertainer dated back to when he was five, when he earned spending money as an "errand boy for prostitutes and pimps." At a young age he was on a radio show from North Philly and on two soap operas, and when he was eleven he sang and danced outside of bars and gin mills, earning enough to help support his family. He very much disliked New Jersey—one of the worst states in America, he wrote, "hate, hate, hate." But he stayed on and enrolled in a business college, then soon dropped out and left for New York City. "In less than three weeks, I became a Broadway Gypsy," he wrote, and he later appeared in productions of *Carmen Jones*, *Finnegan's Rainbow*, and *Green Pastures*. He also claimed to have joined the dance troupe of Katherine Dunham. Characterizing himself as a "chorus boy in all the B'way and Harlem nite spots," he claimed to have worked as a houseboy in between shows. In these years, he lived at the Salle de Champagne and "made more money, turned more tricks." Going out and taking drugs, Payne recalled that he had "such a Ball," and then he moved to Washington, D.C., and by his recollection virtually stormed the Howard Theatre, the Old Rose Social Club, and the Corvins, shocking the "jive spooks at Howard U": "I recked [*sic*] them too, you better believe it." Next Payne moved to Boston and worked as an emcee at the famous Hi-Hat, performing with musical celebrities such as Carmen McRae, Miles Davis, Max Roach, and Dizzy Gillespie, declaring that "they know and love Jason!" Whether or not Jason had in fact achieved this level of success remains something of a mystery, and yet not entirely unlikely. In the film, Jason is prompted to recount a story that involves the famous jazz musician Miles Davis, which comes across as entirely believable.[6]

Clarke's family background and successful career as an independent filmmaker meant that her life was more valued and therefore carefully documented and archived. Born to an elite Polish-Jewish family and raised by servants in Manhattan, she went away to attend a series of colleges, moving on to a new school after exhausting the dance courses at each of them. She later married well and continued to dance at her leisure. After one of her injuries, Clarke's therapist apparently suggested that she try a new career, and in 1953 she produced her first dance film, *Dance in the Sun*, and soon engaged other female filmmakers.[7]

Clarke was more than a decade older than Aaron Payne, and far more fortunate. Her résumé of directorial work and performance is a list of breathtaking accomplishments. By the end of the 1950s, her films earned international recognition, including prizes from the Venice Film Festival and Edinburgh Film Festival. She also produced a film about children for UNICEF, which received mixed, controversial reviews because of its frightening imagery, and an Oscar-winning short on the life of Wallace Stevens. In her first feature film, she adapted Jack Gelber's play *The Connection*, a dark off-Broadway work set in a tenement flat occupied by heroin addicts, featuring intense dialogue and an onstage shoot-up or injection. It had opened to weak reviews and with some difficulty but then gained a cult following—as did Clarke—and went on to acclaim at the Cannes Film Festival, which crowned her a progenitor of the New American Cinema. At home censors stalled the New York premiere because the actors used the slang term "shit" to refer to heroin, initiating months of litigation.[8] As early as *The Connection*, reviewers praised Clarke's innovative technique that mingled documentary with the fictional to create a "feeling of the spontaneous which is so in vogue these days."[9]

In these years, Carl Lee introduced her to new aspects of African American culture and also inspired her next film, *Cool World* (billed as the first theatrical film to shoot on location in Harlem), which probed the pathology of black youth culture. In an interview, she described her intent on showing "what's really happening on the scene in the lives of young Americans." None other than Bayard Rustin wrote to Clarke about the documentary, reading it as an appeal to the conscience of the nation in the face of urban grief: the "a black boy is as beautiful as he is condemned." While some film scholars treat her works as tailored for a white audience, Clarke later spoke of her hope that *Cool World* could inspire black youth to find an "incentive to shift their way of life," observing at one point that "their main problem is a lack of self-identity, of dignity." The film "gave them a sense of pride," she asserted, and yet this seems strikingly naive if not condescending. Her relationship with Lee had given Clarke a kind of entrée into black culture that sometimes read as false entitlement. "I went into the film as a liberal. I felt I had to love all Negroes," she stated, but she then discovered the negative impact of the ghetto environment that apparently produced pathology. At the cutting edge of artistic production, Clarke recapitulated the old analysis of the culture of poverty: "The life the great majority live in the ghetto is untenable—it is impossible to grow up with any dignity." In the end, the production left Clarke drained, and friends bid her to relax. Around this time, Clarke noted the influence of gay films on her, particularly the success of Kenneth Anger's *Scorpio Rising* and Andy Warhol's *Chelsea Girls*, and so perhaps she believed taking up the subject of homosexuality would lead to another success.[10]

Either way, Clarke had gambled—no other major film had depicted a black gay man before—and her intuition to go one step further, beyond heroin addiction and the black ghetto, and shoot Jason Holliday eventually paid off both financially and, more important, in terms of critical acclaim. Some high-profile reviewers, such as Vincent Canby of the *New York Times*, chose not to even mention the subject of homosexuality, but this was rare. They often identified Jason in terms of stigmatized race and sexuality, labeling him a member of multiple minority groups: a Negro and a homosexual, a fag and a homosexual, a black homosexual prostitute, and, in the case of a forward cultural periodical, "no-longer young, not-yet-middle-aged Negro fag who's done the wealthy white's houseboy scene." From one vantage point, Jason was the personal bearer of a "horror story," from another a familiar figure beset upon by "torrential words and gestures." In the former, Clarke becomes a brilliant artist, in the latter, "the unseen but omnipresent second character in this supposedly one-character film."[11]

Clarke's purported objective in making the film was for "Jason to explain himself in his own words," but this was evidenced neither in her directorial style nor in the edited result. The publicity campaign for *Portrait of Jason* claimed that Clarke considered appearing in the film but decided that she knew too much about the camera and directing, and so she wanted someone with less experience who would not seek to overly stage or manage the performance.

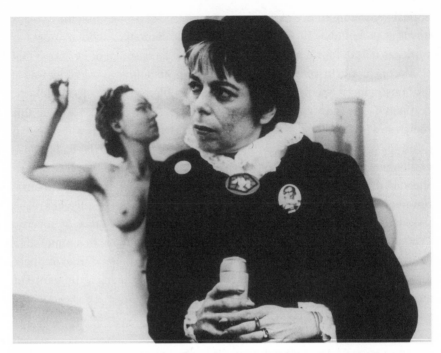

Shirley Clarke, 1967. Shirley Clarke explored cutting-edge themes in a series of independent films. In 1967 she produced and directed the daring black gay one-man performance in *Portrait of Jason* but subsequently entered a legal dispute with the film's subject, Jason Holliday. (Courtesy of Wisconsin Center for Film and Theater Research).

As for Holliday, she "suspected that for all his cleverness, his lack of know-how of film making would prevent him from being able to control his own image of himself."[12] This directorial control turned on the intersecting axes of race and class, and of insider and outsider, not only on technical knowledge. Clarke achieved her cutting-edge vision through the depiction of the marginalized, and this transition toward racialization and focus on African Americans had unfolded in terms of her relationship with Carl Lee.

But Jason's relationship to white power—and to upper-class white women like Clarke—had its own history of laboring under and against objectification. At one point, when the camera runs out of film, Clarke directs the set to keep the sound rolling; Jason's tone shifts perceptibly, and the topic turns toward the shocking and personal. "They keep asking me to speak about sex, but I don't want to talk any more," declares Jason, signifying multiple refusals. In this way, the wisdom of a remarkable man who had led a colorful and daring life becomes reduced to self-denunciation for the camera—"I'm not anything but a male bitch"—edited into the image of artificiality.

Clarke tracked the shifting opinion of her work in the press, preserving the published reviews and notices for many years. Reviewers tended to assume the worst of Jason's character because of his sexual identity, perceiving that "as a Negro and a homosexual, Jason is a habitual actor, playing the roles he must play to maintain his self-respect." Because of this, a reviewer observed that Jason provided the viewer with a "revelation of a kind of life that, mercifully, must of us will never know first hand." It often seemed that the more negative the stereotype or impression of Holliday held by the reviewer, the more likely the critic relieved the director of any responsibility for how Jason appeared. Yet a few reviewers observed his humanity. "Apparently the director felt that Jason could stand on his own—as a human being, not as a freak, with the needs and insecurities shared by all 'normal' human beings." They marveled at the spectacle of Jason as a "monstrosity," while others explained the apparent deviance as a result of his background and of not having been "born into the right race and the right economic circumstances," echoing the image of Moynihan's pathological black men. From their perspective all they could see was deviance caused by deprivation—he had "nothing whatsoever going for him. He is black, queer, and myopic to boot."[13]

The press treated the film more like a fast-breaking news story of cultural change than a standard film to be evaluated for its merit, but why so many mainstream magazines covered an avant-garde film on so marginal a subject remains something of a mystery. *Newsweek* noted that Jason's appearance signaled the end of all the old taboos and at another point attested to the documentary's brutal honesty, for no "writer could ever have imagined the grisly ritual of suffering." In a longer feature labeling him a "black . . . queer," *Newsweek* again commented on the film's shock value but in this case reprimanded Clarke for the seemingly exploitative direction, arguing that "what does not work at all is Miss Clarke's decision to bait and taunt her subject . . . until he cowers, quivers and weeps." Yet NBC's *Today Show* declared the film to be a "completely frank and therefore shocking exposure of a desperate human . . . a throbbing and horrifying and compassionate understanding of what society can make of a man."[14]

Sophisticated film journals also understood *Portrait of Jason* as unmediated, or at least as an authentic portrait of the self, with the director's method justified by the sort of revelations it presented, or as one reviewer explained, "Even though dignity is trampled through sharing inner agonies with strangers, the sociological document provides majestic salute to the spirit of the individual." A number of reviewers did empathize with Jason: "Her film is so clean and precise that it works against—instead of for—Jason," such that she "does not know where to stop with her portrait." Another observed that Clarke "ruthlessly badgers him into disclosing the sore and violated areas of his personality," even as others felt such tactics were justified; one head-line declared, "Scorching 'Portrait of Jason' Strips Homosexual of Pretenses." Another referred to Clarke's "obsessive voyeurism" and to Holliday's "shocking" and "desperate state." Whether in *Newsweek* or in a London Film Festival notice, the excesses of the performance were attached to a sociology of race—in one article's words, "a revelation of what being a Negro can do to this man"—directly countering Jason's strenuous efforts to prove himself a legitimate entertainer and to display his talents.[15]

In his accounting of himself, under the pressure of camera lights, inebri-ation, and the tactics of off-screen interrogation, the final scenes become a series of digressions, ramblings, and nonsensical profanities, punctuated by self-mocking laughter. Clarke intensifies the interrogation: "Jason, did you love your mother?" Jason replies in the affirmative, though he also claims he regretted his neglect of her. "Jason, did you hate your mother?" "Did your mother ever talk to you about fags?" asks Carl. "Jason, did you hate your mother?" Clarke asks again. Jason works up a response, recalling that "white folks was proud of her, because she knew her place, and she tried to protect me." Showing signs of fatigue and delirium, Jason then recounts how his father routinely and ritually punished him and that on a nightly basis he was beaten with a belt, frequently for patronizing the local gay bar. The famous gay poet Allen Ginsberg described the film as "the inside history of a gay negro boy-hood," and perhaps this was the most generous and grounded observation.[16]

And what was Clarke's response to the criticisms of her directorial technique? In an in-depth interview for a book on feminist avant-garde film, Clarke claimed that "no one has ever suggested that Jason was exploited. As far as I know, there has never been anything written about it that doesn't see *Jason* as an exploration of what makes a particular human being tick." When asked about the question of power relations, Clarke observed that "Jason is an expert manipulator" and concluded with the assertion that "Jason ends up winning in that film. . . . That is the point." Yet Jason's ambitions for a career in entertainment evolved in tension with Clarke's purposeful exposure of his inner core. He is directed to perform a repertoire of pathology, undermining himself as an actor, with *Variety* calling him "dreadfully bad when he does impersonations" and the *Nation* proclaiming that Jason "has talent only for exhibiting himself." At best he was manipulated; at worst, a shocking stereotype of the deviance attributed to black homosexuals was extracted and edited for a sophisticated audience with an appetite for the spectacle of abjection.[17]

This is not to suggest that there was no risk or talent on Clarke's part but rather to stress that for Jason the film was a gamble and that this shot at fame was little more than a setup for failure. After having gone into debt for *Cool World*, Clarke was able to rely on her savings to cover the budget of *Portrait of Jason*. After cutting the twelve hours of film down to 105 minutes, she went on to work with Independent Film Distribution to sell rental copies and toured film festivals and other venues to publicize it. In a sense, the economy of avant-garde film had forced her into another trade with Jason, compelling her out onto the stage to promote her representation of him. "I took the film around the country to universities. . . . And I almost blew my brains out. It was the most horrible experience I've ever had. I felt like a record, playing back on myself, and I got to hate the film. And hate me, and everything else about it."[18]

In the end, the two remembered their contractual obligations quite differently. In 1968 Jason Holliday retained Morton Weiner of Grau and Weiner Attorneys at Law to represent him and inquire into the balance due him from the proceeds from exhibition of the film. Weiner requested Clarke's "immediate attention" in order to avoid litigation. Clarke responded the following day, acknowledging the agreement with "Mr. Holliday" to pay him 10 percent of the profits. She sent a balance sheet showing her accounting of the costs and advised that she would remit a payment and send quarterly balance sheets. This particular document of the film's proceeds was not saved in her papers, but a spreadsheet of the film's foreign release indicated substantial profits, showing rental requests from universities in London, Liverpool, France, and Cologne. According to research conducted by a team of film restorers and archivists, the film did not gross a profit in its first run (it ran for eleven weeks with an average box of $1,700 a week, but lost more than $7,000). Yet the lucrative college and art house rental market continued into the 1970s. And Clarke's promotions and lectures about *Portrait of Jason* earned her up to $1,000 a shot. There are no documents indicating payment to Holliday nor further correspondence from his attorneys. A flier in the Clarke papers advertises a nightclub act featuring Jason, but I have found no other evidence to suggest Holliday achieved his aspirations for fame and fortune.[19]

By the late 1960s, on the eve of Stonewall and at the height of the urban crisis that precipitated more and more academic investigations into purported cultures of poverty, social scientists also reoriented theories of homosexuality. In 1968, Mary McIntosh "proposed that the homosexual should be seen as playing a social role rather than as having a condition," justifying decriminalization and more humane treatment. Her main point was that "social categorizations of this sort tend to be to some extent self-fulfilling prophecies: if the culture defines people as falling into distinct types—black and white, criminal and noncriminal, homosexual and normal—then these types will tend to become polarized, highly differentiated from each other." What was happening was probably more complicated from below; Jason's performance of mental deviance, addiction, and the hustler reassembled the black gay repertoire at the intersection of midcentury ideas about black homosexuality. At a space between the edge and the margin, Holliday sought to perform in ways that might gain recognition by both enacting and resisting dominant stereotypes, showing them to be mere performances. Whether or not he could or did succeed remains a matter of debate; but in retrospect Jason's encounter with the filmic representation of his own identity proved ambiguous at best, and it was more likely an instance of objectification.[20]

In some ways, recent history has treated him no better. In 2012, the Academy Film Archive, Milestone Films, and Modern Videofilm mounted a restoration project, involving a search for the existing prints of the film, archival research not only into the Clarke Papers but also into Aaron Payne's background, and biographical research into the crew and others connected to the film production, including a new interview with Wendy Clarke. In 2013, a restored version of *Portrait of Jason* was released and screened at a number of art house movie theaters. But despite their efforts at restoration, brightening, and re-creating the film as it might have appeared some fifty years before, Payne's story remains obscure. What Jason had said but Clarke chose not to cut is lost in outtakes. As for Jason, recent expert digging in Trenton turned up a high school photograph and some clippings from the *Trenton Times-Advertiser* indicating that he had performed locally throughout the 1950s. According to this research, he was born in Trenton, New Jersey, or Montgomery, Alabama, in 1924 (not in 1934 as he claimed in biography for the film). His parents owned a restaurant, Payne's Restaurant, and the Trenton Central High School yearbook shows him in Boys Choir. Recently discovered clippings at the Trenton Historical Society provide fragments concerning his career as an entertainer. An obituary surfaced indicating that Payne had died in Flushing, New York, on June 15, 1998; that he had lived most of his life in Flushing and Jamaica, New York; and that as "as a young man, he was in the entertainment world and travelled abroad extensively, using the stage name, Jason Holliday." The *Trentonian* reported on July 31, 1998, that he was cremated at Oxford Hill Crematory in Chester, New York.[21]

Race and Gay Liberation Pulp

At the intersection of black power and the sexual revolution, an increasingly pervasive media of magazines, television, and film concentrated on the black male body and in the process reconfigured dominant images of masculine sexuality. In this era of blaxploitation, according to film scholars, a stream of black-directed films featured macho black leading men whose actions often reversed social norms and racial hierarchies: black criminals defeating the police, heroes pedaling drugs, and black studs sexually dominating both black and white women. The conflation of normative masculinity with phallocentric power mobilized the reversal of white dominance, naturalizing black male virility.[22]

Into the early 1970s, the blaxploitation phenomenon both mirrored and undermined the struggle for black self-determination, and with the proliferation of this imagery came certain prescriptions for black masculine aggressiveness. In these films, from *Shaft* (1971) up through *Car Wash* (1976), black gay men were associated with the comical—the depiction of black masculinity next to gay men understood as a laughable contradiction—while other gay figures served to enhance the sexual appeal of the lead straight character. What might be termed "black queerploitation"—recurrent stereotypical depictions of hypersexual black men intended for gay readers—came to dominate the pulp pornography of the same era, and like blaxploitation, black queerploitation played on themes of machismo and reversal of power relations in which subordinate black roles, such as a slave or prisoner, take sexual control of white men.[23]

Of the hundreds of gay pulp novels that were published in the late 1960s and 1970s, somewhere between a quarter and a third of them featured scenarios that manipulated ideas about race to heighten the erotic impact of their sexual representations. Unlike the earlier lesbian pulps with veiled romances that titillated through sexual innuendo, the gay pulp plot lines described graphic acts of sexual contact, from kissing and oral and anal penetration to fetishes and group orgies. The standard size of a paperback was five by seven inches, 160 to 180 pages in length, with graphic art of the main characters on the covers; some books included photographs of seminude or nude black men and less frequently of nude white men. In examining approximately 120 boxes of pulp novels held in the Human Sexuality Collection at Cornell University, I selected out plots or motifs having to do with race, racism, and racialization, permitting a systematic analysis of the recurrent plots, depictions, and characterizations.

Despite its obvious significance for structuring desire, few studies of homosexual pornography consider race or racialization. Tracy Morgan's pioneering essay on 1950s whiteness and physique magazines conceives of the absence of black gay men as a "conscious or unconscious strategy employed by white publishers to remain connected to the connotations of class and quality generally associated with whiteness." Whereas white bodies were presented with poses intended to invite homosexual fantasy, argues Morgan, black photographs employed "racialized codes of representation," emphasizing black bodily strength at the same time that they elevated an aesthetic of whiteness. John Howard analyzes both southern sexual images and the life of an author of white gay pornography to understand how his writing related to the "gay erotic archetypes" of jocks, workers, and white-collar men, and a handful of scholars have collected and anthologized the fast-growing pulp novels in postwar America. By the mid-1960s, successful challenges to censorship laws unleashed a wave of increasingly explicit texts. Many of these books skirted the boundaries between respectable and prurient, and in turn some homophiles deemed them unrespectable.[24] In the same period as Stonewall, the black cultural revolution promoted the reaffirmation of sexual expression and yet also disavowed homosexuality, and therefore many black gay men searching for information about homosexuality and pornography would have crossed over into the white world of gay institutions and publications.[25]

Unlike the response to the Moynihan Report or *Portrait of Jason*, there is little evidence documenting the consumption or perceptions of the pornographic material. Nor is it entirely obvious whom the authors of the pulp aimed to pleasure—black men or white men or both—but clearly its purpose was not to address social problems but rather to satisfy desire. If it is difficult to catch readers of such works in the act, a closer historical analysis nonetheless provides insight into something that seems obvious yet remains understudied: the way that race roles structured constructions of sexual intercourse. How were black and white men figured in sexual scenarios, and how might these representations have shaped the interpenetration of race and desire in other contacts and contexts?[26]

The majority of the pulp paperbacks featured exclusively white characters, such as the series from the Blueboy Library that presented blond cover models with a cast of all-white figures, such as jocks and college students, cowboys and truckers, construction workers and priests. Though racial difference was absent, sometimes age difference structured the representations of intercourse, involving scenarios of older men that sexually dominate youthful passives. Some of the pulps accented class differences by attributing masculinity to working-class figures who played the active sex role. If these men were older, bigger, and dominant, their bodies were not colored. In other words, sometimes the covers, illustrations, and character descriptions featured color, but neither brunettes nor blonds were consistently either active or passive. The white pulps often took place in gay bars, featured characters discovering their gayness, and lingered on the beauty of a figure more than on his body size, but they clearly valued large genitals and muscularity.[27]

In contrast, many of the racially themed pulp novels included prefaces that purported to address societal problems—perhaps they were added to avoid prosecution for obscenity by evidencing a redeeming social value. This homoeroticism of the race problem, for example, informed a preface to *Black in White* in which the author explained to readers that historians believed slavery to be less a "racial institution than an economic one" while mentioning the historian Fawn Brodie's research on the affair between Sally Hemings and Thomas Jefferson. Apparently inspired by the discovery of the famed interracial relationship, which supposedly demonstrated underlying racial unity, the author asked, "How could a young white man behave toward a black man who was not merely his brother under the skin, but was literally his half-brother?" What followed was the usual set of sexual scenarios: oral and anal sex, group intercourse, and rituals of subordination and domination. In *Black Meat*, again the preface pretended to the redeeming purpose of broaching a subject too long shrouded in secrecy and declared that "interracial sex is a fact of life" but "rarely admitted." While cross-race sexual relations were stigmatized throughout history, the preface added, this was not the "case in Manhattan. And it isn't the case in most of the homosexual world." Therefore the purpose was to explore one character who was "hung up" on black men and "how that attitude grew and where it led," but then going on to rehearse the usual objectification of race: "He was the most beautiful shade of not-quite-black brown," with a "stupendous cock" and "cantaloupe-like buns of a black beauty."[28]

Perhaps the most fascinating of those works purporting to advance social reform but actually further objectifying their subject, Victor Dodson's *Black and Gay* ("A Barclay House Psycho-Sex Study") claimed to have conducted a "survey of interracial homosexual practices." Referencing the sexology studies by Alfred Kinsey, the table of contents ranged from "Sado-Masochism in Interracial Homosexuality," "Are All Negro Males Basically Bisexual?," and "A First Experience" to "The Negro and 'Drag Queen,'" "Black Stud for Sale," and "Black and White Sex in Prison." Blurring the boundaries between sociology and pornography, it began with the proposition that "the Negro homosexual labors under a double handicap" of racism and homophobia in society but also claimed that he "has no fears of being refused service in a homosexual bar; he is not classified as an inferior when socializing with the Caucasian homosexual." This notion was followed by the even more remarkable sociological misunderstanding that the "cause for homosexual justice is doing more for the advancement of the Negro cause." Although "black homosexuals" were supposedly more open and "readily admitted" their gayness, the author issued the caveat that "it is quite possible that not all of the story of interracial homosexuality is presented herein." What followed were the standard sexual scenarios. One chapter had white domination and racial abuse—" 'Hey, boy, get over here' "—highlighting "the color of our fuckin' skins, man." Mixing genres, the chapter on sadomasochism reported that some masochists were attracted to "the Negro" because of his appearance and belief in black beastlike sexuality. Because black men were "secure" in their masculinity, they were more open to bisexuality, while the homosexual of the Caucasian race had a "certain fear of rejection." In comparative terms, the text concluded that "the Negro male . . . is more prone toward homosexuality than is his Caucasian brother."[29]

Authors utilized racial stereotypes, and even racist epithets, to stimulate sexual arousal, and yet oftentimes their larger portrayals of American society upended or reversed societal conventions of white privilege and black subordination. At one point in Dodson's book, a character's redneck drawl spews racial epithets, and in the next scene a big black man is penetrating him for the pleasure of both. "Those who try interracial sexuality once and not again are strangely rarer than those who continue to practice such relations off and on," the narrator authoritatively reported. In a surprising conclusion, the author referred to Calvin Hernton's tract on desire across the color line, *Sex and Racism in America*, to advance the notion that race "is a scientific construct where men may be classified into more or less exclusive groups on the basis of similarities and dissimilarities." By contrast, the "homosexual white and the homosexual Negro seem to possess far less resentment and friction between one another."[30]

The cover of *Dark Brothers* features a long-haired, muscular white man atop the shoulders of a smiling black man with an Afro. The story concerns Kenny Crawford (white) and Chris (black), who is two years older than Kenny and has just graduated from high school. Chris is also larger, with "matted hair" and a manly odor. When Kenny encounters Chris on the porch of a neighbor, he recalls that his father had taught him "not to look down on black people the way most farmers around there did" and that one of the rare times his father had disciplined him concerned his usage of the term "nigger" (not in quotations in the text).[31]

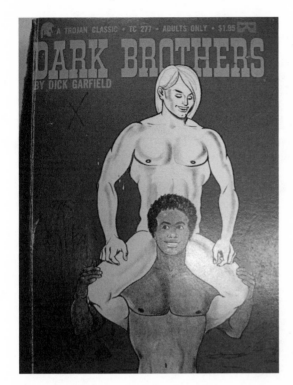

Dark Brothers. In the 1970s, gay pornographic novels proliferated through bookstores and mail order houses. Many featured black characters and black-white sexual encounters that were depicted in a stereotypical fashion. (Author's collection).

After their chance encounter, Kenny begins to long for Chris and meets him again the following day when his father offers him a ride, violating the local taboo against interracial association, and soon this violation becomes a passing touch caused by the bumpiness of the road, leading to Kenny's arousal—"with just the touch of a knee, and a black man's knee at that." Later, when he goes hunting with two friends, they have a sexual encounter but Kenny fantasizes about someone else. After losing his virginity, he decides "he liked male bodies, male cocks," but here coming out becomes intertwined with racial discovery. When he meets Chris again, this time on Sunday (though he does not attend church, to Kenny's surprise), the pair go for a naked swim, and some of Kenny's prior stereotypes about racial difference fade, offering a lesson of racial brotherhood; at the same time, Kenny becomes aroused by the "black, coiled pubes" and "heavy shaft." Next, Chris shows him affection, and in turn Kenny strokes his "kinky hair." Chris is the dominant top; Kenny, the passive white bottom. Rather than further racialization, however, the text presents touching intimacy. Although noting the bodily difference between the two, some of the scenes refuse the scene of brutal domination, and at one point the narrator observes that although Chris has animalistic passion, he also expresses love in his "moist eyes."[32]

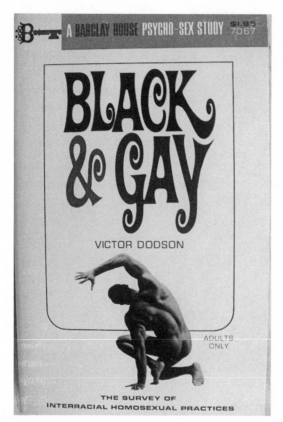

Black & Gay. Many of the new pornographic novels that featured black men purported to present serious information on race relations and the problem of racism. (Author's collection).

But references to scratchy, kinky hair, rough pubic hair, a "sweet musky odor," and the "huge black cock," as well as more racially derogatory descriptors, were repeated throughout the interracial pulps. The body was always racialized—"the black dick," "black asshole," "black stud," "huge black dork," "slumbering black prick," "mighty black oak," "beautiful black ass," and "black balls." The word "white" almost never appeared in these texts but was instead silently assumed. The vast majority of pulps depicted black men and white boys, or group sexual scenes of black men, but almost never an older or dominant white man with a passive black man. In the full range of texts, all men's penises were depicted as large, with the understanding that the average was eight or nine inches, but black men's penises ranged from twelve to fourteen inches in these works.[33] The roles were often rigid and unchanging—white, younger, passive, effeminate, gender transitive. The frequent reference to queer, gay, clone, and femme suggest an increasing homosexual taxonomy against the backdrop of homogenizing racial roles. In a culminating scene in one of the pulps, Tommy explores his masochistic impulses and is tied up in a men's bathroom, where numbers of black men penetrate him in a "wild degradation scene." In the end, the white character experiences the "best orgasm" of his life, but when black characters are dominated—in the few texts that fantasize about slavery in terms of bondage and discipline—their pleasure is rarely described or emphasized.[34]

In heterosexual pornography involving black-white scenarios, the animal-istic black man served to excite and yet also reassure the white male gaze, permitting them, in the words of pornography scholar Linda Williams, "to maintain the sexual-racial hierarchy of white men over black men." Yet as more pornography reached larger and more diverse audiences, such rep-resentations might also have become sources of pleasurable consumption. Or, in other words, following Jennifer Nash's position on black female por-nography, depictions of black eroticism presented possibilities of pleasures within a "white-dominated representational economy."[35]

The plot lines of gay fiction purposefully reversed hierarchy, fetishizing military rank, racial order, and class relations. For instance, in the midst of a slave revolt and revenge mass murder, *Master Black* extensively depicts vio-lence, grotesque deformation, and erotic exaggeration. In this fantasy, the black master controls the white slaves in scenes of sexual domination and physical punishment, alongside the promiscuous use of racial stereotypes and epithets. In ever-more elaborate plots of slavery and sex, the fantasy of black mastery and white enslavement anticipated or at least intermingled with the emergent subculture of sadomasochistic bondage and discipline.[36]

The rise of black power had secured more recognition of African American culture, community, and beauty and promoted representations of black machismo that clearly appealed to diverse audiences. In the gradual shift in homosexual definition from the social deviant once prevalent in *Jet* maga-zine to that of pulp's black gay aggressor, from straight black–produced rep-resentations of pathology to gay white–produced erotica, the figure of the black gay man remained the object of the dominant gaze, still little more than a projection oscillating back and forth across the color line. There were hints of subjectivity and pleasure in these representations, but not until black gay men spoke and wrote for themselves was there a substantial historical advance beyond stereotype and objectification.

Chapter Four

The Limits of Liberation

The rise of black power not only catalyzed significant shifts in African American culture but also influenced Left activism and urban countercultures and in turn inspired many gay radicals. No single figure better symbolized the revolutionary charisma of the times than Malcolm X, though his relationship to and meaning for black gay history remains complicated and in a sense emblematic of the fraught encounter between black radicals and gay liberation. With the publication of Manning Marable's 2011 biography, *Malcolm X: A Life of Reinvention*, a major controversy resurfaced over the young rebel's sexual identity, sparking numerous negative and often-heated reviews. Marable's critics acknowledged that he had uncovered a wealth of new information that expanded readers' understanding, but a significant faction objected to the claim that Malcolm Little had engaged in homosexual relations. In the 1940s, after manipulating a 4-F exemption from the military draft, Little became a hustler and drug runner, Marable contends, and at this time he offered his services as a masseur and companion to at least one wealthy homosexual. According to an interview with the recipient of the services, Dennis Newman, he "paid Malcolm to disrobe him, place him on his bed, sprinkle him with talcum powder, and massage him until he reaches his climax." Malcolm alluded to this transaction in his famous autobiography published in 1965 but identified another male prostitute who serviced Newman.[1] After Malcolm was convicted of theft and sentenced to more than five years in prison, he converted to Islam and left no trace of a record of homosexual relations (unlike Bayard Rustin, for example, whose prison records reveal several sexual infractions). Yet during his incarceration, records do indicate that Newman visited Malcolm, and another document showed that he had once planned to go to Newman for assistance and accommodations upon his release. In the end, once he converted to Islam, Malcolm had no place for Newman, given Islamic tenets that reject the practice of homosexuality.

A series of negative reviews of Marable's book sought to defend Malcolm against putatively "salacious" accusations, treated homosexuality as a sign of disgrace and perversion, and dismissed Marable's research as a false "allegation," likening the attribution of homosexuality to criminal charges that must be rebutted. Although several reviewers defended Marable and pointed out the historical significance of black gay figures, such as Bayard Rustin and James Baldwin in African American history, a significant pattern in the published reception to the volume was to avoid the issue. At one point Malcolm X's grandson made a public appearance to decry the homosexual interpretation, and then in a public forum on the topic speakers argued that communities "need icons" and that this justified their protest against Marable's portrayal, but why homosexuality disqualified him from iconic status or hero worship went both unexplained and largely unchallenged.[2]

Marable's interpretations were preceded by a 1991 biography that presented a number of examples of Malcolm's bisexuality, including an early incident in which Malcolm "stumbled" upon a young man masturbating and persuaded him to engage in sexual activity, as well as the relationship with Newman. The author, Bruce Perry, portrayed Malcolm as a product of a broken home and domestic abuse—reminiscent of the emasculated black son in Daniel Patrick Moynihan's report—and generally remained on the surface of the man, and his book was nowhere near as exhaustive in research or probing in interpretation as Marable's. But for reporting on Malcolm X's bisexual experiences, Perry too was attacked, his book remained controversial, and a major scholar dismissed him for misunderstanding black culture.[3]

More important than whether or not Malcolm X engaged in homosexual activity is to contemplate what the historical possibilities of a gay Malcolm, and what the pushback against this imagery, reveal about the contours of black gay history. While Lorraine Hansberry's passion for women set her on a path in and out of the black Left, animated her (largely unpublished) gay- and lesbian-themed writing, and played a role in mobilizing her several activist interventions, Malcolm disavowed homosexuality and converted to the position of a moral conservative. As a leader, he advocated a particularly straight black masculinity and heteronormativity, even though James Baldwin greatly admired him. He was commissioned by the Warner Brothers film company to adapt his autobiography into a screenplay, which he did while holed up in Truman Capote's Los Angeles estate. Yet Malcolm's popular appeal, and the tendency to contrast him with the puritanical Martin Luther King Jr., must have stimulated a level of black gay identification. In a 1992 published dialogue, prominent black gay writers Ron Simmons and Marlon

Riggs discussed at some length rumors of his "homosexual experiences" and complained that they were "a little disturbed—actually a lot disturbed—by the idea that we can't discuss the complexities of Malcolm's life . . . for fear that it will be used to tarnish our hero and in turn tarnish Black America." While they did not entirely agree on the significance of Perry's revelations, neither sought to prove Malcolm's homosexuality. Rather they felt the whole matter underscored the repressive and unequivocally straight definition of black masculinity.[4]

Rustin and Baldwin may have admired Malcolm X, but neither shared his political outlook. Rustin rejected racial separatism and even the intimation of violent self-defense, but he was not entirely dismissive of the militant leader. In a 1960 debate between the two, Malcolm spoke eloquently and at length, putting Rustin on the defensive to a certain extent. In turn Rustin criticized Malcolm's advocacy of racial chauvinism, while Malcolm argued that integration was little more than hypocrisy. The dialogue concluded with Rustin's halfhearted accusation that Malcolm and the Nation of Islam practiced anti-Semitism.[5] Rustin published an essay after the assassination of Malcolm and another upon the publication of Alex Haley's collaboration with the slain leader, *The Autobiography of Malcolm X*. He argued that Malcolm's life was characterized by far more continuity than represented in his professed conversion narrative and that he was not "entirely reborn" after his release from prison, though Rustin probably was not aware of his prior history of male hustling.[6]

On the one hand, Rustin could position himself quite strategically, and prophetically, on the need for a coalition between civil rights and labor and argue for a change in strategy from public demonstrations to greater participation in the electoral political process. On the other hand, in assailing Malcolm X even after his assassination, he needlessly provoked and alienated himself from the black Left. At one point, Rustin distinguished between the charisma of Malcolm and the qualities that make for a truly great moral leader, drawing a far-fetched comparison of him with Booker T. Washington, pointing to their rhetoric of self-help and separate economic development. At a meeting of religious leaders and scholars in New York, Rustin suggested that Malcolm was in the process of renouncing violence, but in a memorable phrasing critical of separatism he observed that "Malcolm X-ism is here to stay unless the nation is ready to revolutionize its spirit and its institutions."[7]

In response to one of his essays on Malcolm, the Black Arts movement writer Lawrence P. Neal charged that Rustin had absorbed white values, wielding the well-worn tactic of refuting a political position by questioning the racial authenticity of its advocate. He reminded readers that Rustin worked with a white leftist coauthor, Tom Kahn, and commented on the "bad vibrations from the effeminate projections of the Rustins" and "the flabby orientations of the Farmers, and the shuffling act of King." Here was the powerful trope of black masculinity that cast racial integration as a form of submission to white (sexual) power, fusing together black power manhood, rejection of assimilation, and homophobia. In defense of Malcolm and in the name of political revolution, Neal continued, the "Bayard Rustins who flirt among us must not be allowed to speak of our blood with so much disrespect."[8]

Despite the political fallout, Rustin remained a harsh critic of black power, or of what he described in an essay in a special issue of *Ebony* magazine as "The Myths of the Black Revolt." Of the myth of black capitalism, he argued that it benefited only a few entrepreneurs and exacerbated separatism. The problem with reparations was that it condemned white people rather than advocated on key black issues, isolating black activists from their liberal allies. He went on to attack the academic enterprise of black studies, in part because "second-rate programs will threaten the professional status" of scholars: "If such a situation is permitted to develop, Black Studies will become little more than a haven for opportunists and ideologues." In critiquing the black power and black studies movement, Rustin was joined by a number of liberal African American leaders, including Roy Wilkins of the NAACP. But the same issue of *Ebony* featured a long essay by the leader Huey P. Newton, with striking photographs of members of the Black Panther Party (BPP). What was even more striking was the extent to which, in Newton's political comments, Rustin had become irrelevant, not eliciting even a mention; instead he wrote as if the debates on the merits of integration were over and the real dialogue now turned on cultural versus revolutionary nationalism. Finally, in response to Rustin's condescending critique, Leonard Harris wrote an angry retort in the *Liberator* titled "The Myth of Bayard Rustin" in which he sought to refute each of Rustin's positions, from his opposition to reparations to the repudiation of violence to his rejection of black separatism.[9]

Rustin's conservative political turn—the product of alienation, miscalculation, and stubborn ideological commitment—has been clearly delineated in the historiography. A pacifist and nonviolent tactician to the end, he completely rejected the black power call to arms (even as a rhetorical gesture) and did not envision racial separatism (even as a temporary organizing strategy). It is also quite possible to see Rustin as painfully aware of his vulnerability as a gay man in the midst of black machismo and therefore to understand his reaction against identity politics, including the black studies movement, as a defense strategy to remain relevant at a time when black power expected a certain level of ideological conformity—and straightness. As a result a number of cultural nationalists conflicted with Rustin, attacking both his manhood and his racial identity or authenticity; but revolutionary nationalists simply ignored him, and I found no discussion of Rustin in the BPP documents that I surveyed or in the party newspaper, *The Black Panther*.

To a far greater extent than Rustin, Baldwin found a way to make common cause with the new youthful radicalism. He attended meetings of Students for a Democratic Society on black power and its challenges at the University of California, Berkeley, and spoke at a memorial service for Malcolm X. By 1968 he appeared in Newark with black power leaders Amiri Baraka and Maulana Ron Karenga and again demonstrated his capacity to gain support from more radical political groups, even though some black nationalists, such as Daniel Watts, editor of the *Liberator*, publicly criticized Baldwin as unrepresentative of the race. He also took part in an event to celebrate the first anniversary of the black power "invasion" of the California state legislature, along with Huey Newton and Bobby Seale, to commemorate a demonstration in which the BPP appeared armed and outfitted in military garb in the legislative chambers to protest the passage of new legislation on guns and ammunition.[10]

Yet like Rustin, Baldwin was also marginalized by a politics of masculinity that circumscribed his engagement with black power, particularly the conception of black masculinity advanced by Eldridge Cleaver. After 1968 perhaps no figure came to signify black power more broadly than Cleaver and his famous memoir, *Soul on Ice*, and no single figure so vehemently criticized James Baldwin. Written from his cell in California's Folsom State Prison, *Soul on Ice* presented a scathing critique of the civil rights movement not only as politically misguided but also as defeatist and sycophantic. Recalling the 1963 confrontation between Kennedy, Baldwin, and Hansberry, Cleaver summarized the historical moment as one where "Attorney General Robert Kennedy called together a group of 'influential' Negro entertainers and athletes to meet with him in secret, to get the message from the Man and carry the gospel back to the restless natives." His satire bordered on condescension, referring to "that Queen of the Mellow Mood, Lena Horne, and Harry Belafonte, quarterbacked by James Baldwin," who "were qualified—not to say 'willing,' which they weren't—to say or do something to make the black and white hordes of insurgents 'freeze' for a cooling-off period." From Cleaver's perspective, the political climate had changed and the old strategies of nonviolence had failed, and so "Kennedy's attempted cool-out was greeted with hoots of scorn and contempt from Negroes—entertainers and athletes included."[11]

Eldridge Cleaver addressing an audience at American University, October 15, 1968. In 1968, Cleaver published his best-selling memoir, *Soul on Ice*. A leading member of the Black Panther Party, Cleaver attacked black homosexuals in general and James Baldwin in particular. (© Bettman/Corbis).

By the late 1960s, in many ways black power politics gained more adherents than the project of civil rights suasion, and now black radicalism not only filled the city's streets but flowed onto the pages of best-selling tracts, dispersing ideas about race and identity into ongoing debates over the next phase of the movement. As one paper reported, "Black is marketable," pointing to the soaring sales of books such as Frantz Fanon's *The Wretched of the Earth* and *Malcolm X Speaks*. Major texts that spoke directly to questions of masculinity and sexuality—H. Rap Brown's *Die Nigger Die!*, Fanon's *Black Skin, White Masks*, and Claude Brown's *Manchild in the Promised Land*—were widely available in growing numbers of black-themed bookstores in cities across the nation, from Los Angeles to Chicago to Detroit to Boston to New York.[12]

The *New York Times* hailed *Soul on Ice* as one of the most important books of 1968, and the *Wall Street Journal* reported that the publisher had anticipated a record first printing of 40,000 but had sold 121,000 copies; eventually more than 300,000 copies were printed that year with another 300,000 expected. In September the book entered at number three on the *New York Times* best-seller list. In *Soul on Ice*, Cleaver juxtaposed the infamous 1955 lynching of the black fourteen-year-old Emmett Till (for allegedly whistling at a white woman outside a store in Money, Mississippi) with his calls for the rape of white women as a revolutionary act. Sexual revenge and misogyny remain among the most memorable themes of the historic text. For Cleaver, the civil rights establishment had failed to respond adequately to the assassination of Malcolm X, and "the bootlickers, Uncle Toms, lackeys, and stooges of the white power structure have done their best to denigrate Malcolm, to root him out of his people's heart." Integration—"this sickness between the white woman and the black man"—and its tactics, interracial cooperation and "bootlicking," were to be repudiated. Drawing on one of his favorite authors, Calvin Hernton, who had written a major manifesto that denounced black-white sexual relations and promoted homophobia, Cleaver first offered a confession of his own internalization of racism, observing that "a black growing up in America is indoctrinated with the white race's standard of beauty."[13]

The thrust of the narrative was driven by his imprisoned desire, his sexual longings in the context of involuntary celibacy, and this helps to explain why he became so enraged when prison guards ripped down the pinup photograph of a white woman from his prison cell wall and declared that he could post pictures only of black women. "I was genuinely beside myself with anger: almost every cell, excepting those of the homosexuals, had a pin-up girl on the wall and the guards didn't bother them."[14] If there was any doubt that Cleaver was straight, his memoir powerfully claimed his manhood through a shocking denouncement of homosexuality, a disavowal that was articulated in terms of race.

Cleaver at first seems to approve of Baldwin's writings, but the turning point was *Another Country*, which he read in prison: "There is in James Baldwin's work the most grueling, agonizing, total hatred of the blacks, particularly of himself, and the most shameful, fanatical, fawning, sycophantic love of the whites." Self-hatred defined his desire: "The black homosexual, when his twist has a racial nexus, is an extreme embodiment of this contradiction. The white man has deprived him of his masculinity, castrated him in the center of his burning skull, and . . . he submits to this change, and takes the white man for his lover." He calls Rufus Scott, Baldwin's bisexual protagonist in *Another Country*, "a pathetic wretch who indulged in the white man's pastime of committing suicide, and who let a white bisexual homosexual fuck him in his ass, and who took a Southern Jezebel for his wife. . . . [He] has completely submitted to the white man."[15]

Baldwin sidestepped Cleaver and never directly addressed his harangue in his voluminous writing at the time, but in 1969 he was asked about the statements in a forum at the University of Illinois and was reported to have said,

"I didn't like the attack. No one likes that sort of attack. But let me say that he was using me to make a point. And if you take me out of it—he was right." Without further elaborating, Baldwin may have agreed with his views on white sexual dysfunction and other matters concerning the depth of U.S. racism, but it was also true that Baldwin understood Cleaver to be a favorite among both black radicals and white youth at the time. As he explained years later in 1984, Baldwin did not want to talk about the attack because he felt overwhelmed: "My real difficulty with Cleaver, sadly, was visited on me by the kids who were following him, while he was calling me a faggot and the rest of it. . . . I had to try to undo the damage I considered he was doing." Since both men often appeared on the same speaking circuits, Baldwin felt particularly constrained "because what I might have said . . . would have been taken as an answer to his attack on me. So I never answered it and I'm not answering it now."[16]

Considering the immense popularity of *Soul on Ice*, acquiescence to Cleaver's homophobia may have been Baldwin's only option. Reviews of *Soul on Ice* ran along a spectrum from neutral to laudatory, but perhaps the most striking were found in the mainstream press, which consistently acknowledged the renunciation, radicalism, and rage but never the scapegoating and victimization of Baldwin.[17] In a major review of the book, featured in the *New York Times*, Charlayne Hunter, the black civil rights activist and journalist, linked his rage to the so-called Kerner Report, the recently released government account of the causes of massive urban rioting, and on the question of rape, Hunter highlighted the racial repression that silenced most convicted rapists (due to white male subordination). She identified Cleaver as an "involuntary participant-observer" in the race-sexual system of incarceration and described his homophobic rants as a "highly critical piece on James Baldwin" without finding the words with which to denounce it as far more than that. In point of fact, only one major review lit upon the treatment of Baldwin—in the *Baltimore Sun*—characterizing it as a "vicious and brutal attack against a helpless target," though even here the effeminizing and victimizing of Baldwin lingers.[18]

Over the years, a number of libraries and booksellers refused to loan or sell *Soul on Ice*, reflecting a surprisingly long series of censorship contests over the permissible limits of racial discourse. In 1973, the Teacher's Association of Ridgewood, Connecticut, and the Fairfield County school board debated a law to ban *Soul on Ice*, in the belief that their community rejected violence and refused to endorse a fugitive (since Cleaver had fled bail). The objective of the book banning remained amorphous, but commentators called it "erotic" and "trash" and spoke of its "intricacies of sex," while writers in the *Chicago Defender* pondered obscenity and censorship. In 1977, a New York high school banned *Soul on Ice*; conservatives identified it as inappropriate for youth and as "pornography" and yet others as unpatriotic. In Maryland, it was reported, "a number of disputes" had "arisen over *Soul on Ice*," and a Montgomery County panel debated banning the book in response to increasing complaints that the text would corrupt the youth. However, the effort failed, Cleaver's book was retained, and teachers were commended for defending the freedom of ideas.[19]

In turn, the superintendent of schools in the state of California, arguing that legitimate social commentary becomes unpalatable when couched in "obscenity" and "pornography," cautioned teachers from assigning the texts and at one point reportedly threatened revocation of teachers' credentials if they did so. Perhaps the most interesting turn in the controversy came from a distraught substitute teacher who not only criticized the tactic of censorship but claimed that works by black radicals were read by nearly every "literate black student" and that "often these are the first books that they have read with real zeal," while another article reported that Cleveland high school students—white, black, and Puerto Rican—were enrolled in remedial reading programs that assigned Cleaver's text. The American Library Association honored it as one of the six best books that reflected the "turmoil of the times." In the end, Cleaver's words had divided America in new ways around race and sexuality, gradually reversing the popular embrace of James Baldwin's *Another Country*, with its seemingly naive utopian dreams of infinite mutations of social difference leading to recognition of black and white interdependence. The extraordinary controversy sparked by *Soul on Ice*, perhaps most especially the conservative backlash, had transformed a deeply homophobic text into the *Catcher in the Rye* of the sixties generation.[20]

After his arrest in a police shootout and release on bail, Cleaver fled the United States and settled in Cuba, a guest of Fidel Castro, but soon became disillusioned under the authoritarian regime and traveled to Algiers, where he again dissented from governmental control and repression. By 1976, Cleaver had returned to the United States to stand trial and in the process managed to convert a number of his former targets into supporters of him—even Rustin and Baldwin. Rustin led efforts to organize a defense fund for Cleaver, ironically so, for as he observed, "there were perhaps no greater or more total political opponents" than he and Cleaver. The irony was also that the alliance revealed just how far to the right Rustin was leaning; he quipped that "there will be no 'Free Eldridge' campaign," referring to Left mobilizations for the prison release of highly visible black power activists such as Huey Newton and Angela Davis.[21]

Rustin's criticism of black power and of Cleaver found significant support among liberals who remained uncomfortable with the new radicalism. A distinguished scholar of African American history, August Meier, congratulated Rustin on his analysis of Cleaver's public prominence as a function of changing political fashions but wanted to note that liberals were not the problem, instead blaming Communists for promoting the mystique of the black revolutionary. The writer of another letter claimed to have met Kathleen Cleaver, who had asked for his advice on how to deal with her husband's incarceration, and he had counseled her to make bail because otherwise, he believed, Cleaver would be killed. Like Meier, he agreed that "white liberals and 'intellectual revolutionaries'" were his largest audience and added that Cleaver felt he had to play a prefabricated role: "If he spoke in detail and with serious intent to an audience they yawned. But if he said 'mother fucker' several times, they gasped and went into spasms of absurd joy." The writer also criticized Cleaver's preoccupation with the attainment of black manhood, without mentioning the homophobic attack on Baldwin, and suggested that Cleaver suffered not from hypermasculinity but the "reverse." He asked rhetorically, "How did one prove his manhood? A man is such by the size of his balls."[22]

Race and Revolutionary Faggots

In 1970, one of the first post-Stonewall gay newspapers ran a story, "Eldridge Cleaver's Missing Balls," to criticize the radical author because he "has swallowed hook, line and sinker the myth of white American masculinity." According to the article, Cleaver believed that "if the black man would only be given back his balls . . . the thorough collapse of the effeminate, corrupt, impotent and often homosexual white rules would be assured"; through such statements, "Cleaver's hatred of homosexuals is made unmistakably clear." While the gay columnist disclosed that he shared "many of his views of the corruption and venality of American life," he rejected the rhetoric that aligned liberation with the attainment of true black manhood. In disavowing Cleaver's representation of masculinity, liberationist writers gradually discovered critical issues with his treatment of women. Milwaukee's *Gay People's Union News* observed that the "awe for Cleaver and his work has not been wrong, but that his sexism must not be accepted or overlooked." Although Baldwin probably felt quite alone in the pages of *Soul on Ice* and in the ensuing celebration of Cleaver, after Stonewall gay liberationists did debate the text and criticize its sexual polemics.[23]

That the Stonewall riots erupted in the shadow of the black urban crisis is more often implied than explored in the scholarship on this watershed event. In his landmark study, *Stonewall*, Martin Duberman constructs one of the first, and still influential, narratives of the gay urban disorders that transformed increasingly militant homophiles into gay liberation radicals. In Duberman's telling, the 1969 police raid of a gay bar signaled not only the usual violent repression but also an emergent coalition of the respectable activist, the street drag queen, and the barfly, alongside black and Hispanic gays. Despite their different locations and status, a range of gay men thereby became oriented toward a shared public culture that Martin Meeker refers to as "contact zones." In turn the new gay consciousness energized activist organizing and sustained both the Gay Liberation Front (GLF) and the Gay Activists Alliance (GAA), as well as numerous attempts at coalition-making with black radical causes.[24]

Between 1969 and the early 1970s, the rise of the GLF in major cities, from New York and Philadelphia to Boston, Chicago, and San Francisco, crucially transformed the political orientations of the new generation. Gay liberationists agitated for the declassification of homosexuality as a mental illness, achieving reform by the American Psychiatric Association in 1973, and throughout the 1970s in cities and college towns they introduced, debated, and sometimes passed antidiscrimination ordinances.

When a faction of GLF-New York suggested that the group donate five hundred dollars to the BPP for a legal defense program, others in the group objected because of the party's reputation for homophobia. After the GLF eventually voted in favor of the move, a predominantly if not entirely white faction withdrew and formed the GAA, with the founding principle of pursuing exclusively homosexual objectives. Whether or not this new single-issue agenda precluded the consideration of race remained unclear, but it was the case that the GAA gained a reputation, among black gay men at least, as insensitive to other issues of inequality. The controversial split influenced future debates of the GLF, but eventually it donated the sum to the BPP fund.[25]

In expressing the "desire of members of the GLF to free all oppressed minorities," a gay columnist had asked a straight black acquaintance to inquire about the Black Panthers' view of gay activism, reporting that "my friend called back and reported to me the disappointing news that most of the Panther leaders, at least those in the Bedford-Stuyvesant section of Brooklyn, responded either with hostility, bewilderment, or both." In the 1960s and 1970s, a series of recurrent interchanges between the BPP and the GLF became more a matter of publicity than useful political connection; at one point a leading activist from the New York GLF spoke at a New Haven rally for the Black Panthers and attempt to defend Cleaver's use of the term "faggot," describing his encounter with Huey Newton as one of the "greatest thrills." It may be to their credit, as well as reflective of their inexperience, that gay liberationists hoped to show the Panthers "how we are all brothers and sisters because we all suffer oppression," and yet this sentiment hardly appeared sufficient to meeting the challenge. When one writer suggested that the GLF stage a huge orgy in honor of the Panthers, agreeable since "many Panthers are no doubt well built and well hung," he belied the undercurrent of white objectification of blackness clearly visible in the sexual culture, especially pulp pornography.[26] Perhaps humorous in retrospect, the gay liberation rhetoric appeared naive about what was at stake in black power while at the same time blind to the realities of racial subordination.

According to Marc Stein's rich study of Philadelphia, many white gay men and some lesbians identified with the issuing of Newton's 1970 manifesto "A Letter from Huey Newton to the Revolutionary Brothers and Sisters about the Women's Liberation and Gay Liberation Movements." In this challenging command to the rank and file of the BPP, Newton chastised members whose stereotypes and prejudice clouded their vision of revolution and argued that the party must relate to the "homosexual movement." Newton proclaimed that homosexuals "could be the most revolutionary" and instructed members to judge their presence and contributions as they would any other faction. Yet Newton's explication of gay desire—the point where he asks, "And what made them homosexual?"—suggests a certain disavowal and claim for his own redoubtable straightness. His formulation of liberation—"A person should have the freedom to use his body in whatever way he wants"—stayed a safe distance from gay liberation's advocacy of polymorphous perversity. While Newton also claimed that he accepted lesbians, perhaps his most important intervention concerned homophobia: "The terms 'faggot' and 'punk' should be deleted from our vocabulary," he declared, seeming to refute Eldridge Cleaver and his rhetoric of revolutionary manhood.[27]

Newton issued the letter in conjunction with the BPP's Revolutionary People's Constitutional Conventions in Philadelphia and Washington, D.C., staged to unite the African American community and to create an alternative strategy for the 1972 federal elections, which the Panthers believed symbolized the rise of racist, fascist rule. "And the Revolutionary People's Constitutional Convention will be our last—and our greatest attempt to peacefully implement All Power To The People," the BPP declared. In inviting white gay men and lesbians, the party opened new possibilities for coalition, and yet reports on the event were mixed. Lesbians had vocalized their views that stressed the need for fundamental economic and social change in order to promote women's full autonomy and had questioned gendered institutions, such as marriage and the family, but also had reported considerable resistance from the other participants in the convention. White gay men generally fared better, perhaps because they sought to struggle alongside, rather than partially beyond or against, the BPP's revolutionary convention.

That the BPP was headquartered in Oakland and therefore close to the ferment in San Francisco meant that it had significant exposure to gay politics and to the possibilities for coalition. Into the 1970s, *The Black Panther* followed news of local sexual politics and rightward backlash. It reported that members regarded conservative reformer Anita Bryant and her crusades to repeal gay rights and remove gay teachers to be a threat to the entire progressive Left. "The Extremists Exploit Homosexual Issue in Right-Wing Surge," declared one headline in the paper while running a public announcement for a Gay Freedom Day Parade and Fair in San Francisco in another issue, and endorsing later the openly gay city supervisor Harvey Milk. In strategizing against the New Right and Republican-led activism, *The Black Panther* observed that "gays and other left minorities have reason for concern" while identifying gay rights as one of the "hottest" cultural issues. At a 1977 rally of more than 300,000 for human rights, Black Panther Ericka Huggins denounced the rising "climate of fear and violence," reportedly proclaiming that "I would like to point out that shouting 'faggot' while ruthlessly stabbing a gay human being several times closely parallels this country's historical pattern of shouting 'nigger' while cruelly lynching, raping, or castrating a black victim."[28]

Another site of interchange between black and gay radicalism was the burgeoning political mobilization within and around prisons. With the outbreak of the Attica prison riots in New York that rocked the nation, public concern over the penal system and its inhuman conditions had sparked a protest movement, and this was particularly the case for black activists. In the spring of 1971, the *Black Scholar* published a long essay by Angela Davis on the Soledad brothers, the imprisoned radicals whom she was accused of aiding in the shooting death of a guard, and in the following September issue, the journal ran an unusual essay on homosexuality in prison. In this remarkable account, "Love: A Hard-Legged Triangle," Billy "Hands" Robinson, incarcerated in Cook County Jail, begins with the assertion that he "couldn't resolve the contradiction of masculinity theme Eldridge Cleaver was later to write about so well." More explicitly than Cleaver, Robinson describes the sexual dynamics and hierarchy in prison, where "the black dudes have a little masculinity game that they play. It has no name really, but I call it whup or fuck a white boy—especially the white gangsters or syndicate men, the bad juice boys, the hit men, etc."[29]

His story recounts the desire of a black protagonist, Tank, for Jerry, a white, blue-eyed inmate with "a clean freshness about him that gripped Tank's heart." When they steal away and have sex, which Robinson describes in graphic detail, another inmate discovers the pair and laughs at them. While Tank becomes angered at the mockery, he refrains from violence because the interloper is a twice-convicted murderer, serving life. Next, he returns to his cell and looks at a photograph of a woman, Christine, his girlfriend, and then spins a fantasy-memory of his sexual encounters with her. As he continues to fantasize about Christine, he realizes that his sexual partner in reality is "a faggot." The story returns again to the pervasiveness of prison sexual encounters, recounting a dialogue between inmates about oral sex and references to homosexuality outside of cell and prison life. Some years later, public attention returned to Cook County Jail when *Ebony* ran an article on sex problems that stimulated a number of responses, including a letter complaining that the author had failed to distinguish between sexual assault and consensual homosexual relations. Running against the stereotype of effeminate and weak, he portrayed men unable to "sublimate" their desires who "continuously foment prison riots, rape fellow prisoners, and kill guards and fellow inmates." In the context of black power, writings from prison had mobilized a new politics of masculinity, even as incarceration fostered a traditional dichotomy between effeminate, passive gay and masculine, straight penetrator.[30]

Therefore the genealogy of black pathology—the constellation of ideas that designated the homosexual as deviant, criminal, and emasculated—persisted into the 1970s. Yet across the racial and sexual divide, in the radical gay press the strategy of queering black power signaled a level of serious engagement with black liberation ideas and served to prove the revolutionary potential of black gay men. Published by a Boston area collective of predominantly white gay radicals, *Fag Rag* advanced revolutionary critiques of sexual ideology, argued for a polymorphous perversity (that all men were naturally bisexual), and extolled the profane and pornographic as modes of self-expression and collective affirmation. One of the founding members recalled that *Fag Rag* started in part because of exclusion of radical men from lesbian publishing ventures, such as *Lavender Vision*, and it ran from 1971 to 1978. Each issue featured news, political essays, and poems, as well as photographs and drawings, with many shots of nude men, and a significant number of these were black gay men.[31]

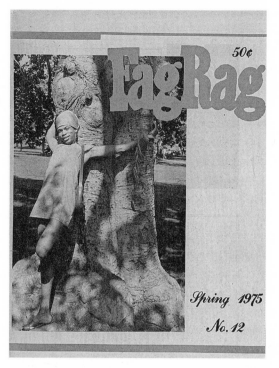

50¢

Spring 1975

No. 12

Fag Rag. After Stonewall, the rise of gay liberation sparked a revolution in journalism. By the 1970s, every major city had its own gay newspaper, and some, like the radical *Fag Rag*, pushed the envelope even further by featuring black gay writers and poets. (Author's collection).

Fag Rag ran a major story on the assassination of George Jackson to demonstrate that "these events concern gays because in the eyes of Amerika we are 'sex' criminals. Many of our Brothers are suffering under the conditions which led to the explosion in Attica," aligning gay liberation with a challenge to "straight white Amerika [that] will not allow anyone out of its norms (i.e. John Wayne, Superman, woman slayer, plantation owner consciousness) to be free and exist." In addition, the journal featured black gay men, some self-identifying as "black flaming faggots," such as Freddie Greenfield, who recounted that he had left home at the age of twelve "to live with an older man" but that when his father discovered his sexuality, he was confined in a juvenile delinquency facility. "The first place I was sent was to the Reception Center in Joliet," but he later moved to other facilities, and guards then came to his cell, handcuffed him, and sent him to Sheridan prison, where at one he point he spent ten months in "the hole." "An awful lot of gay people were committing suicide, hanging themselves. They eventually gave us a building," but he sometimes chose to have open homosexual relations, a violation of the prison rules, in order to be sent to isolation.[32]

In this context, coming out was a matter first of safety and community, not only of political consciousness. According to an interview with a black prisoner featured in a 1973 gay anthology, "It's true that in jail straight men force people into homosexuality, but most of the gay people who were overt about it were all put into the same tier. . . . Anyone wanting to attack one gay person would have to fight thirty or forty others first." But those who were gay but refused to self-identify or who could be pressured into the role of the "faggot" suffered. Hall reported that "one boy was gang-raped. . . . There's a lot of that: I think institutions encourage things like gang rapes by keeping the tension between homosexuals and straight people there." In the integrated areas, consisting of equal numbers of heterosexuals and homosexuals, "nobody would even utter faggot, even the guards were very careful about what they said. I was playing a role, a passive, feminine role. Had I not played a passive role and gone into the institution and been put on a straight tier, and had a homosexual relationship with one person on that tier, the whole tier would have known about it, and I would have had to have homosexual relationships with everyone on that tier because I was an overt outlet, so to speak."[33]

As the prison became a site of political mobilization, black gay men sought to connect through reaching out, reforming masculinity, and, in their own words, building on "links with brothers behind bars" to forge a "communication network with brothers in captivity," while "faggots on the outside can also gain access to valuable knowledge about how handymen of the law carry out their witchcraft." These black gay men argued specifically on behalf of the numbers of effeminate inmates who accepted favors from masculine men, or who were sexually victimized by them, and critiqued the pervasive racism operating in prison culture. Their critique explained that the racial division between black and white inmates reflected the will of prison authorities— they "divide the prison population between black and white, favored and unfavored, straight and gay." In turn, they proclaimed solidarity—"I am a gay prisoner like so many other gay prisoners"—while complaining of internalized homophobia. "We are always referred to as she, her, miss thing, etc., never being given any sort of identity or humanity."[34]

The circulation of prison narratives in U.S. society—from *Soul on Ice* to *Soledad Brother* to the features in *Fag Rag*—represented just one example of the impact of mass incarceration on gay identities. Inmates found discarded copies of the gay newspapers and placed classified advertisements, hoping to find a pen pal or lover or someone to sponsor their parole. In "Letter from Rahway," published in *Fag Rag*, a self-described black "communist-anarchist" serving a seventeen-year sentence wrote that though he preferred women, "if I see somebody who's of the same gender I am, and their physical presence stimulates me sexually, I'll dick them down." Prison sex followed an active/passive model in which men taking on the female sex role not only became effeminate but were also subject to violence, and some black prisoners therefore may have absorbed a conception of gay men as the penetrated and dominated figure. In another letter to *Fag Rag*, a prisoner reported, "I was into a role thing, where I was a homosexual and he was a straight man, and I related to him that way." In this role of the active-dominant, some prisoners found it possible to engage black power: "I was in jail when I first heard about the Black Panther party, and related to it very positively, but out of a black sense, not out of a gay sense, because they were offing gay people, verbally offing gay people, saying things like, 'this white man who is fucking you over is a faggot,' and that was getting to me, because I was a faggot and I wasn't no white man!"[35]

In response to the contradictions and omissions of sometimes cooperating but often conflicting liberation struggles, in the early 1970s radial activists formed the Third World Gay Revolution (TWGR) and produced a manifesto reprinted in a number of gay papers under the heading "What We Want/What We Believe." The TWGR adapted the BPP's model of drawing up an official platform that declared its political objectives and social demands. Like the Panthers, members of the TWGR sought "self-determination . . . as well as control of the destinies of our communities" and called for liberation of women, drawing on second-wave feminist efforts to change patriarchal institutions. As students of socialism, they called for full employment, and equal employment at all levels of production, as well as socialized public housing. Their manifesto argued against dominant norms of feminine and masculine because "third world men have been denied even these false standards of 'masculinity,'" recognizing the rage fueling someone like Cleaver.[36]

Black gay liberationists shared the main tenets of sexual pleasure and revolutionary challenge but also felt caught between often uncompromising ideological positions. One author, for example, recited the standard litany of liberation rhetoric: coming out "brings the righteousness of spirit that comes with the truth" and that "it is not the negative definition of others (homo, lezie, queer, pansy, fruit), but a positive term we can call our own." The problem was that the stress on gay identity sometimes contradicted the larger message on human liberation. "I am reminded of a Puerto Rican gay brother—see, even that phrase 'Puerto Rican gay brother'—reeks of dehumanizing rhetoric," said one writer, who then discussed the assumptions that one category, or even intersecting categories, could effectively expressed uniqueness of each individual. "Some of us saw in him our fulfillment of our fantasy of the right-on-gay-Young Lord," referring to the Puerto Rican nationalist activist group the Young Lords. In another nationalist reference, the writer pointed out that "'Revolution in our lifetime,' was the Black Panther slogan we often espoused. It was with this sense of immediacy that we joined with the Panthers and a melange of white radicals at the Revolutionary People's Constitutional Convention."[37]

Black gay radicals too stood up, and spoke out, and fought back: "I am a black faggot"; "Everyone who comes in contact with me knows that I am a black faggot," proclaimed one *Fag Rag* columnist. In a queer inversion of the profane, or a valorization of the stigmatized, a number of black gay writers explored and recuperated the experience of degradation: "Since twenty years ago, at work and play, people have referred to me as 'punk,' 'sissy,' 'nigger queer'—not faggot, not gay comrade, not revolutionary or counter-revolutionary." In this critique not only of straight society but of some sexual radicals, the author recalled how he had once conformed to the norms in society and that the "norm was and is heterosexist, middle-class conscious, male supremacist whites." First and foremost, liberationist discourse valued the declaration of identity because it supposedly brought one psychological health and personal freedom, and yet black gays asserted that racial subordination preceded, and informed, sexual identification. Before gay liberation, the experience of white supremacy led the writer to the insight that "shame was a farce, a ruse of the ruling class. They, the powerful, the rulers, were never ashamed to sell good food to whites and garbage in the supermarkets in Black neighborhoods." At the same time, the bitter reflections on his experience of African American poverty colored his views of white men in gay liberation. As "some nigger queer," he resented white gay men who avowed liberation—"all walking around looking, sounding and smelling like the straight men they've been all their lives." For black gay men, there was a longer experience of racial oppression that prefigured coming out: "They're the boy next door that the queers dreamed and creamed about, the new left would-be heavies, the confused, repressed sons of white middle (or higher class families who could have had anything they wanted, who spent years learning that they belonged to the master race). . . . So it cannot be surprising that drag queens and other flamboyants are unwelcome, that third world gays don't abound, that the age and beauty standards are the same as they are in straight white Amerika."[38]

In the gay liberation era, theoretician of this intersection Charles Shively, a white Harvard-educated professor of history, wrote in the pages of *Fag Rag* to advocate for "more than a social transformation" and for greater attention to how "in the areas of sex, race, or class, the powerful use language as an instrument to keep the many in place." Drawing on his experience in antiracist campaigns, Shively also argued that "white people have used language, particularly written language, to keep Black people subordinate," and then announced that none of the members of the *Fag Rag* editorial collective was black and that radical liberation, including the Good Gay Poets, had failed to incorporate or "integrate," as he put it, the new energy of radical black consciousness. He pointed out that the poetry of Adrian Stanford, an important black gay poet, had not been accepted for publication without argument, even though his volume, *Black and Queer* published in 1977, was both radical and gay. It eventually would become a classic, but "the left gay and lesbians . . . objected to his poem on tina turner on the basis of its supposed sexism."[39]

Stanford's poetry inflamed, transgressed, and testified, appropriating his designation as pathological by identifying with and therefore transforming it. In the poem "tina turner (after hearing her sing)," Stanford pivots toward the profanity of revolutionary rhetoric: of her "asshole murmurings splashing in honkie faces" and "her music: always full of resentment and glories long forgotten" and "rural south or sophisticated philadelphia (the colored sections), wooly haired bitches getting laid. big black cocks that press on and on." And in the title poem, "black and queer," Stanford gestures to black power, "the hate ridden excrement of three hundred and fifty years of 'master race' philosophy is not to be flushed from the American white mind by a few half-hearted applications from the 'integration' eyedropper."[40]

The local mobilizations and rhetorical extravagance of black power inspired a generation to challenge the inherited wisdom that achieving equality meant cultural assimilation into the mainstream of U.S. society. Raised fists and military-style actions signaled a real challenge to the order of things at a time when gay activists searched for ways to break out of the closet and find both personal and political liberation. On the ground, gay liberation fronts agitated for broad changes in the way people organized sexual relations, powerfully inspired by the radicalism of the times. Yet they also had to confront the uncomfortable contradictions of a black radical tradition that criticized figures such as Hansberry, Baldwin, and Rustin for their sexuality. Few if any black gay men appear in the voluminous writings and activities of black power, but some did speak out in the pages of the gay press or in meetings of gay organizations. At the same time, so powerful were the writings and accomplishments of black power that generations of black gay activists would take up their call for self-determination and collective revolution.

Chapter Five

The Disavowal of Brother
Grant-Michael Fitzgerald

In the era of civil rights, as a result of ongoing demands for black respect-ability and heightened concern among African American leadership about maintaining a morally upstanding profile, it could be assumed that black gay men, should they choose to come out or if found out, were at risk of losing their place in the movement. In that sense, the fates of Bayard Rustin and James Baldwin were representative. At the same time, even as gay liberation called for coming out in a way that resonated with black power—pioneering activ-ist Frank Kameny proclaimed "Gay is Good" and Jim Owles advocated Gay Power—few black gay activists appeared on the front lines of the movement. In New York and Chicago significant numbers of gay men of color formed the Third World Gay Revolution, and black gay men joined Gay Liberation Front chapters in other cities, but these formations were, like gay liberation itself, fairly short-lived.

The black power movement's construction of a militant masculinity included a forceful rebuttal of white authority, a refusal of racial assimilation, and the advocacy of black eroticism for black people. In politics and popular culture, black male sexuality became more visible and celebrated, encour-aged and expressed, aggressive and potent. At the same time, although the number of Stonewall-inspired organizations dwindled, new gay sexual institutions continued to proliferate. By the 1970s, for any gay man, black or white, looking for a place to connect was as easy as going downtown. Every imaginable type of bar opened, including black gay bars; nightclubs offered elaborate dancing facilities; and gay saunas and sex clubs abounded. Virtually overnight, gay newspapers appeared in every major city, and the pulps and other pornography continued to be sold in bookshops, each site providing "contact zones" in which a range of desires might be fulfilled. Yet none of these institutions of gay culture provided a viable site from which to articulate a black gay political agenda or form a black gay activist network. The dilemma of sexual vulnerability and repressed self-expression faced by Rustin and Baldwin still persisted, only through evolving and shifting forms of prejudice and sites of objectification.[1]

Called from the Closet

Like Bayard Rustin, the relatively unknown black gay activist Brother Grant-Michael Fitzgerald initially chose to dedicate himself to struggles for social change through religious organizations, and both were committed to and in turn shaped by the civil rights movement. Rustin as a Quaker and Fitzgerald as a Catholic, both relied on their faith to locate not only a higher power but also a sense of community. Their sexuality disrupted and transformed their relation to these formations, with different results for each of them. After his trouble with the law and disastrous public exposure, Rustin withdrew into a safety net of interracial liberal civil rights and union networks, remaining largely in New York City, and for him the politics of gay liberation must have seemed somehow distant, too youthful, and perhaps politically undisciplined if not illegible. By contrast, Fitzgerald left his hometown of Philadelphia for New Jersey and eventually settled in Milwaukee, Wisconsin, to join a religious order and through this body become a leading advocate of social justice—and black gay liberation. Into the 1970s, Rustin lost battle after battle in frustrating confrontations with black power activists in Brooklyn, Maryland, and Washington, D.C., but Fitzgerald understood himself to be active in the black power movement at the same time that he served to challenge organizations that marginalized his sexual identity.

Born in 1947 in Kingston, New York, and baptized in Philadelphia in May 1953, Grant-Michael Fitzgerald had two sisters and apparently lived with both his father, Eugene (a bar and restaurant owner), and mother, Mary (who worked for a time for RCA Victor). He shows up in an official archive in the 1960s, when his name appears in the institutional records of a religious order. At the age of twenty, recently graduated from a Philadelphia Catholic high school, Fitzgerald contemplated joining a seminary and eventually chose the Order of the Salvatorians, a Catholic community of brothers and priests who lived together and devoted themselves to religious faith, scholarly work, and community service. The Salvatorians' seminary in Blackwood, New Jersey, had a theater troupe that performed in Philadelphia, and perhaps Fitzgerald had attended one of their productions, piquing his curiosity about their community. He recalled that after "leaving home I had always lived in community with the Salvatorians." His first venture into youthful independence led toward a world of men with a strong sense of brotherhood.

According to his résumé, Fitzgerald "entered society" in September 1967 at the seminary in Lanham, Maryland (soon to be closed and sold off), and advanced to the status of novitiate in July 26, 1969, after moving to the new headquarters in Milwaukee during his first year of undergraduate studies. He commenced studying for a bachelor's degree at St. Paul College in Milwaukee, which also soon closed because of financial difficulty. By the time he made his profession of vows, which were renewed annually thereafter, to uphold the values of the Salvatorians, serving in the Spirit of Christ, he had relocated to Dominican College in Racine, Wisconsin. He majored in sociology and psychology in order to pursue his interests in questions of social processes and deviance, perhaps recognizing his own deviation from what was expected of a young black man in 1960s Philadelphia, the city teeming with black power activism that he had left. As a young member of a devout order, he was expected to mature quickly and convey an air of religious seriousness, devotion, and selflessness. As a supervised novitiate, he was also expected to practice the virtues of chastity. In the recollection of one of his classmates at Dominican, it was during these years that Fitzgerald seemed to discover and cultivate his gifts for counseling and working with youth. He taught theology at a local high school, practicing a vocation that he pursued throughout his life.[2]

In college he forged a variety of significant personal relationships, including with another young man who would become a historian of the Salvatorians, Steven Avella. Avella's first and enduring impression of Fitzgerald was that of someone soft-spoken, kindhearted, and sensitive. He was one of the few black men in the Catholic order and one of a small but not inconsiderable number of gay members. Studying at Dominican, Fitzgerald attracted the attention of a young black woman, Louvenia Butler, also known as Lu-Lu. According to Avella's recollection, Lu-Lu developed a crush on Fitzgerald, and at some point Fitzgerald felt compelled to reveal to her his sexual orientation. Lu-Lu may have been the first female amour that Fitzgerald had to confront, but they remained friends. In the following months, Fitzgerald's other friends in the community were told. As Avella recalled, "I knew comparatively little about homosexuality and sexual identity in those days, and he was one of the first openly gay people I had ever met. I learned a lot from him."[3]

Fitzgerald could have fabricated any number of cover stories about his sexual identity or simply rejected the advances of Lu-Lu and continued on in secret. His sexuality stood in contrast to his race, at a time when the leadership of the progressive Salvatorians admired the civil rights movement but had far less experience with homosexuality. Being one of the few African Americans in the community in what were once described as "race sensitive days" cleared a path for him into social activism. At the same time, many in the Salvatorian community showed considerable tolerance for his sexual identity, in part because of flux and crisis among Catholics and within the Salvatorians. Even the official history of the Salvatorians featured Fitzgerald's photo and rather casually noted that after "'coming' out in 1973, he became involved in gay rights activism in cities around the nation."[4]

Yet, if the Salvatorian narrative depicted a relatively unproblematic and effortless gay identification, Fitzgerald also spoke of a more painful revelation. In a short memoir essay intended for juvenile readers, he wrote that he explained his same-sex desire to his mother as early as high school, recalling that "she cried and said, 'It's okay if I know, but don't tell your father.'" However, he did eventually come out to his father, about a year later, remembering that he was not particularly surprised and had suspected as much since Fitzgerald's adolescence. At another point, he suggested that some of his school friends had rejected him because of his coming out. If his seemingly early realization of his gayness prompted him to join the Salvatorians, he did not say so in print, but he did often refer to the Salvatorians as a community, and perhaps while coming out he sought communal belonging. It could be that he felt that being both black and gay destined him to a solitary existence and that the Salvatorians could save him from this fate, or perhaps his homosexuality left him with a felt sense of guilt that religious devotion could assuage.[5]

His was a difficult and conflicted decision, in no small part because the Catholic church expected celibacy of its clergy, as did the Salvatorians, and the average Catholic probably rejected homosexuality as a sin. Fitzgerald's friend Avella recalled a dramatic incident during a meeting of the Catholic Charismatic Renewal, a short-lived movement of ecstatic prayer groups in northern Wisconsin, while they were in college. These meetings were held at Saint Mary's Parish in Racine and emphasized a kind of ecstatic version of Catholicism in which members were moved by a communal spirit to share with the group, inspire others with their professed faith, and confess their sins before God. During a moment of personal revelation, Fitzgerald stood and announced to the meeting that he was gay, apparently expecting affirmation. Instead, a number of members criticized him and called homosexuality a sin, even demanding that Fitzgerald leave the worship group. Avella remembered that at some point, he felt forced to stand up and defend Fitzgerald, saying something to the effect that, like the men and women in attendance,

Brother Grant-Michael Fitzgerald pioneered activism on several fronts at once. A member of a Catholic intentional community, he fought for reform of the church, the passage of gay rights, and greater tolerance for homosexuals in a variety of settings. (Used with the permission of the Society of the Divine Savior—USA Province Archives).

Fitzgerald was called to faith and experienced the salvation of Christ. Afterward, Fitzgerald became demoralized by the incident in part because it demonstrated a kind of religious bigotry from which he had been shielded, and so he did not return to the meetings. The incident became a matter of concern for one of the heads of the ministry, Father Ramon Wagner, a leading progressive visionary who sought to direct the Salvatorians' participation in local community affairs.[6]

Brought to the attention of Wagner, Fitzgerald gained important recognition and was invited to join new outreach programs established during the Salvatorians' period of renewal. Several leading Salvatorian scholars had called for openness and engagement in response to mobilizations around poverty, war, and racism, while a number of theologians began to reconsider the church's core values around sexuality, including the supposed intrinsic evil of homosexuality. When the American Psychiatric Association declassified homosexuality as a major mental disorder and revised the *Diagnostic and Statistical Manual of Mental Disorders* in 1973, the move prompted a kind of liberalization toward the question of homosexuality that filtered into some theological circles. Rather than a moral problem of good and evil, theologians talked about homosexuality as a fixed constraint, something inborn or inherent, and less a matter of personal or moral failure.[7]

Since the sexual revolution and the Second Vatican Council, more American Catholics were ignoring the pope's prohibition on birth control and advocating the right of conscience or latitude for personal choice. In several religious journals, theologians argued that Vatican II promoted a distinction between the individual and his or her mental condition, as well as a view of sexuality as an expression of deep, enduring intimacy. Religious authorities also entertained the idea that both gay liberation and antigay theology suffered from an overemphasis of identity. At the same time, the rise of the first gay churches, particularly the Metropolitan Community Church, had advocated for a sex-positive response to homophobia and taught that sexuality was one of God's gifts and a source of spiritual fulfillment. In the context of gay liberation, the liberal reading of Catholic teaching now extended to homosexuality—that gay people too shared in the grace of God.[8]

While gay founders of churches referred to the civil rights movement or identified with African Americans as a social minority, black religious leaders worried over a crisis of faith. In an essay called "The Black Religious Crisis," Joseph R. Washington warned of something "tragically askew" and referenced the increasing numbers of black college students who were religiously inactive; he identified an "erosion of middle-class church membership" caused by integration, rising economic status, and loss of direction. Around the same time, James Tinney, a gay academic teaching at Howard (and the subject of chapter 7), reported a similar trend in his article "Black Catholics: Is There a Future?," which recounted alarming statistics indicating a shortage in black priests and incomplete educational materials (though a black Catholic group worked to reform the curriculum to address issues of race). Across a range of denominations, black revivalism had dissipated, becoming less radical, as the "political tone of the former years was gone."[9]

Yet the liberalizing effects of Vatican II had not necessarily moved Catholic orthodoxy beyond the official, and undoubtedly largely held, view of homosexuality as sinful. In 1974, the Roman Catholic Archdiocese of New York issued strong statements opposing the passage of a local gay rights measure, and a representative of the Archdiocese of Philadelphia testified against such a measure in that city. The church issued a pamphlet titled "A Menace to the Family Life," blaring the usual warnings that homosexuals would "propagandize" and that the passage of antidiscrimination legislation would "damage true civil rights causes in the city." But the same year the *New York Times* also ran an op-ed by a professor of religious history who argued for greater tolerance, admitting that he found homosexuality personally problematic but declared there were worse evils. This kind of shift in opinion provided Fitzgerald with more latitude and space for mobilization.[10]

In a series of exchanges in the Catholic journal *Commonweal*, a number of writers, most prominently Michael Novak, weighed in on the question of the sinfulness of homosexuality and rejected gay liberation by arguing that Catholicism stressed family life and its reproductive purposes. But in response to his view that sinful acts stain the sinner, a sister submitted a letter to the editor that asserted "what [the gay person] does with his gift of homosexuality will determine his moral character."[11] It was reported that *Commonweal* itself had endorsed the passage of gay rights measures, as had the National Federation of Priests' Councils, and a priest criticized both the archdiocese for homophobia and conservatives for assuming that homosexuals were of a "fundamentally *different* human condition." A leading theologian, Norman Pittenger, surveyed a quarter century of religious change and advanced the argument that both homosexuality and heterosexuality were rooted in expressions of love, the essence of human experience, and that therefore genital expressions were right if directed toward love, becoming sources of joy. Perhaps more to the point, random survey data and studies indicated an unexpectedly high percentage of priests were in fact homosexual—by one account, based on a "network" of contacts established by University of Chicago doctoral students, as many as "48 percent of priests known to them were homosexual according to some definition of homosexuality, while 55.1 percent of seminarians were." Up until the 1960s and 1970s, students of Catholicism had rarely thought to ask such questions, but even if exaggerated, these and other statistical findings suggest that Fitzgerald's orientations—toward both men and political activism—were becoming more common among Catholic orders into the 1970s.[12]

In practice, however, reconciling homosexuality and celibacy, and particularly both of these with gay liberation, proved a challenge for Fitzgerald. In retrospect, several gay Philadelphians remembered Fitzgerald as unusual or odd, and some were skeptical of his religious authenticity. Fitzgerald had taken vows of chastity while claiming a sexual identity but also recalled how his own fears of gayness had led him to his faith: "I realized that being celibate had been a way I could handle being gay without dealing with it." By the time he returned to Milwaukee from rural Wisconsin, Fitzgerald clearly began to have sexual experiences. By 1973, Fitzgerald explained in his narrative that "he declared his gayness to his religious congregation two years ago," in this instance describing himself as "bisexual." According to Fitzgerald, "As I became fully aware of myself as a gay male, I did have sexual experiences. But my commitment to the ministry is more important than personal relationships. The vow of celibacy is a goal I still hold, and my board has accepted me on those terms."[13]

As recorded in the official history of the Salvatorians, during this period of liberalization, leading theologians sought to distinguish between homosexual orientation and the homosexual act, with the former increasingly understood as a mental disease. According to Avella, moral theologians influenced by new psychological data began to refine Catholic thinking on homosexuality, with some drawing more careful distinctions between homosexual orientations and actions, forgiving the former. As the Salvatorians framed the issue, the church stressed the value not only of family but also of filial affection, and members considered themselves brothers cooperating in a spirit of fraternal love.[14] It would seem that they unintentionally opened a space of implied homosociality—a space where gay men (or men who felt certain homosexual desires early on) sought community and the support of male companionship. If their vows to chastity and religious values deflected or dimmed the homoerotic implications of "fraternal love," the embrace of the brotherhood remained intertwined with his observance of faith, the gift from God that Fitzgerald had discovered. At the same time, despite the Catholic church's stance against avowed homosexuality, it seems unlikely that Fitzgerald experienced much overt hostility from among the Salvatorians. In reflecting on this question, the archivist for the Salvatorians commented that he very much doubted that Fitzgerald had "ever concealed that from them. . . . He certainly was open about it to everyone in our Formation program, and . . . their heads would not have been in the dark about it."[15]

Though raised in a black neighborhood in a black social milieu, Fitzgerald apparently had few connections to the traditional black community. His interest in working with youth emerged in his own youth, perhaps substituting for a sense of personal loss. In college he taught three classes in New Testament scripture to freshmen at St. Catherine's High School in Racine and volunteered as assistant to the chaplain in counseling teenagers. Some time later, he announced that he planned to adopt children in the state of Wisconsin as well as serve as a foster parent. Perhaps he admired or even identified with the innocence of youth or with their seemingly infinite potential to change through growth. Also, for some the label of "troubled youth" or delinquency probably resulted from maladjustment as young gays, and perhaps Fitzgerald wanted especially to reach out to them.[16]

After finishing college and returning to Milwaukee, he searched for an opportunity to be of service in the community and found a teaching post at a predominantly black high school. In 1972 Fitzgerald signed a contract with "Harambee Education Center, Inc." to begin teaching social studies in August. Formerly a church, the Harambee school served primarily African American students with instruction in Afrocentric subjects and advocated a community centered, local control approach to curriculum and pedagogy. In a sense, Fitzgerald had returned to where he had come from—to an urban black community, teaching and learning about human relations, sociology, and politics, among black youth. After having traveled a long and seemingly triumphant road from Philadelphia and Racine, however, Milwaukee presented again powerful challenges to his standing and sense of belonging.

At some point, the principal of the school was, in the words of Fitzgerald, "made aware of my gayness" and then "started monitoring my classes every day" through a kind of an intercom or "sound system [that] was left open . . . so she could hear what I was saying." Under his supervisor's close surveillance due to his sexuality, he faced an unusually stark example of the dilemmas occurring at the intersection of social difference.[17] While continuing with his teaching, Fitzgerald recalled that "one day last December, in a class that had already discussed frankly and at length subjects like venereal disease, sexuality, and 'That Certain Summer' on TV, a high school co-ed put it directly: 'Brother, are you gay?'" As described in the gay magazine the *Advocate*, he "asked the class's permission to decline the question, and the classroom fell dead silent," but "later, I told Sister Carol that I couldn't keep silent about the oppression of my gay brothers and sisters. . . . I told her I'm proud of my blackness and proud of my gayness." He wrote of the hypocrisy of working in liberation and remaining silent about gayness, coining the term "Black-Gay Liberation" to describe his political purpose. He would not pick and choose in the dilemma that he faced at the Harambee school.

By this time, Fitzgerald was regularly attending meetings of a local gay liberation group, the Gay People's Union (GPU) at the University of Wisconsin at Milwaukee, where he discussed the incident, observing that his open "avowal of gayness" had brought "pressure from his employer to resign from a teaching position." The group's newsletter quoted him as proclaiming, "I cannot and will not be hypocritical and support only those aspects of liberation which are socially comfortable for me or you."[18] Before he eventually left, he told his "students about the oppression that I was getting" and found that even "the parents rallied around me and told me I should stay." Fitzgerald explained his resignation to his superiors in the Salvatorians by quoting from the original letter of resignation and claimed that he made the decision without "undue malice or regret, but out of an honest recognition of the present incompatibility," and yet there was lingering bitterness.[19]

The incident at Harambee had exposed not only the burden of multiple identifications but also what Fitzgerald realized in his letter of resignation to be their internally conflicted nature. He had failed to bridge the new black urban terrain with his gay activist commitment to advocate for full social justice. Perhaps any Catholic institution, beyond the unusually tolerant Salvatorians, would have rejected such a position. Fitzgerald had not sought to enact change or reform as much as to teach and guide his students; but under the circumstances he would have felt the closet particularly constraining, and therefore he had to answer their questions. When Fitzgerald later offered a recollection of the incident, he noted that a black student had said, "Father so-and-so's a faggot," and recalled that he had "tried to reduce their bigotry by inviting a lesbian or gay priest to speak." However, the school refused to permit the appearance. He also remembered his sense of alienation from most forms of what were becoming recognized as identity politics, claiming that he felt alienated from both the "drag queens," whom he did not mean "to put down," as well as from "the radical blacks, the militants, because they consider gays decadent and don't see that we're all fighting the same battles." To further complicate the dilemma, he observed that "gay men are much more racist personally and socially." In these and other accounts, quite remarkably, Fitzgerald rarely questioned his purpose or doubted his strategies but rather understood the barriers to progress as external, embedded in movements or institutions founded on a singular cause and category of identity.[20]

The Gospel of Gay Rights

After leaving his position at Harambee, Fitzgerald returned to the Salvatorian headquarters at Hi-Mount, Wisconsin, to reestablish his connections and gain support for the painful process of moving on. In the immediate aftermath, he found work at a local book bindery, earning less than three dollars per hour. The period 1972–1973 became one of recuperation and then reimmersion as he returned to the local gay community, specifically the GPU and the Milwaukee branch of the Council on Religion and the Homosexual (CRH), a national gay religious organization founded in San Francisco with branches in many major cities. He also landed a new service position as a counselor in rural Wisconsin, within driving distance of Milwaukee.

An examination of Fitzgerald's longest single position of employment, for three years from 1973 to 1976, opens a window onto how he negotiated his religious vocation, dedicated service to youth, and gay activism. Fitzgerald supervised so-called delinquent youth at the Southeastern Wisconsin Homes in Milwaukee, serving as a resident counselor for a group home for teenage boys, aged thirteen to nineteen. He worked twenty-four-hour shifts, acting as the "live-in house parent," performing duties such as cleaning, counseling, recreation, transportation, cooking, arranging medical appointments, and so on. If, in retrospect, those on the staff at Southeastern worried over the impact or effect of his gay identity on the youth, they recalled neither a significant problem nor need to reprimand. Particularly in the wake of the controversy at Harambee, Fitzgerald may have tried to remain in the closet in his new position, though at one point he also claimed to be out to his colleagues.[21]

Despite his marginal status as a black gay man, Fitzgerald achieved a modicum of success, and holding this position for a sustained period structured a routine in his life that had been missing. At the same time, though he worked there for three years, neither of his supervisors recalled much personal information about Fitzgerald, suggesting the limited extent of his connections in these years. Lynn Oehlke remembered him as focused, relaxed, and easygoing, also describing him as rebellious and disorganized. Another of his supervisors, John Molenar, described Fitzgerald as visibly or noticeably gay and perhaps effeminate, and if Oehlke thought him to be impatient with bureaucracy, Molenar described his working habits as focused and bold. Similarly, he was characterized as a born reformer, more interested in social change than in scholarship, or as the history of the Salvatorians phrased it, "by his own admission, he was uninterested in theory."[22]

If Fitzgerald proved to be an effective counselor, his work environment was still not an entirely comfortable one. Of four male employees, he was the only gay counselor. His supervisors knew of his sexuality, describing it as obvious, but also observed that "there was a balancing agent" with the other workers at the home so that gayness became less problematic. Oehlke recalled, "I can remember talking with Grant, and telling him that my expectation was that he didn't use the group home as a bully pulpit. I think he separated his life. We didn't make a big deal out of it . . . and [asked] him if he could keep it separate." Because he worked with youth, who felt increased anxiety concerning their own masculinity and identity, his supervisors appealed to Fitzgerald to exercise a kind of self-censorship. At the same time, his homosexuality was clear to Oehlke: "I kind of vaguely remember that it would percolate to the surface; it is not unusual for teenagers to wonder about their own sexuality. The issues would have come up." At one point in these years, Oehlke recalled consulting with Fitzgerald and counseled him on the separation of the professional from the personal. At a time when he was more involved in activism that advocated just the opposite, this likely felt restrictive, and yet for his part, Fitzgerald apparently followed the instructions.[23]

Around the time that Fitzgerald turned back toward his religious community, the National Federation of Priests' Councils (NFPC), a body that convened its first national meetings of the nation's dioceses (115 of 150 attended) in 1968, began to consider a wider array of social issues. Stimulated by Vatican II, the NFPC experimented with democratic processes, debate on resolutions, and votes on major church positions and embarked on programs that revolved around both expansion and reform of the church and collaboration with social justice causes. The NFPC also furthered the organization of an urban ministry, published a monthly newsletter for priests, and lent financial and moral support to Cesar Chavez, the Latino agricultural activist. In 1973 meetings, among the NFPC's mandates for the year was a call for a "task force of theologians" to make a "'critical and contemporary Catholic theological analysis of homosexuality." The mandate also declared its opposition to "civil laws discrimination against homosexuals in employment, housing, etc." The NFPC planned to cooperate with the Catholic Theological Society of America (CTSA), whose task force on homosexuality was under way, and the chair of the CTSA advised the NFPC to postpone appointing members until the CTSA had published its report. In explaining that the CTSA expected its project to extend for up to three years, perhaps the chair was discouraging the more progressive, and increasingly forward, members of the NFPC from too hasty a move on the matter of homosexuality.[24]

In the same spirit of outreach and social justice, about fifteen Salvatorian priests and brothers and one sister formed the Commission for Justice and Peace, which convened in Milwaukee, and established a variety of action-oriented task forces on education, nonviolent action, human rights, and youth advocacy, any of which would have drawn in Fitzgerald. However, following his increasing engagement with gay liberation, he chose to form the Gay Ministry Task Force, and this particular group would soon move to center stage in the community's justice and peace initiatives and overshadow every other program.[25]

Because of his work with the GPU—at one point he was featured on a cover of the group's monthly newsletter—and with the CRH, the national gay magazine the *Advocate* ran a long story on Fitzgerald, greatly increasing his visibility. Fitzgerald told the interviewer that the key question was "How do I show the gay person that God is love, not a bookkeeper tabulating sins?" After describing the mission of the Gay Ministry Task Force, the reporter observed that Fitzgerald's "personal style leans more to gentle firmness than loud confrontation." In this instance, Fitzgerald proclaimed himself to be a bisexual, loving both a man and a woman (was he referring to Lu-Lu?), but then also reported that he practiced celibacy. The article highlighted Fitzgerald's plans to take his ministry into gay bars and saunas in the city, but perhaps he had pressed the envelope too fast and too far. Was the reader to imagine that Fitzgerald's outreach was entirely divorced from cruising or that the patrons were welcoming? In either case, Fitzgerald was becoming a national gay rights activist whose unique personal vantage point as devout, black, and gay increased his political visibility.

At the same time, the conservative priest Guy Charles sent a clipping of the *Advocate* article to the NFPC, along with a copy of a letter he had sent to the Salvatorians questioning Fitzgerald's credentials. Charles, "a former leader in Gay Liberation," was the head of Sanctuary House, a church retreat designed to convert homosexuals into nonsinning believers; he now offered "true conversion," to change from gay to straight, through personal salvation in Jesus Christ. The counselors at Sanctuary read the gay press and reportedly contacted some "3000 homosexual men and women who have advertised in gay magazines and newspapers for partners," claiming that "more than half of those . . . contacted [are] really seeking for a lasting love, the love which Jesus Christ can give." Charles explained that he was "in Gay Lib for a number of years" and reported that "I checked on this Brother Fitzgerald. From what I am told, he is a 'johnny-come-lately' to the Lib scene."[26]

It was true that Fitzgerald was new to the politics of gay liberation, but soon he would emerge as a leading voice for reform of the church at the highest level. Yet Charles signaled a more foreboding set of interests and theological orientations, which emerged in opposition to the sort of outreach to the laity and liberalization of theology that the Salvatorian task force sought to promote. Apparently disturbed by the *Advocate* article, Charles sent a typescript to the director general of the Society of the Divine Savior to draw his attention to Fitzgerald. Since he "has not yet taken his final vows as a religious, serious doubts are cast upon his acceptance of the Evangelical Counsel of Chastity, as well as doubts cast upon the Salvatorians themselves in allowing such freedom of living accommodations and life for a non-professed as reported," probably referring to the article's coverage of gay clubs. Charles then went on ·

to mention Troy Perry (the founder of the first gay Catholic order, identifying him with "rip-offs" in the "gay ghetto"). In the end, his point was that "Theology and Holy Scripture are not in error"; rather, human weakness and, by inference, succumbing to gay desire were to blame. In concluding, Charles observed that the "surge of interest in the Church, during the past decade of 'social action' and social justice, have brought about many painful discoveries regarding the weakness of men and women in religion."[27] The questioning of Fitzgerald's celibacy, the reference to a correct theology, and the alignment of social activism with weakness were all of the same fabric, and the progressive Salvatorians were under increasing pressure to respond.

But Fitzgerald decided to mount a campaign for reform of the Catholic church and continued work with the local branch of the national CRH, which only recently had begun meeting regularly in the evenings at the Church for All People in Milwaukee. The CRH began by adopting the ten goals of the original San Francisco group and proposed an additional one: "to work with existing homophile organizations in the community in the area," referencing the GPU. Outreach to the community meant that relatively traditional gay members of the CRH were confronted with the open eroticism of 1970s gay culture, leaving them with the task of explaining the proliferation of bars and bathhouses and pornography to the larger religious community.[28]

Fitzgerald appears in the CRH archive for the first time in the March 1973 minutes, when he volunteered to serve on what was known as the Committee for Periodical Review "to review the Catholic Periodicals," with another member assigned to do the same for Jewish materials. This gave Fitzgerald a reason and place in which to study seriously religion and sexuality, and for more than two years the CRH sustained him with an apparently close-knit learning community. Fitzgerald began assembling a study guide or informational packet to explore the issues involved in gay ministry, and then he coauthored with Louis Stimak a preparatory unit that explored the operation of homophobia within and outside the church. In what they termed a module, Stimak and Fitzgerald linked homophobia to the imperative to reproduce and argued that homophobia stemmed not only from rigid expectations of masculinity and femininity but also from "certain values—like marriage and good family name—that heterosexuality teaches are basic to a normal life."[29]

The module also explained, and defended, the institutions of the gay subculture to the religious leadership, even admitting the existence of tearooms, or public restrooms where homosexual encounters took place, and claiming that "the dark dingy bars were the only other places" where gay men could congregate. Yet the authors concluded that "homosexual people do not enjoy promiscuity and 'quick sex,'" attributing such behavior to "living under fear and oppression." Even as it sought to deflect critical stereotypes of gay culture, the document deployed negative views of its own by categorizing as disturbed those "who are forced by the homophobia around them to hide their sexual identity and pass as straight." In searching for the middle ground between gay liberation and religious rejection, the CRH endorsed a kind of normative respectability. For his part, Fitzgerald had set out "to develop a program of ministry to the Salvatorian community in the area of human sexuality" and argued for the "dignity of all persons whatever their sexual orientation."[30]

In combining liberation with Christ's "loving self-sacrifice," Fitzgerald's vision in the document in some way flowed from religious commitment, which had long provided him with another world or community through which to articulate his black gayness. Promoting a kind of gay respectability, the CRH modules advanced the objectives of inclusion in the church and freedom from oppression, helping gays to become integrated persons. Beyond this invocation of equality and social justice, Fitzgerald studied the gospel itself and outlined the differences between a literal and a more liberal reading of the Bible. He argued that the church has always recognized that scripture requires interpretation, opening ethical possibilities for sexual justice.[31]

The emergent intersection of liberation and liberalism offered a significant strategic opening for Fitzgerald to bring together—to bridge—two otherwise disconnected communities. With perhaps less vigor than secular gay liberationists, he articulated the value of sexual expression and counseled against personal denial or sexual abstention as a treatment for homosexuality while calling on members of the clergy to put aside their biases and to recuse themselves if they were unable to consider the issues objectively. Echoing Fitzgerald's own personal journey, the module employed religious terms to describe the process of coming out for gay men and lesbians, terming it a "discernment of their homosexuality," and observed that "as the individual becomes increasingly aware of his/her sexual nature, there comes a time when that individual begins to feel the need to 'come out.'" In a sense, the new medical model in which experts deemed homosexuality a mild psychological disorder was adapted to a religious injunction for tolerance of the individual, and both clearly focused on the health and personal well-being promised by coming out. The authors defined this in quasi-religious terms—at a "time" when the individual "feels" such a need, eventually "he/she will publicly identify him/herself as a homosexual person." When such persons remain in the closet, they suffer from lack of integration, and "the longer the homosexual lacks integrating personality, the greater is her/his potential to disintegrate, to

break down and develop a myriad of psycho-social difficulties." In these asser-
tions, Fitzgerald referenced "personal crises" resulting from not "receiving a
positive response from co-workers and employers" about his homosexuality,
presenting his painful experience at the Harambee school for consideration
by the Catholic church. Not surprisingly, in light of Fitzgerald's work in the
Southeastern Wisconsin Homes, the document also advocated the counseling
process, religious services, and affirmation of a "believing community."[32]

In 1972, the governing body of the NFPC, the House of Delegates, had
directed the membership to "establish a task force to aid priests in extending a ministry to homosexual persons," and the report under construction by
Fitzgerald would be presented at the annual meetings in April 1974. In the
months leading up to the convention, however, the report was sent out for
review, and a leading scholar at the Catholic University of America, Charles
Curran, sent back highly critical comments. Curran began by noting that
theologians disagreed on the question of homosexuality and that probably
a majority "maintain the traditional opinion that homosexual acts are always
wrong and that the homosexual must strive by whatever means available
(treatment, sublimation, etc.) to avoid such genital, homosexual activity."
He then outlined a range of positions, developed his criticism of the liberal approach, and reiterated the clear preference for heterosexuality. Most
objectionable were calls for "the right of gays to develop a full and integrated
sexual identity." Because Fitzgerald's mentor, Father Ramon Wagner, also sat
on the board of the NFPC, he was aware of the criticism addressing the commissioned report. Only weeks before the annual meetings in San Francisco,
correspondence circulated regarding the "Task Force Paper on the Ministry
to the Homosexual," and one commentator lamented that a "balanced view
of homosexuality is difficult to achieve in these days of rabid causes," likely
referring to gay liberation. He went on to call for an overall pastoral approach
and concluded that Fitzgerald's report needed "a great deal more work before
it can be presented to the House of Delegates."[33]

After Fitzgerald's formation of the Salvatorians passed a resolution in
support of the task force and educational modules, news of the pro-gay initiative "was picked up by the national newsletter, *Crux of the News*," and
members from at least twenty-three states and three other nations requested
information about the module on homosexuality. As the initial spark by the
Milwaukee group flared, it was reported that the task force sent "a general
mailing . . . to all the members in August," and by the end of the year, several
months before the next annual meetings of the NFPC, the Gay Ministry Task
Force had secured a mailing list of 150 and monetary donations.[34]

Studying and organizing for reform, Fitzgerald and Wagner traveled to the national meetings of the NFPC in San Francisco, and Father Wagner formally presented the proposal for a Gay Ministry Task Force and for the publication of guidance materials. According to a study of the NFPC, some theologians felt that "the theological aspects of the report were undeveloped."[35] The Salvatorians' presentation also encountered some procedural obstacles. When they planned to distribute the model ministry (what they referred to as the "Resource") to all convention delegates, the NFPC Executive Board (by a vote of 13 to 9) "delayed its distribution until it could be included in an 'informational packet.'" It was reported that an "advance copy has been given to moral theologian Charles Curran who criticized it for its lack of theological rigor and because its working assumption (i.e., that there is no real moral difference between homosexual and homosexual orientations) was difficult to sustain in the light of traditional teaching." By withholding the module that the task force had constructed, the board had diminished the case for the task force. It was a difficult setback, and Fitzgerald declared at the time, "We were shafted."[36]

During the main session in San Francisco of the Ministry and Priestly Life Committee, Fitzgerald and others submitted a number of items to vote on, including proposals for broad support of civil rights and for outreach to gay and lesbian laity. In an interview with a Milwaukee gay newspaper, Fitzgerald explained that his task force was "really surprised at the support. All of a sudden, I thought that maybe we had a chance to get something passed." The first proposal called for the repeal of laws that criminalized homosexuality between consenting adults, calling for freedom of "consensual" sex, and the second endorsed a standard civil rights measure prohibiting bias in response to the problem of "severe discrimination." However, the call for action, including a subresolution advocating open discussion of homosexuality in dioceses and the church, was returned to committee, and the call for nondiscrimination in employment in the church similarly failed. When a delegate called for reconsideration of the vote on this issue, he pleaded that "it is the height of hypocrisy for us to call on civil government and business to end discrimination, and then do nothing about it in our own church." For Fitzgerald, there was a palpable sense of contradiction: "They were willing to deal with civil rights, but most are still convinced that being gay is unnatural, and a sin."[37]

Yet the work of Wagner and Fitzgerald, along with the NFPC's ongoing efforts to address sexuality, had a considerable impact. At the meetings the Ministry and Priestly Life Committee adopted a resolution to establish a formal task force to formulate a "critical and contemporary Catholic theological analysis of homosexuality" and further recommended that this task force include a "number of gay men and women." The NFPC boldly announced a $5,000 start-up foundation to fund the new project. The language in the resolutions used the term "gay," and not only "homosexuality"; termed gays "a significant minority"; acknowledged that gay men and women had children; and recognized the wrong of discrimination, which represented a major shift in the church's position. While the minutes of the proceeding suggest minor disagreement over terminology, the record suggests that after considerable deliberation, key resolutions had garnered much support. Fitzgerald found the process of advocacy empowering and a sign of liberalization—"when the convention started, we had to demand to be heard. By the end, they were coming to us asking for input and direction." In May, a San Francisco member of the CRH wrote to thank the president of the NFPC, indicating the CRH's approval of the NFPC's "courageous Christian stand for justice" without broaching the subject of the church's own institutional stances or prohibitions.[38]

Though the religious press cast a "wary eye" on the discussion of homosexuality at the meetings, several influential Salvatorians continued to support the gay task force proposal and referred to its opponents as purveyors of prejudice, a remarkable condemnation. But upon returning from San Francisco with a partial victory, Fitzgerald found diminishing support for his activism. Despite the defense by progressive brothers, by 1975 the Gay Ministry Task Force was, in the words of the Salvatorians, "effectively finished as an agent of change in the province. It even became a liability." Some observers believed that their entanglement with gay issues had irreparably polarized the Salvatorians, tarnishing subsequent progressive initiatives, even after the task force had disbanded. In their travels around the country, several leading Salvatorians heard much of the discontent firsthand. In late June 1974, they attempted to respond with a letter: "Both Ramon Wagner and Myron Wagner supported the Ministry Task Force document, and defended it at the national convention of priests, and referred to the critics of extending outreach to gays and lesbian laity as the view of out-of-touch homophobes," according to the Society of the Divine Savior historical account. But the official history also reported that the visibility of the initiative caused a backlash when open and active gay men began applying to the community, resulting in a number of unpleasant episodes in formation communities. In Wisconsin plenary meetings of the NFPC, no organizational initiatives were announced regarding the new resolutions just debated in the spring, while the following year, in 1975, the steering committee of the Wisconsin conference met at

Stevens Point, Wisconsin, apparently without taking up the topic of how to address the needs of gay Catholics. Fitzgerald's efforts at San Francisco had not led to an invitation to serve on the planned task force, nor to local dialogues between the NFPC, the Salvatorians, and other groups working on the issues, such as the CRH.[39]

Meanwhile, as rightward religious opposition intensified and commitment to gay liberation declined in the mid-1970s, the Milwaukee CRH reported that it had decided to disband due to the "lack of support we feel from both our professional clergy and our Gay people." The group found it difficult to establish a dialogue between the church and the gay community, concluding its business by drawing up a list of recommendations for future endeavors. Members complained of a lack of action and decided that future activities ought to have some affiliation with a church in order to bridge the divide, suggesting that perhaps not enough of the membership was religious. In addition, they noted the necessity to develop additional means of financial support.[40]

As the possibilities for reform from within the church evaporated, Fitzgerald returned to the gay community and made public appearances to advocate for what he now termed black gay liberation. In Milwaukee he was a guest on a public television program with the GPU, the CRH, and an allied lesbian organization. Their purpose was to convene "representatives of a group in society that feel that they are misunderstood," but their attempt to secure recognition through discussion did not necessarily permit them to examine in depth the nature of sexual or racial oppression. Several years later, Fitzgerald recalled the impact of his performance on television: "Seeing gay men and lesbians on TV had a profound effect on my life. It helped me to see myself." Yet sporadic and isolated interventions were never enough to overcome the forces of repression that had derailed Fitzgerald's activism over and over again.[41]

Fitzgerald was the only black speaker on the Milwaukee TV show, and he invoked the black civil rights movement to facilitate his advocacy for gay equality, comparing the divide between integrationists and black power to the divide between the closeted and those who came out. On the program, Fitzgerald corrected and clarified the teachings of the church, arguing that many theologians were reforming their views of homosexuality and that sexuality ought to be viewed as a gift from God. He summoned authority from his voice and his rhetoric as well as from his religious garb. In this sense, the purpose of the white religious collar he wore was not only the official function—"the outward sign of one's inward commitment to Christ"—but also a multifaceted symbol that Fitzgerald strategically deployed to secure a certain public legitimacy. It contradicted the normal assumptions about a black man with an Afro haircut and an advocate of gay liberation, signifying religiosity, commitment, seriousness, and celibacy.[42]

In his final major political appearance on record, Fitzgerald presented a singular response to what appeared to be a unified front of black religious opposition to gay rights. Traveling to his hometown of Philadelphia, Fitzgerald joined advocates to press for a gay rights measure and to lobby city council members to pass an ordinance to extend antidiscrimination protection to gays and lesbians. The city council hearings commenced in late 1974. A large contingent of African American conservatives turned out to oppose the measure, led by several local black religious leaders, including Rev. Melvin Floyd and Rev. Sam Hart. They had mobilized dozens of black evangelical supporters and spoke fervently against the recognition of antigay discrimination. For example, a number of women associated with the evangelical churches of Hart and Floyd expanded a kind of religious maternal argument that relied on a vernacular distinction between good and evil, right and wrong, and detailed their duties to protect their children from the corrupting influences of homosexuals. Several women believed the ordinance to be a sign that public schools would hire openly gay teachers.

Though white religious leaders testified on both sides of the question, reflecting the impact of both the liberalization of Protestantism since the 1960s and the rise of gay churches, black religious leaders almost universally denounced the granting of rights to homosexuals and did so based on their interpretation of the Bible, arguing that homosexuality was morally wrong.[43] Because of the unexpected level of controversy and higher-than-expected turnout by religious opponents of the measure, the chairman of the city council extended the hearings to a second day, when Fitzgerald was called to testify. He opened his testimony by identifying his membership in the Salvatorians, spoke out for black gay liberation, and set out to address the arguments advanced by the previous black religious testifiers. From the beginning, he established a personal foundation of experience that served to refute much of the antigay testimony, speaking in a characteristically soft voice with a pattern of speech that gathered urgency as he testified to his background: "I am also gay, and I want that to be part of the record. I am a born again Christian who is black and is gay." It is unknown if he faced the council members or the audience, but he was one of the few pro-gay witnesses to address directly the black religious members in attendance.

Drawing again on this authenticity of stylistic gestures of black power and a profession of religious devotion to God, he questioned the validity of the other black religious testimonies that preceded him. At least one of the dailies noted that he declared himself to be both gay and celibate and claimed to be a member of a religious order. Yet even this report did not identify him by race or mention the racial context in which Fitzgerald was responding to a long litany of attacks by black ministers. Unlike them and other evangelicals, however, Fitzgerald refused to speak for God: "What I will say is, because Jesus Christ has imbued me with love, and Jesus Christ is my lover, and because I am a lover of Jesus Christ I will speak to the issue." Fitzgerald referenced history and recounted his own experiences as a protester, locating sexual equality along the same path as the black struggle by arguing that "this is a civil rights bill." He spoke of the freedom to "hold hands in public, to be publicly identified as a gay or lesbian person," and pointed out that "black people can do that today. Interracial couples can do that today. But not more than fifteen years ago white ministers were saying very much the same thing that these black ministers are saying today." Finally, like many of the black witnesses and virtually all of the black women, he recited scripture, professing his mission to spread the news of the love of Jesus, who would take away one's sins: "And I would like to say to my gay brothers and sisters that you are loved by God because you were called into existence by God."[44]

At the time, in the Philadelphia city council hearing, Fitzgerald appeared as a singular figure that emerged out of thin air and seemed to speak transparently from his own personal experience that he presented for political purposes. Yet, as I have tried to demonstrate, this important performance rested rather on a longer labor of activism and a careful study of issues such as racism, social inequality, homophobia, and theology. As he deftly deployed the comparison of sexual struggles with African American history, his position sometimes appeared to be overgeneralizing and essentialist: "I am gay from birth," he declared. Again, the analogy of gayness with race may have served to secure the pro-rights position and de-legitimate homophobia, but the political context had pressured him, and many other witnesses, to claim a predetermined and uniform gay identity that proved ahistorical. In the end, their valiant efforts—whether sophisticated or pragmatic—had not prevailed, and the gay rights measure went down to defeat in 1975.[45]

Fitzgerald apparently returned to Milwaukee, and after this string of losses he retreated from the political spotlight for reasons that were not entirely clear but probably reflected his own fatigue as well as rightward shifts in politics more generally. He departed the Salvatorian headquarters for a period of discernment around 1977–79, returning to Philadelphia, and continued to perform the same kind of work geared toward youth counseling. He traveled to Germany, working on a U.S. army base in Stuttgart; returned again as a teacher at the Philadelphia Day Care Center for several months in 1978; and then worked as a community facilitator for immigrants, performing home visits and case work in 1979 while searching for more suitable employment. (He compiled a typed résumé at this time.) He worked in New York at a nursery and at a Catholic charity for teenage boys while he remained on leave, and the Salvatorian records reported that he was "still considered under vows, [during] a period of discernment."

Fitzgerald continued to immerse himself in community life, according to a Philadelphia friend, Jefferson Keith, who first met him at "a gay men's rap group in West Philly." By that time he had earned a reputation as an important activist, and Keith recalled that he "had heard of him, since we were both active in gay groups in the city, and it was unusual to have a Catholic brother, doing that sort of thing." In the rap group that both later attended, Fitzgerald had caused a stir by accusing some of the white members of acting in racist ways.[46] Here again, only traces of Fitzgerald appear into the late 1970s, and by the summer of 1981 he reported he was tired of Philadelphia and wished to live again with the others from his Catholic order.

From 1982 to 1984 Fitzgerald returned to the fold of the Salvatorians and was assigned far from a gay urban subculture in Huntsville, Alabama, where he assisted with maintaining a Society of the Divine Savior house with a senior priest and brothers and performed the daily activities of a pastoral assistant in a parish of five hundred families, St. Joseph's Catholic Community. After he moved to Alabama, he wrote that "the doctors told me I have Aids [sic] and about two years to live," but Fitzgerald claimed that "there is no pain physically." However, "emotionally I get depressed lots." In reaching out and writing, he found something to "help my depretion [sic]." As he was no longer teaching or counseling and was no longer in contact with youth, depression seems like a reasonable response to the darkening situation. A loyal friend and correspondent, Jefferson Keith brought him the relief of friendship as they exchanged a series of letters beginning in 1984. "Today I got your letter—and Boy! Was I happily surprised (sp?) to hear from you," Fitzgerald wrote. "I needed to hear from you and you came through—Thank you!" Keith had sent him what he described as a "lovely meditation," which was "hanging on my bedroom door, so I see it and remember you often as I pass by." Relying on these personal anecdotes to sustain him, he called Keith a "a loving, caring, and faithful friend!!"[47]

To cope with his depression, he engaged a therapist and at the same time felt the spark of romance in a casual relationship with younger man from the West Indies, whom he described as "very Christian and straight, Seventh Day

Adventist & Black." Fitzgerald fantasized about the love interest, who was only nineteen, and noted that he "has been abel [sic] get me to share some of my years with him—Irvine is very straight and caring." Perhaps because Irvine was straight, Fitzgerald felt comfortable bringing him on a family visit to Philadelphia. But his work in the isolated, rural South and the seemingly platonic friendship with Irvine did not fulfill his fundamental desires regarding gay life and identity that he had cultivated over the past decade of struggle. "I love the people [and] they love me," he wrote. "However, I do feel like I only let them see 1/2 of me at times."[48]

By this time, Fitzgerald was aware that he had contracted HIV but apparently moved in and out of a kind of denial about his health, admitting himself into local hospitals and then claiming he was well and disease-free. What he called Fitzgerald's stories about his "miraculous cure" weighed heavily on Keith—they "made me feel very sad while he was wanting me to be happy for him"—and were a sign of Fitzgerald's continued resistance to coping with a terminal illness. In the year following his diagnosis, he told Keith that his "health is much better; so much so I feel the doctors have made a mistake. My depression has passed, so I feel at peace and happy!" Perhaps his closest friend and only openly gay friend known to the family, Keith received a brief letter of thanks from Fitzgerald's mother, Mary Mosee, in the final months before his death. A letter he had sent to her had "made her day," but she also noted that her son's health varied daily between decline and stabilization. Fitzgerald began to suffer more from the symptoms of full-blown AIDS, and intestinal infections sent him to the doctor. The deterioration of the body surprised Fitzgerald, according to Keith, and he talked of returning Philadelphia to live with his family.[49]

Keith wrote in his diary of Fitzgerald on several occasions in 1986, at a time when the number of cases of AIDS was outpaced only by soaring national apathy. In fact, Keith considered living abroad, after traveling to Puerto Rico and Spain: "I've wanted to get more involved in Central America issues but I keep getting drawn back to gay things. Particularly now with the gay 'community' going through so many difficult changes (and also my own group, BWMT [Black and White Men Together]), I feel like I want to stay involved." In return for his service to others, Keith believed that the community offered "emotional support," quipping that there was "sometimes a little sex on the side." But his entries concerning Fitzgerald also demonstrate the stresses and anxiety of such involvement and the worry of a dedicated friend. When Fitzgerald returned to Philadelphia at some point in the summer of 1986, Keith encountered him and planned to introduce him to his new friend, a black gay activist. "A week ago Grant-Michael came to town and I decided he and Guy really should meet each other," Keith noted, but he became "pretty disgusted and wanted to drop the whole thing" when the meetings fell apart. When the veteran Fitzgerald finally did meet Guy, Keith saw that the "two of them knew a lot of people in common, and they would be both in national Black Gay circles and in the gay religious circles (Guy is very religious and identifies with the Gay MCC [Metropolitan Community Church] . . . although his attendance there is sporadic)."[50]

On the same occasion, Keith reflected on his own anxiety in the face of the crisis: "I guess have health on my mind a lot lately because Grant-Michael was in town," he wrote. And their reunion served only to increase his concern about his friend's well-being: "[Fitzgerald] feels tired and weak a lot and it's obvious he is not 'well' at all. But he hoped it was partly my own difficult attitude. . . . I'm very skeptical about all that." After he saw Fitzgerald, Keith read an article on AIDS in *Newsweek*, a "very emotional and human-interest type writing, and very scary," that reported on the continuous spread of the infection into new population groups. In addition to the prognosis of his friends, then, "all that sort of talk really keeps me on edge."

In the final months, Keith recalled, "it was interesting for me to see some other sides of him, such as the Black Activist side or the Gay Religious Side," and he reported that Fitzgerald could "still have animated conversations on these subjects." Fitzgerald presented various effects of the illness, exhibiting loss of both his ability to read and his memory. "I was nervous that he was kind of living on borrowed time," Keith wrote. But he continued to telephone his friends, moving back and forth between the hospital and hospice; in the end he suffered a great deal of pain ("in spite of the morphine"). Keith noted in his diary, "And then: on a Monday night his sister called me to say he had passed."[51]

The newspapers treated his death in different ways, with the gay press reprinting his eulogy and honoring his contributions and the city daily, though running the story of his death, becoming intrigued by the fact that a clergyman had died of AIDS. In addition to its story on Fitzgerald, the *Milwaukee Sentinel* reported on another clergyman who had recently passed and mentioned that he had "known Brother Grant-Michael Fitzgerald, who died here last November of AIDS." The paper added that "in a few cases, priests with AIDS have been given money for medical expenses and then told to leave their dioceses, according to Brother Rick Garcia of Chicago, who has ministered to the gay community for eight years." From the perspective of the church, the death signified a lapse in the performance of the clerical duties, with the consolatory observation that "priests are human and priests fail."

The Salvatorians, however, had stood by Fitzgerald in his return from Europe and then through his illness.[52]

The service for Fitzgerald opened with "I Am the Resurrection and the Life, Says the Lord," and the hymn "Keep Your Eye on That Prize" and included readings from Isaiah, followed by a section in which "friends remember[ed] the life of Grant-Michael." Two members of his biological or traditional family, his grandmother Jane Smith and sister, Gerri Fitzgerald, also attended. After several personal testimonies, they played what was believed to be his favorite hymn, "Victory in Jesus," followed by a "litany of prayer," including a call and response between one and many, and this litany of prayer was then followed by a "scripture and homily delivered by Reverend James Tinney of Faith Temple," a gay black congregation in Washington, D.C., who is the subject of chapter 7. Tinney read the official Catholic biography of Fitzgerald, describing him as "the first openly gay black Christian in a public role in the U.S.," and reported that Faith Temple was considering giving an annual award to the individual who represented "one or some of the causes for which Fitzgerald stood."[53]

Keith recalled the service as "beautiful" and that Fitzgerald's sister, Gerri, "was very much in charge." He also commented, "Imagine three white priests conducting a service for a congregation that was about 90 percent black in a black neighborhood in West Philly!" Here it would seem that Keith mistook one of the priests, Tinney, for white, though he identified as black. Keith went on to note that "at least one of the priests had known Grant-Michael for 20 years since college and was very positive about his liberation work and call[ed] him the 'conscience of the Salvatorians'!"[54]

The day after Fitzgerald passed away, Keith had decided to publish an obituary or memorial tribute in the *Philadelphia Gay News* and went to see Tommi Avicolli, the news editor, to ask him about the possibility. Keith's decision to write something reflected not only his sense of vulnerability but also his desire for the correct narrative, a prospect that left him "worried": "Grant-Michael liked candor, I know that much. I didn't name his family or his religious orders but I did say a lot of other stuff." Meanwhile, Keith recorded in his diary that his friend Michael, who lived downstairs, "was coughing all week and had a high fever last before he went to the hospital. We're afraid for him because he too is at high risk for AIDS."[55]

At the end of the day, Brother Grant-Michael Fitzgerald had lost far more than he had won—the Catholic church retrenched, the Harambee school never rehired him, and his campaigns for gay rights proved insufficient to win passage. And, of course, he lost his life. But here one sees a turning point, where a stronger and more developed gay community stepped in to recognize and honor Fitzgerald, and another moment when a black family and white gay community came together, even if only temporarily in mourning. Fitzgerald had pioneered black gay liberation on several fronts at once and championed this cause from a vantage point of virtue that few had ever imagined possible for a black gay man. To speak of gay rights and civil rights in the same breath, to explain the indignity of homophobia in terms of the experience of racism, and to call for the reform of the church, education, and the state were struggles always already destined for failure. But this was not an ordinary loss, rather the beginning of a search for recognition and community that would move along a path first charted by this courageous young man.

Chapter Six

In the Life of Joseph Beam

By the 1980s, long after gay liberation impulses had mobilized post-Stonewall activists, and the rapid proliferation of bars and clubs, pornographic paperbacks and magazines, and bathhouses and cruising seemed to undermine or at least divert commitment to the gay revolution, the erotic metropolis had more fully expanded into black lives. Racial, social, and political isolation continued to define the black gay experience, and yet second-wave feminism, particularly work by black lesbian feminists in the 1970s, opened up new frontiers of activism. The founding of the National Black Feminist Organization; the issuing of the Combahee River Collective Statement (1977), the black feminist manifesto documenting simultaneous oppressions; and the prominence of lesbian feminist writers helped to sustain the production of new knowledge and institutional networks.[1]

The expansion of black lesbian feminism brought the elaboration of the concept of the intersection, invented by leading activist-scholars Barbara Smith and Audre Lorde, with Smith perhaps becoming more important to academic theorizing. In the classic 1982 anthology *All the Women Are White, All the Blacks Are Men, but Some of Us Are Brave*, the editors reprinted Smith's 1977 essay "Toward a Black Feminist Criticism" in which she argued that "a Black feminist approach to literature that embodies the realization that the politics of sex as well as the politics of race and class are crucially interlocking factors in the works of Black women writers is an absolute necessity." Although black feminists gradually advanced in literary and academic circles, their success in gaining recognition was only partial. For black gay men, it was perhaps even slower and less successful. Rather than a location of interconnectedness and multiplicity, or of fluidity and coalitional possibility, the intersection just as often confined activists to isolation.[2]

Perhaps no figure better illustrates the importance of intersectional strategy, its difficulty in adapting to shifting terrain, and the complications of negotiating multiple sites of identity than Joseph Beam. Beam represented the aspirations of a generation of black gay men for self-definition and cultural invention and pioneered a collective voice and visibility, leading dozens of black gay poets and writers. Unlike black feminists of the 1970s and 1980s, however, just at the moment that these men were poised to revise the literary canon and have an impact on diversity in the university, many fell in the AIDS crisis.

Loneliness and Loving Black Men

Like Grant-Michael Fitzgerald, Joe Beam was born in Philadelphia to a working-class family in West Philadelphia, and he entered into a predominantly white world of elite education and religious institutions. Beam was also a scholarship boy and attended Malvern Preparatory School. Beam recalled that he was "the only Black student in [the] freshman class of over 100," while at home the "brothers in the neighborhood" questioned his choice not to attend their local school. In these years, Beam transferred from school to school (attending six different ones), and his adolescence involved a daily routine of negotiating the predominantly white institutions, and his predominantly black neighborhood, where he spent some time with his parents and a series of boarders in their home, and long hours in solitude studying and writing.[3]

Beam was closest to his mother, Dorothy Beam, who had completed her high school diploma at age thirty, the same year that he was born, 1954, and eventually went on to Cheyney State College to graduate in 1966 with a degree in education, the first to do so in her immediate family. Beam described his father, Sun Beam, as a "warm brown man" who could be distant, silent, and detached. Born in Barbados, Sun Beam had worked as a janitor at a Philadelphia bank for at least ten years before retiring. Beam understood their class or economic status in anxious terms: "My background is not middle-class. . . . If forced to describe my upbringing, I would call it aspirant." He also appreciated the advantages he had earned working hard in school, while at the same time he felt ambivalent about the distance that had grown between him and his father. He appreciated his parents' financial support—"they have never spared me creature comforts"—but believed that they were "hurt people and move from that hurt place within themselves," a recognition that helped him understand himself.[4]

But unlike Fitzgerald, for Beam the church played a relatively minor role in his upbringing as well as later in life—he did not mention attending church beyond Sunday school or refer to religious faith in his large corpus of political and personal writing. Even so, he attended a Catholic private high school at one point and, after graduation, won yet another scholarship to Franklin College, which he described as "a nondescript Baptist college in Indiana." He too majored in psychology and enjoyed working in media, especially radio and television broadcasting, and earned solid grades. He appeared to be a sociable joiner: he was a member of a recently formed group known as FIM, or Franklin Independent Men, and the Student Activities Council, contributed to *Apogee* literary magazine, and served as treasurer of the Black Student Union. His involvement in a black student group would have been new to him, and Beam later observed that "I have always been different, prior to being gay . . . in high school I was too smart and too white, and in college I wasn't Black enough, although and in spite of massive amounts of work I did with the Black Student Union." Few other documents during his college years concerning his friendships, romance, or other personal crises have been preserved, but his sense of being a racial outsider certainly persisted after graduation. Unlike Fitzgerald, he remained in the closet throughout his undergraduate education, and yet he would not have been in a state of total sexual denial. Beam saved a neatly organized notebook from a course in adolescent psychology and from another course in experimental psychology in which he studied Erik Erikson, Sigmund Freud, and Erich Fromm, noting the latter's emphasis on "acceptance" and the "unity and integration of self." Given his future investment in the recognition of black gay lives, it is striking that in college Beam underlined with a highlighter the question "What is identity?," listing its "components of identification w/individuals, parents, teachers, friends, models to simulate, as well as capacities, opportunities, and ideals."[5]

Studying psychology did not spare Beam from his own difficult challenges with personal development. Like many college-age men, he chafed at the contradictions of student life, yearning for independence and yet remaining financially dependent on his family. Trying to fit into the social scene at Franklin, Beam overspent his budget, found himself broke before the end of the month, and wrote desperate, pleading letters to his parents for financial help, despite his understanding of them as barely middle class. After his first year, he debated leaving Franklin and transferring to his mother's alma mater, Cheyney State. At another point he wrote to his parents and threatened to kill himself if they did not send money, and this was not the first time he countenanced such an act. Some of his correspondence suggests that he had attempted suicide at a younger age.

His emotionality and impulsiveness continued to guide Beam's decisions through the Franklin years, and after graduating in 1976 he followed his heart and set out on the trail of a love interest from college, a man referred to in his papers only as Joel. Beam once identified the impulsive move as his coming out: "I came out in Portland, in my 1970 VW bus. It was not that I had sex with a man, but it was the first time I had been willing to recognize that feeling."[6] The romantic interest with whom he "had gone to school . . . for a year in Indiana" had transferred at the end of the "year (freshman) to a school in Portland." It is not clear if Joel was white or black, but the odds are that he was white, since Franklin was a predominantly white college.[7]

What happened to Beam's fleeting attempt to relocate with his erstwhile boyfriend remains difficult to discern with precision. In correspondence dating from a later, longer relationship, he again mentioned the Portland experience: "I am sure you are afraid of me like I was afraid of Joel many years ago in Portland, Oregon. But I never communicated that fear to him, I simply ran—in this case drove—as fast as I could away from him, back to the security of Mom on the east coast." Beam recalled a telling image of personal anxiety that would complicate and undermine future intimate relationships, saying, "God, I was so scared, oh so scared, but I wanted to be with him so much. But I couldn't handle it. I jumped on the highway and at 70 mph raced out of Portland as quickly as I could." For Beam, this moment of indecision seemed to indicate a deeper fear of his own desire, and so in a sense he had not really come to terms with his sexual orientation yet.

Judging from his intellectual interests and pursuits in college, Beam had already embarked on a course toward some kind of cultural activism. He had followed his interests in journalism, media, and social networking at Franklin and then in 1977 moved on to Iowa State University in Ames to earn an advanced degree in communications. Under this financial pressure, according to Beam, he "managed a job and apartment and car amidst incredibly wide mood swings" and failed to enjoy or excel at the university because "all of my waking energy focused on this constant vigil against being perceived as gay." Years later, he recalled that in the "winter of '79, in grad school, in the hinterlands of Iowa, I thought I was the first Black gay man to have ever lived. I knew not how to live my life as a man who desired emotional, physical and spiritual fulfillment from other men," and therefore he recalled the closet as a distracting burden, vigilantly controlling how he gestured or was perceived. "I spent so much energy in self-observation that little was left for classwork and still less to challenge the institutionalized racism I found there."[8]

After withdrawing from Iowa—Beam felt that he had failed—he sought the security of home and his mother, rarely mentioned his father, and on occasion encountered his brother, Charlie, whom he described as an "almost bag-man." From Philadelphia his writings suggest disappointment, depression, and fatigue, even as he spent downtime writing, immersing himself in literature, and studying social issues. More immediately, however, Beam had to cope with the urban crisis and endemic unemployment, especially for black men. In President Ronald Reagan's America, the unemployment rate increased to record highs for black men and was even higher for young black men in Philadelphia. In a tightening economy in which deindustrialization dictated flows of capital, segregated residential growth, and chronic underemployment, Beam confronted the intersection of racism and late-capitalist flexible accumulation, in which consistent forty-hour workweeks with benefits and dependability were replaced by part-time and temporary stints, wage stagnation, and little job security. He found employment at Sam Goody's, a retailer of musical instruments and records, and at the end of December 1980 Beam wrote that "I'll be glad when the Christmas season and Sam Goody's is over. Still feel kind of out of tune with myself, w/my environment, etc. Not really making any money at work." Beam went on to complain, "There seems to be little time for anything but work and that consumes too much of my energy [and] at the same time offers no psychic reward." "Bills piling up . . . these are hard times for me as well as others," he noted. And his romantic connections further drained him because he felt that he always gave more than he received. Perhaps the only positive note was a letter from a man who called himself Ombaka (Percy Tate), a straight black man incarcerated for life with whom he would commence a five-year correspondence.[9]

Eventually he saved enough money for a deposit and first month's rent and found a studio apartment in Center City, Philadelphia, on the fourth floor of a large house at 2039 Spruce Street that Beam described as "a rather shabby brownstone . . . near fashionable Rittenhouse Square." Paying the rent continued to be a challenge, as he often cobbled together cashier's checks and postal money orders, but Beam had finally arrived, on his own, and settled into the gay ghetto. Despite the fact that he had pursued the possibility of a gay relationship from Indiana to Portland, Beam understood this new venture as paving the way out of the closet that stifled him in Iowa: "I came out on January 25, 1981. I remember it because it was the first meeting of Phila. BWMT, and the first time that I went into an openly gay environment and declared myself as gay." The organization Beam referred to—"Phila. BWMT"—was the local chapter of Black and White Men Together, a gay interracial social group first formed in San Francisco in 1980 to explore issues of racism and foster friendships (discussed in greater detail in chapter 8). To explain his choice, he wrote, "I have never had propensity for white men, although on some levels

Joseph Beam, ca. 1986. Joseph Beam led a new generation of black gay activists in seeking greater visibility and a collective voice. Inspired by black lesbian feminists, Beam advocated for the making of a brotherhood that could bridge differences of sexual orientation in the black community. (Photographs and Prints Division, Schomburg Center for Research in Black Culture, New York Public Library, Astor, Lenox and Tilden Foundations).

it is easier to connect with them then [*sic*] the brothers." Given the still-pervasive stigmatization of homosexuality as well as the complications of race, it was not surprising that Beam had struggled to come out. "I've spent a lot of time running," Beam wrote to a friend. "In college I was so afraid of my gayness, that I ran to the west coast after graduation. When the shit came up again I ran to the Midwest for graduate school. I flunked out of graduate school because so much energy was going into keeping those feelings down that I couldn't do anything else."[10]

If Fitzgerald found community in the church, with his sense of identity evolving at a distance from a gay neighborhood, Beam immersed himself "in the life," with clubs and discos, bathhouses and cruising just outside his doorstep. Beam drank whiskey and Coke and patronized the local gay bars—the Steps, Allegro, and Smart Bar—but also reported that he sometimes felt bored by the nightlife and offhandedly remarked, "The bar is my home, my second around the corner home. I am a regular. . . . The drinks are strong, which is perhaps more a disservice than a benefit." His new urban routine also presented him with a vibrant political community, including the Gay Coffee House and Gay Activists Alliance, the *Philadelphia Gay News* and the Philadelphia Lesbian and Gay Task Force. The promise of Stonewall was realized and celebrated, and yet Beam remained isolated and alienated because of race, specifically because of the politics of the intersection. In an essay that he later published for a gay newspaper, "Black Gay History: Act Like You Know," Beam had complained that too often his teachers of history failed to include material about Africa, while others overlooked the fact that the Stonewall rebellion "was instigated by Latino and black drag queens." Conflicting, divergent, and partial narratives of gay life had substituted for the whole; gay communities formed in tandem with the exclusion of gay men of color. Rather than a seamless migration into gay community life and sexual liberation, Beam focused on marginalization: "We, like those outrageous drag queens who started it all, are the fringe of the movement—relegated to 'color' supplements, minority task forces, and workshops on racism."[11]

Beam's move into the gay ghetto had not therefore satisfied his longing for a community, which became a key theme in his writings on the vicissitudes of black gay identity. "I keep searching for home. When I'm in Black neighborhoods, I feel safe in my Blackness, but know that I'm seen as queer and as a faggot. In white areas, I'm perceived as Black and therefore despicable. Where can I go where these large segments of self can come together and flourish?" he asked. "I've always been too white, or too Black, or too much like a sissy, or too smart, or not smart enough, or too dark, or too poor," wrote Beam.[12]

In the context of his epistolary labor—writing, receiving, and collecting letters—Beam considered the ways in which the construction of black masculinity demanded a pose of cool strength, hip bravado, and invulnerability. He observed how black men "gather in public spaces: barber shops, street corners, pool rooms, basketball courts," and yet Beam felt that they never truly connected on a personal level. It was a sphere of performance or competition where they "can talk about dick and ass and pussy, but not about the fierce competition among our selves for the few jobs and scholarships." His sense of manhood originated in his relationship with his father—the "warm brown man of seventy . . . from Barbados." Beam conveyed his gratitude and acknowledged that his father had "worked hard for me so that I can write these words on this page," and yet he felt that their relationship suffered from the divide of black masculinity—of generational and experiential differences. Since his adolescence, Beam moved with some ease between black and white social worlds, but his father had not enjoyed these options for mobility.

Beam's academic success separated them, and yet Beam felt connected: "his past is my present, our present the future." Later in life, when coming out to his father, he did not expect affirmation or even understanding, and he accepted the fact that "he does not ask me about being gay or why I wish to write about it."[13]

By the 1980s, after coming out, Beam could explain his estrangement from family in terms of his status as a black gay man, and not only in terms of their disparate social opportunities and endeavors. In turn he sought to explicate and address contemporary crises of black masculinity, particularly the intersection of economic discrimination, unemployment, and social stigma: "I dream of a time when it is not Black men who fill the nation's prisons; when we will not seek solace in bottles and Top papers." Despite these racialized social pressures, Beam observed, black men were expected to remain "silent and stoic rather than acknowledge just how much my life and experience is discounted each day." Yet when Beam pursued a sociological analysis of the contemporary crisis, he encountered misconceptions concerning homosexuality. In one essay, for example, Beam refers to the "noted sociologist" Robert Staples, whose books on black masculinity treated homosexuality as a pathology or a moral failing, and therefore Beam sought to develop his own antiracist and nonhomophobic analyses.[14]

In a society that continually obsessed over the problematic nature of black manhood, Beam sought to foster the expansion of community through appeals to a shared racial experience and social position beyond differences of sexuality, departing from other black gay critics. The Washington, D.C., activist and educator Ron Simmons criticized the homophobia of black nationalists, but Beam would not directly address black homophobia until relatively late, and even then with a more conciliatory tone: "There are so many issues that divide us as Black men. Answer this: when was the last time you had a 'heart-to heart-talk' w/another Black man?" While gay radicals critiqued the homophobia of black power radicals, such as Eldridge Cleaver, they also appropriated ostensibly hostile political discourse to their causes and concerns. "Bobby, Huey, and Malcolm gave us that rhetoric in the 60s," declared Beam, referring to the famed black radicals Bobby Seale, Huey Newton, and Malcolm X. Later Beam clipped and saved a review of the *Autobiography of LeRoi Jones* that appeared in the *Philadelphia Tribune*, at the same time that he wrote more about the antigay sentiments of black nationalists. At this intersection of reflecting on his relationships with his father and other men and of studying texts of the ongoing crises of black masculinity, Beam's instincts were communal and collective, reflecting his driving desire for connection. The phrase with which he became widely associated, "Brother to Brother," appeared first in his diaries: "Brother to Brother; I have for a long time felt estranged . . . [from] my father, my gay brother, uncles, cousins. . . . I often love these men very deeply but could not find the words or actions that would bridge the chasm of fear and anger that lay between us."[15]

For Beam this space could foster "the silent love that Black men give to other Black men" and replace a homophobic "silence" that was enforced by "a world where we are not meant to survive" (a phrasing that echoed Audre Lorde's haunting poem on the fate of gay and lesbian marginalization, "A Litany for Survival"). Beam's inquiry into the meaning of black manhood led him to the problem of African American incarceration and the growing prisoners' rights movement. In his writings, he had explored both the sociological and erotic interconnections of the prison: "I did not know that one of every four Black men would experience prison in his lifetime. Nor did I know that my motivation for writing to prisoners arose from a deep sense of captivity as a closeted gay man rather than [an] act of righteousness [that] would become an integral part of my life and a place for dreaming." In a partially filled diary, he compiled a kind of archival list of his correspondence with several prisoners, including David A. Keely, whom he wrote to in 1980, and another prisoner in Angola, Louisiana, Morris Gyles, at the same time that he subscribed to *PROSCRIP*, a newsletter published by a prisoners' advocacy group devoted to stopping sexual assaults in prison.[16]

The longest correspondence he had with a black prisoner lasted more than five years and included many long letters (some of which remain restricted in the archive). Beam's relationship with Percy Tate, who changed his name to Kenyatta Ombaka Saki and went by Ombaka, was both passionate and intellectually serious. They "began corresponding under unusual circumstances." "I had been writing to another prisoner named Morris who was transferred or released, but in any case had vacated this particular cell which was to become Ombaka's new home," and he found a letter left behind, probably hidden, that featured "a photograph of me, read it and responded." At the time that Beam described the incident, the correspondence had been ongoing for three years, involving some forty letters that revealed substantial commitment to the long-distance friendship. The letters to Ombaka began at a moment of directional change, according to Beam. In the beginning he was "fresh from graduate school and thoroughly naïve," and from that experience he was gaining a sense of how to relate to differences and of the "necessity of acknowledging others different from ourselves." He explained the current state of economic problems and cultural possibility in an early letter: "I am 26 yrs old, & enjoy reading, photography, the arts, and when I get a chance I play basketball. I sell stereo equipment for a living, although recently it's not been much business, considering the expense of necessities. And although I don't play a musical instrument, I enjoy music with a passion—everything from classical to disco and in between."[17]

Beam's close friend and black gay activist Max Smith also corresponded with a prisoner, but his relationship eventually turned amorous. Born the same year as Beam in Hickory, North Carolina, into a Baptist and Methodist family, Smith played basketball at Jefferson City High School and graduated from Michigan State University with a degree in communication arts in 1976, the same year that Beam did. But Smith was more out at Michigan than Beam was at Franklin, and he participated in the first successful effort to pass an antidiscrimination legal ordinance protecting gays and lesbians. Smith went on to work for Democratic Party campaigns in Missouri and Michigan and in 1976 moved to Chicago, where he remained politically active, joined the Metropolitan Community Church, and worked in advertising and sales.[18]

Both Smith and Beam had also joined organizations dedicated to the discussion and reform of masculinity, but now Smith was pursuing the romance, and "instead of going to the Boston Men's retreat weekend, I went to Mississippi in July" to visit his epistolary lover, Eddie Howard, incarcerated at the notorious Parchman prison. So invested in the potential relationship was Smith that he attended Howard's parole board hearing and agreed to serve as a sponsor as well as provide a home, but the parole board denied the appeal. Perhaps disheartened by the realization that his lover might never attain his freedom, Smith reported in a letter to Beam that Howard had been convicted of two rapes and had committed an assault again while on parole only five years later. Smith had gone to extraordinary lengths to secure his release again, including presenting a letter from one of the first victims forgiving Howard, but it had not convinced the board. Despite the dim possibility of release, Beam encouraged Smith and wrote at one point that "I support you wholeheartedly in your risk taking." For Smith, the relationship was not only emotional but practical. As Smith put it, "Eddie has become my personal solution to the AIDS crisis." Before widespread awareness of the HIV epidemic, black gay men frequented any number of cruising sites and bathhouses, but now the authorities remained unsure about the safety of oral sex while definitely advising the use of prophylactics for anal sex. With Eddie Howard, Smith declared, "the safe sex rule will be broken because it must be broken and I say it must be broken."[19]

In his many letters, Beam kept Ombaka apprised of the progress of his endeavors to become a professional writer, listing each completed piece and publication, and boasted that he had landed a position as the author of a biweekly column in a local gay paper, *Au Courant*. "Too many nights these last few years I've wished Ombaka were here, holding me, telling me that everything is going to be all right," he wrote to Max Smith. For both Beam and Smith, these pen pals substituted in some way for lovers they could not find, for desires that remained unfulfilled, and for companionship unavailable to them in white gay communities. Beam often compared his life to a prison cell while his feelings for Ombaka deepened; their long correspondence had become "one of the most important friendships in my life," and he confessed to Smith that "there are many moments when I thought of us as lovers and we've talked about that a little bit."[20]

Through theses dialogues with Ombaka on questions of incarceration, nationalism, and masculinity, Beam came to understand "how my work simply isn't radical enough": "I've been reading James Forman's *The Making of Black Revolutionaries*, which on some level speaks to the development of a revolutionary consciousness, but says nothing to me as a gay, pro-feminist man. The homophobia and sexism of the 1960s Black liberation struggle, in part, caused that movement's demise." At one point, Beam had the idea of coauthoring a piece with Ombaka and wrote to the novelist John Edgar Wideman for advice after reading his memoirs, *Brothers and Keepers*, on the incarceration of his brother. He described their backgrounds as very different: "Perhaps most notably, he identifies as heterosexual and I as a gay man. He is Muslim, I'm agnostic." Beam then requested an autographed copy of the book for Ombaka and sent Wideman copies of his key writings on black gay identity and masculinity. In the midst of the urban crisis, Beam envisioned the possibilities for building a new sense of brotherhood that fused love and politics. In turn, he acknowledged his alienation from whiteness. "It seems like white men will make it without my assistance. Doors will fling open—seas will part w/o me by his side," he quipped ironically. And then he concluded, "A Black man will need, will want my help," and this need originated in deeper shared exclusions—"Smashed fingers in doors attest to that. Brown man on brown sheets on a brown night."[21]

At the same time, the satisfying erotic connections of some of his personal relationships were not easily reconciled with the refusal of several of his amours to come out or to appear with him in gay places. His sense of isolation and distance continued to feel like incarceration, and this painful void motivated his activism perhaps more than any single issue or problem.

"I sometimes think that I'm searching for the love my father didn't give me, but that's far too simple[,] perhaps too Freudian," Beam wrote to his closest friend, Essex Hemphill. "The man I've connected to most deeply, Stanley, resembles my father. Darker than me, husky, strong but gentle." The lost brother, the distant father, the alienating white gayness—each had motivated his search for community that took the form of the most resonant black vernacular of family, particularly brothers and brotherhood. To address the alienation of straightness, Fitzgerald had sought a brotherhood and religious community where love, solidarity, and purpose aligned belonging with faith but not with his sexual identity. What does it mean that Beam arrived at the same site of alienation through coming out, and where was he to turn for a new direction? "Please stay well in spirit, and believe that love will come to you and make you stronger, but be strong, now, while it seems love is not near. And please know, we're brothers," wrote Hemphill to Beam. Such assurances recurred throughout Beam's correspondence, indicating that Beam had discovered not just brotherhood but also a community of love.[22]

If coming out brought Beam the institutions of a gay community and the pleasures of nightlife, he also lucked into an offer of employment at a neighborhood bookstore that would satisfy his hunger for literature and point him toward his vocation. Ed Hernance, one of the owners of Giovanni's Room Bookstore at Twelfth Street and Pine, established in the early 1970s, ran into Beam at the Steps, a popular Center City nightclub that primarily attracted a young, white clientele, and the two started up a conversation that ended with a job offer to clerk at the bookstore.[23] After Beam accepted Hernance's terms and began working in January 1982, he became responsible for purchasing in certain specialties, especially feminist and multicultural lists, and coordinated the public readings by featured authors. The bookstore offered Beam an opportunity to learn the titles in gay and lesbian literature and to make contacts with prominent writers; the store was a "positive environment" and a "warm, supportive nurturing place."[24]

So much of his passion went into his cultural activism and authorial ambitions, and in turn this commitment seemed to alienate him from the community that surrounded him. Beam gained broad social recognition but remained alone, endlessly searching for a lover, while dating men who were unwilling to commit. Beam wrote of his ideal relationship and how this would enhance his writing, but his correspondence often reveals a combination of self-sabotage and a tightening schedule. He had not stopped to breathe or to take stock of his situation and figure out how to sustain a romance until several years after coming out. "It's only been for the last year or so that I've been the least bit interested in an on-going committed relationship. It has something to do with AIDS, with me approaching 30. . . . A year ago a white lover might have been a possibility, today I wouldn't entertain that notion at all," he wrote.[25]

If Grant-Michael Fitzgerald was encouraged by a liberal strain of Catholicism, Beam was buoyed by lesbian feminist culture. As he stocked the store shelves, he found the inventory's limitations both frustrating and inspiring and sought out a perspective of feminists of color, perusing catalogs from the groundbreaking publisher Kitchen Table: Women of Color Press.[26] Because black male authors "almost always have real awful stuff to say about gay men," Beam declared in a letter to one of his lovers, "writers like Cherrie Moraga, Barbara Smith, Michele Parkerson, particularly Audre Lorde, inspire me to continue writing." He was reading and recommending *Jonestown and Other Madness* by Pat Parker, *Living as a Lesbian* by Cheryl Clarke, and *Black Lesbian in White America* by Anita Cornwell. He understood Moraga's influential *Loving in the War Years* to "speak of being loved unconditionally," a state of being that had eluded Beam. In 1984 at Giovanni's Room Bookstore, he organized a reading and reception for Moraga, who coedited with Gloria Anzaldua the pathbreaking multicultural and feminist anthology, *This Bridge Called My Back*, that would transform Left activism and the culture wars of the 1980s. At the reading he observed that her performance provided a "strong way to reveal secrets." On his day off, he telephoned Moraga, wrote up an interview with her, and finished up the week with a Sunday party for Mary Daly, the radical lesbian feminist. Writing to one of the most influential black feminists of her time, Barbara Smith, Beam declared, "I should say from the outset that it is your work and the work of Audre Lorde and Cherrie Moraga that have given me the courage to begin doing the kind of Black gay activism and coalition building in which I'm involved." In searching for a "role model," Beam found himself crossing gender lines and adapting the strategies of exercising voice and promoting representation that black feminists had developed over the past decade. At the beginning of 1984, preparing to interview Audre Lorde about her latest collection of poems and essays, *Sister Outsider*, Beam proclaimed half-jokingly, "I'm such a woman-identified gay man; friends chide me about secretly desiring to be a lesbian."[27]

Beam also interviewed Audre Lorde for a piece in *Au Courant* and then began a significant correspondence with the influential and important author in 1984. By the spring he congratulated her on the fact that the *Philadelphia Gay News* agreed to run two full pages for his interview of her, sent her a copy of *Painted Bride Quarterly* (an arts journal) hoping to solicit an essay or poem, and bid her strength for her ongoing struggle with cancer. For her part, she wrote a quick note to congratulate him and particularly complimented him on some writing. Again, like in his relationship with Moraga and Smith, Beam testified to the importance of black feminist writings and personally thanked Lorde for being a "source of inspiration . . . [that] enables me to begin speaking." One year he received a surprise from Lorde: "Dear Joe: Income Tax Refund time, and a small contribution to *Black/Out* [a new national black gay and lesbian magazine]. I'm really looking forward to the next issue. Have a good summer and keep in touch!"[28]

What in retrospect may appear as obvious and organic to his condition—that "I am Black & gay"—for Beam gained meaning and intelligibility only haltingly and sometimes painfully through sustained thought and study, experimentation and revision. "There are moments that I feel invisible as I imagine Black lesbians have felt up until recently," he mused, and through this insight he came to disavow white gayness, withdrawing across the literary color line: "I can no longer read the gay male press or gay male literature. It is white, it does not apply." A major source of change, therefore, was an increasing sense of alienation from yet another community—the Center City area that only two years prior he had moved into—but this time, there would be no easy resolution. With more fervor and bitterness than in anything he had written of black straight men, Beam shot out, "I have grown weary of the blond blue eyed protagonist for whom everything resolves into a neat package," and he had also become "tired of the Fire Island, the clone moustache, and cropped hair."[29] Beam now refused a supposedly universal admiration for the white body that, since the days of pulp pornography, always figured as the aesthetic ideal, contrasted with the objectified and oversized, aggressive, and rough black sexual stud that only ever engaged in sexual relations with white men.

Though Beam found inspiration and support from black lesbians, his political work necessarily focused on addressing the immediate barriers confronting black gay men. "Black men loving black men is the revolutionary act of the 1980s," Beam proclaimed in one of his most important essays. Its revolutionary nature stemmed from its conflicted relationship to "60s revolutionaries such as Bobby Seale, Huey Newton, and Eldridge Cleaver [who] dare not speak our name." It was also a clear expression of one of Beam's key theoretical and strategic programs: sustaining a nurturing and supportive community for black gay men by embracing their diversity as well as by reaching across the gay-straight divide. In the midst of urban crisis and the demonization of all black men as criminal and pathological, Beam recommitted to building a new black brotherhood, writing, "Black men loving black men is an autonomous agenda for the '80s, which is not rooted in any particular sexual, political, or class affiliation, but in our mutual survival."[30]

In the Life

For three and half years at Giovanni's Room Bookstore, Beam managed the accounting, coordinated author appearances, ordered products, and processed and shipped book returns. He wrote and edited copy for advertisements, sorted domestic and foreign mail, and created in-store and window displays. What this meant was that Beam both read and did—he absorbed articles, books, and scholarly conferences; actively engaged amateur writers; joined the major black gay and lesbian organizations; and labored in community institutions. "Perhaps I'm a cultural worker which seems to better define the kind of stuff that I do. Activism seems to be more legalist, more of working with the powers that be," Beam wrote. Around the same time, he received a letter from a veritable literary soul mate—one of many writers whom he met and heard from—complaining that "he had grown weary of reading literature by white gay men who fell, quite easily, into three camps: the incestuous literati of Manhattan and Fire Island, the San Francisco cropped-moustache clones, and the Boston-to-Cambridge politically correct radicals." Several years later, a Yale undergraduate introduced to him by Essex Hemphill grumbled that "I have been given the names of many different publications but I have found them all to have a predominantly Gay White Male focus." Over and over again, what he saw and heard reiterated the pervasive silence of the black gay condition, even as he recommended other publications to friends and acquaintances. Perhaps to a greater extent than black lesbians, black gay men suffered from their stereotyping as neither literary nor intellectual—as his friend put it, in a "world where it is assumed that I can not read and can only afford picture books of naked men, you introduce me to a literature of bare souls."[31]

Another turning point that spurred Beam toward a new literary project was the publication in 1984 of *Black Men/White Men* by the founder of Black and White Men Together, Mike Smith. Beam and other black gay men participated in BWMT, but tensions of race and what many perceived to be white insensitivity had alienated some black men, and Beam himself had decided to stop attending Philadelphia-BWMT meetings. One of his closer friends, Max Smith, renamed the group "Black and Cracker Men Together," suggesting the level of suspicion of white members' motivations.[32] The book *Black Men/White Men* presented a collection of essays and poems by both black and white gay men that featured several spreads of erotic photographs of black men, some of them nude, but no nude shots of white men. Beam and other black gay writers criticized the book for its objectification of the black body. Smith had bitten off more than he could chew, objected Beam, and in the process "perpetuated age old stereotypes of the black man as dumb-hung stud and docile object who desperately needs and desires affirmation from whites." In response Beam predicted that "black gays are soon to follow the lead of black lesbians; our voices, from a whisper to a scream," would soon be recorded, collected, and published. If the other reviews by black gay men were any indication, Beam was correct. Sidney Brinkley, a Howard University graduate, wrote that he had anticipated Smith's book on black and white men together, though he "looked askance at such relationships," and found that it confirmed his view that inter-racial relationships were "fostered by white men who think of Blacks as nothing more than walking, talking phalluses, and by Blacks filled with self-hatred and an acute case of white fever." Whatever the merits of this commonly held view, Brinkley signaled a broader intervention evidenced by engagement with a politics of representation in which a new generation of black gay men rejected the cultural legacy of decades of objectification. In the 1960s, Shirley Clarke's portrait of Jason Holliday was seen as authentic and shocking, but now black gay critics could call out the white gaze, expose its bias and homo-geneity, and mobilize to reverse the negative effects.[33]

As early as 1984, Beam jotted down the idea of conducting interviews with others like himself, and in his diary in block letters he sketched an advertise-ment, "Wanted: Black Gay Men," seeking those who would represent experi-ence and fill in the gap of silence. In his words, "our story has not been told," and from the beginning he planned to emphasize social differences—"age, class, educational background, hue, and other barrier are important"—in this new project. As important as representation was authenticity, giving voice to the silenced. By April 1984 Beam "approached Alyson Publications with the idea of an anthology of writings and art by Black gay men," and in 1985 Beam began to solicit submissions for a volume on the "black gay male experience in America," with possible topics including "coming out, interac-tions with family, rural living, youth, religion, prison life, aging, the arts, gay activism, oral history, the military, and erotica." It would be titled *In the Life*, a phrase that located the formation of black gay identity in the underworld of vice districts, prostitution, and mildly criminal deviance. Many of the first submissions for the volume came from black gay men in the Northeast and other urban areas, so in order to shape the volume into something more representative, he traveled south and into rural regions to collect a wider swath of experiences.[34]

Upon his return, in addition to clerking or waiting tables for at least forty hours a week, Beam sent stacks of neatly typed letters to friends and lovers and took in mail from black gay men around the nation, establishing a network that facilitated the production of the anthology but also provided a scaffolding for future activism. Beam worked largely in isolation in his studio, with friends and lovers providing a necessary sounding board for his ideas and the writers among them lending intellectual support. He continued to write journal pieces for the *Philadelphia Gay News* and *Au Courant,* whose editor offered Beam the "hope [that] everything is well with you" and reported that he continued to "welcome any input you be able to offer." Midway through the heaviest period of work, Beam reached out again to Barbara Smith to explore his sense of being overwhelmed by the totality of the project: "What I realized when I started 'living' with this manuscript for the anthology was that I didn't know a whole lot about what I was doing." There were constraints of time and the problem of the delicate egos of writers and their attachment to their own prose, and some of the pieces, particularly the essay on AIDS, proved "heartbreaking" to Beam. His own sense of working as a pioneer and moving down an "untrodden" path weighed heavily at times, as he confided in Barbara Smith. "I keep looking around for inspiration from other Black men, gay or straight, ain't nothin' out there."[35]

Beam envisioned the anthology as a turning point in the history of black gay identity, signaling a new era of purpose and collective recognition. As such Beam had in fact once identified James Baldwin and Bayard Rustin as potential contributors; their celebrity and fame could bring more attention to the project, their acknowledgment ushering in the next generation. Beam's discussions of Baldwin always reflected a kind of ambivalence—even a resentful attachment to the iconic figure. In his studio he hung a picture of Baldwin and wrote that he "was and continues to be a writer whose work I appreciate and . . . come[s] the closest to where I am in my life." In March 1985 Beam attended a lecture by Baldwin in Philadelphia at the Afro-American Historical and Cultural Museum and reported that he was "not impressed," though admitting that "perhaps there was no way he could live up to 20 years of expectations." He criticized Baldwin on a number of levels—as "speaking to white people," as tired, and as too closeted—clearly angered by Baldwin's refusal to be more out or clearly identified with black gay life. Writing to his lover Fred, Beam declared that "I wanted him to address me, which I feel he did not do," and he then vowed to put his feelings in print by "writing a piece called 'An Open Letter to James Baldwin.'"[36]

At the end of 1985 Beam finally wrote to Baldwin to announce the anthology and request an endorsement. He described it as a "first of its kind" and disingenuously showered the author with compliments, telling Baldwin that the contributors "have used your life and writings as a model and witness to our experience: your work has informed our work," and likened praise from him as a seal of approval. In private, Beam had been concerned that "no one has written anything at all about James Baldwin, which is curious considering that I'm sure most of us have read his work." But Beam told Baldwin that "metaphorically, you are handing us the baton. May we run this race with you?" Not surprisingly, given his failing health at the time, Baldwin never apparently responded and ultimately did not contribute. Beam sent him a copy of the manuscript nonetheless, and a month before the scheduled release of the anthology he wrote to Baldwin again to relate that he was "deeply disappointed" that he had heard nothing from him. He made good on his promise to pen a poem, "Go Tell It to This Country / for James Baldwin," that begins:

> another black queen
> is
> digging up
> shit
> cursing & talking
> loud
> I can't be stopping.

Beam was coming into his own, and his circle of friends and writers hailed him as their cultural leader. When a mutual friend returned to Chicago for a visit with Max Smith, he reported that he had heard "that when your manuscript is completed that it will be the best thought-out writing on Black gays since Baldwin's work 20 years ago."[37]

Yet Beam's ambitions increasingly conflicted with the very work that had fertilized his talents, in the bookstore, and so Beam decided to reduce his hours to devote more time to the anthology and other activities. But in the summer of 1985 some conflict emerged as a result and became a "point of contention," and Beam reported that "after several 'summit' meetings of Ed [Hernance], Arleen [Olsham, a co-owner], and I it was decided that it best that I leave immediately." The bookstore needed to begin training a new clerk, and Beam received an acceptable severance package, leaving him the remainder of the summer to work on the anthology. Beam described the compromise as "amiable."[38]

"I've quit my job at Giovanni's Room to devote my full energy to the book, so amidst all of this I'm looking for work and sending out resumes," Beam wrote, and now he trained his ambitions on gaining recognition as an activist and writer. But it proved to be a decision that came with a price. By July 1985 Beam contacted the real estate company that managed his apartment to request that it use one of the months of security deposit for his August rent, and he would remit the additional amount, which the company eventually granted. He explained to the agent that he had been working on the anthology for more than a year, it was soon to be published, and he therefore could "solemnly promise to continuing paying rent." In his own excitement over the anthology, he assured the agent her name would be listed "among these good people who have helped me," but he was continually late with the rent in 1985, falling ever further behind, and he could barely makes ends meet, cobbling together paychecks from Barnes and Noble, and the restaurant Bread and Company.[39]

Beam had pinned to the success of the anthology project his ambitions for a career in writing and speaking, and yet the odds were against a black gay cultural activist at the time. Leading black British gay filmmaker Isaac Julien wrote to Beam with moral support, "Hope your spirits are up! And that the demand of being a 'front-line angel' isn't being too tough on you." For Julien, this connectivity served as a buffer against the "lack of support from our black straight friends, be they feminist or pan Africanist," at the same time that he decried the lack of "*positive images of black men.*" Worn down by the culture wars of London—"the black back-lash is well on its way"—like Beam, he too believed in the importance of finding a collective voice to resist objectification. At one point, writing to Julien, Beam brought up the controversial photographs collected in *Black Book* by Robert Mapplethorpe, the avant-garde artist. In the conservative 1980s, Mapplethorpe's work touched off a national controversy when the Corcoran Gallery of Art refused to display his collection of provocative photos of nudes. *Black Book* featured highly stylized shots of black male bodies, nudes, and penises, many of which were censored or condemned as obscene and derogatory. If Clarke's portrait of Jason Holliday had stirred controversy, distaste, and shock, by the 1980s many white gay critics defended Mapplethorpe's oeuvre against the moral Right. In lieu of the museum exhibit, LGBT and art activists and the Washington Project for the Arts projected the photographs on the walls of an alternative space to large audiences. Beam characterized Mapplethorpe's controversial project as "the ultimate coffee table objectification picture book." Within a few years, a number of black gay critics, especially the London-based art critic Kobena Mercer, would apply a cultural studies approach to reframe the Mapplethorpe photos in ways that suggested greater ambivalence and possibilities for desire.

Despite the similarity between U.S. and UK rightward regimes on the one hand and gay liberation objectification on the other, Julien benefited from a social welfare state that managed to retain some local funding for arts and cultural initiatives while Beam faced overwhelming obstacles. He had applied for a fellowship from the National Endowment for the Arts but was unsuccessful, delaying his plans to travel to England and reconnect with members of the London Black Gay and Lesbian Center Project and attend the International Radical and Third World Book Fair.[40] In the gay public sphere of Philadelphia, Beam had excelled in the vocation of journalism, writing numerous pieces for a range of publications, from *New York Native*, *Advocate*, and *Gay Community News* to those periodicals aimed at black gay men, such as *Blackheart 3* and *Blacklight*, and later he became editor of the magazine for the National Coalition of Black Lesbians and Gays, *Black/Out*. But his contributions to black gay visibility went largely unpaid or paid very little. Without an advanced or professional degree and without other kinds of social service experience, Beam languished in a tight job market, and he lost several bids for jobs for which he was clearly qualified. He was not alone; Essex Hemphill reported to Beam about his own economic woes. For the first time, the economy had forced him to leave the city and commute to Alexandria for work (to a place that "hides its racism beneath a healthy dose of southern hospitality"). "Times are lean pretty baby," Hemphill wrote. Beam saved more than a dozen applications for a number of jobs with similar qualifications with increasingly depressing outcomes. With a degree in psychology, not surprisingly he applied for a position in gay and lesbian peer counseling, stressing as well his experience with the bookstore, but lost out again. He was keen to get a position with the American Friends Service Committee, for which he had worked temporarily in AIDS outreach, and when he did not receive the offer, he vowed to pursue legal action.[41]

Although Beam resigned from Giovanni's Room with a sense of triumph, in the end he failed to find a better-paying position in Philadelphia. He continued to search for work as a waiter but complained of racism in the gay community, which was exemplified by an incident that he discussed in an essay titled "Ways of Seeing": "Several months ago I applied for a job as a waiter at a white gay owned restaurant, one which I patronized daily. I filled out their application and attached my resume. The owner, who knows me by name, never even acknowledged receipt of my application." Beam continued, "The ways of seeing: I don't want to see you. Months later he asked me why he hadn't seen me in his restaurant. Obviously still pretending to not have received my application." For him, race, not class, explained his experience—"as a Black man, all too often I am perceived in that fashion"—and despite his concerted efforts to find "more time to write," he had not landed better employment; his latest position was waiting at a restaurant in Center City, Salad Alley.[42]

Although *In the Life* was scheduled to appear in the late spring of 1986, the press delayed publication of it until around Thanksgiving, and it then climbed to number five on the *Washington Blade*'s best-seller list, where the volume received positive reviews and letters of praise. Beam reported that "Giovanni's Room sold about 120 copies during the first three weeks, and they tell me it's selling briskly. I've been receiving a letter almost every day from brothers around reading the book." A momentous high point was that both his mother and father attended the book reception, with Beam reporting to Julien, "I was so pleased and thrilled that my father had the courage to come out and support his gay son. Those few moments with me made up for so much in the past."[43]

The same year, Beam penned a letter to both his parents, announcing that "in a couple of hours I'll be interviewing Bayard Rustin," whom he described as an "openly gay black civil rights activist." After years of silence and stoicism performed as black masculinity—poses that he had studied, puzzled over, and worked through—Beam explained that "I will probably not bring any children into this world so perhaps I can leave some books behind that say my life moved Black people a millimeter closer to liberation and that I didn't devote my existence to the acquisition of goods." What was next? Telling Ombaka about the anthology, Beam said that "I need to begin thinking about having a source of income which is not derived from working everyday and I think a book would sell . . . and that as Black people we need to be about setting up and maintaining our own institutions."[44]

At the celebration for his anthology, Beam had reunited with his family, returned to the bookstore, and brought out a black gay voice and community. A sometimes debilitating sense of personal loneliness—perhaps endemic to his personality—did not stymie the important work of building a platform from which black gay men might secure recognition. Objectification had sometimes operated as a racist dismissal, sometimes as homophobic refusal, sometimes as erotic attraction. Rustin and Baldwin had pioneered these strategies of organizing and personal expression to create meaningful change, and Beam had given to black gay men a volume of essays documenting ways of life that had not been written about before.

A BLACK GAY ANTHOLOGY

IN THE LIFE

EDITED BY JOSEPH BEAM

In the Life. In 1986, Joseph Beam realized his dream of creating an anthology of writings by and for black gay men. *In the Life* was an overnight gay classic and launched Beam's career as a writer-activist. (Courtesy of Alyson Press).

In 1987, the members of the BWMT invited Beam to address their annual conference meeting in Milwaukee, and he agreed, drafting a keynote speech titled "Our Life, Liberty, and Happiness" that not only served as a call to action in the midst of crisis but also acknowledged real progress. Beam recalled that the Philadelphia-BWMT had formed in 1981 and that he "attended that meeting, which I consider my official coming out." He had met a young man at the meeting, Michael, and his memories of both remained fond. Yet in the intervening six and a half years, Michael died from complications arising from AIDS, and Beam had renounced interracial groups and opted for black separatism. He called the attendees of the conference to action—there were crises everywhere: prison and AIDS, homophobia and racist backlash, liberal lethargy and neglect. In chapter 8, we return to the fate of Beam in the context of this crisis, at a time of mourning and memorialization.[45]

Chapter Seven

The Last Crises of James Tinney

The only trace of James Tinney in Joseph Beam's extensive personal archive consists of two clippings—one from the *Washington Afro-American*, a black newspaper, and another from the *Washington Blade*, a gay newspaper—about his efforts to establish the first black gay church. He had contributed to *In the Life* with an essay on creating community titled "Why a Black Gay Church?" A Washington, D.C., minister and Howard University professor, Tinney pioneered the study of the African American origins of Pentecostalism, agitated for the recognition of gays and lesbians in the church, and, after meeting intense resistance, organized the alternative Faith Temple Christian Church. For him, as for Beam, the 1980s proved to be a time of tumult—of cultural challenges, personal setbacks, and professional anxiety—so much so that the fact he was HIV positive was probably the least of his immediate worries.[1]

A discussion of the life of Tinney inevitably raises a comparison with Brother Grant-Michael Fitzgerald's struggle to achieve recognition in the church, and yet the two narratives remain quite disparate. A pioneer ahead of his time, Fitzgerald sought gay liberation when the movement was in decline, and in a largely white context. And although he stood for black gay liberation, he was by all accounts often a singular figure. By contrast, Tinney worked within key African American institutions at a time of significant gains for gay men and lesbians, and yet the obstacles proved just as immovable. Drawing on reports of attitudes of seven thousand respondents to thirty-one national surveys conducted between 1973 and 2000, scholars have found that African Americans tend to support gay and lesbian legal rights but diverged along racial lines on questions of homosexuality and religion. They were ten percentage points more likely to support antidiscrimination legislation than whites but eleven percentage points more likely to view homosexuality as a sin or a punishment by God. One reason for these disparities has to do with black appreciation of the burdens of discrimination and the importance of civil rights, while at the same time more black respondents were religious fundamentalists or evangelicals. A closer historical examination of the issues confirms not only the negative impact of religion on tolerance toward gays and lesbians but also the role of interrelated social institutions, such as historically black colleges and universities, in perpetuating homophobia. The story of James Tinney's travails also reveals the persistent desire of black gay men for a place to congregate and locate a sense of community.[2]

Searching for Soul

James S. Tinney was born in Topeka, Kansas, in 1942 in a family of five, making him somewhat older than either Fitzgerald or Beam. Like them, he cared about social problems and political change and sought out a vocation in which he could reform problems of racism and injustice. But his journey into the life of a gay activist was more conflicted and personally transformative than the others' journeys. In 1962 he married Darlene Wood, and soon the couple moved from Farbus, Missouri, to Cleveland, Ohio, and then to Jonesboro, Arkansas, where he matriculated as an undergraduate at Arkansas State University, majoring in journalism and English. Throughout these years, a monthly subscription to *Faith and Truth*, the official organ of the Pentecostal Fire Baptized Heaven Church, followed him around the country, from his college in the South back to his home in the Midwest. As a student, he also recalled the powerful impact of the civil rights movement and reported that he had participated in a local organizing of the black creole community about one hundred miles south of New Orleans. Tinney did not often reference these years of intensive mobilization in the South against segregation and disenfranchisement, but perhaps his efforts among the creoles were inspired not only by the movement but also by his own identification with mixed-race people.

As several archive and newspaper photographs attest, Tinney was very light-skinned—he had a full head of black hair shaped into an Afro-style haircut and a beard, but otherwise he had white-appearing facial features and fair skin. In the interviews that he granted and hundreds of articles that he authored, he rarely discussed his family background or drew attention to what might be termed his racial physiognomy. The few exceptions are tantalizing. In 1984 Tinney delivered a keynote lecture for the Third National Third World Lesbian/Gay Conference in Berkeley, California, titled "Claiming Our Identities," which began with personal reflections on his anger and pain at not quite fitting in or feeling connected: "I was stuck in a rut in which the rehearsal of the wrongs of the past and the injustices of the present left me suspicious of everyone who didn't share my analysis." Almost offhandedly, Tinney reported that "I didn't like Whites because my mother (who had passed for white) had given me up to others to raise." He said little else about his personal background but left the impression that he was raised by a black family. Years before, in 1969, Tinney wrote a pedagogical essay for the periodical *English Journal* titled "A Unit on Black Literature" that opened with the admission, "I hesitate to say that I am white. Biologically I would be classified as an Anglo-Saxon, but in terms of a frame of reference, a state of mind, I more readily identify with Negroes. I share in a 'black mentality.'" For Tinney, this identification had less to do with ancestry than with sensibility, and he went on to suggest that such a stance ought to be adopted by every white teacher "who would teach Negro literature." Because whites misunderstood black culture, he argued that white teachers must learn more about black vernacular that originated in music and performance and noted that "the smallest amount of whitish sensitivity or prejudice will 'out.'" Tinney's suggested bibliography referenced Eldridge Cleaver's *Soul on Ice* and J. Saunders Redding's literary articles, as well as James Baldwin's *Go Tell It on the Mountain*. But he would not have thought to recommend Baldwin's gay novel, *Giovanni's Room*, nor to note the conflict among these three authors over the representation of gay men in African American letters.[3] Having chosen to align his identity with his mixed heritage, Tinney wrote that he purposefully moved into a "Negro-majority neighborhood" and attended a "racially mixed church of the emotional 'sanctified or Pentecostalist' variety."[4]

It would seem that for Tinney, the category of race was essential, inheritable, and perpetual, even though he recognized the distinction between physical appearance, or what he referred to as the "biological," and individual variations of culture and background. In these years, he and his wife raised two children, and after earning his baccalaureate he returned to the Midwest and began teaching at Central Senior High School in Kansas City, Missouri. At the time, the school was transitioning from a white to a majority-black institution, and Tinney wrote a paper that explored the role of racism and segregation in fueling African American discontent, focusing on what in 1968 he described as a riot at the high school.

Without dwelling on the circumstances at length in writings or interviews, Tinney discovered his gay sexuality and came out to his wife. According to a 1981 report on him in the *Washington Blade*, Tinney confessed to his wife in part because "he found he loved a man he was secretly seeing," and this made speaking up necessary. But the result was traumatic—"his wife and their

James Tinney faced considerable opposition in his efforts to reform Pentecostal churches and come out as gay at Howard University. After his excommunication from the Temple Church of God in Christ, Tinney established the first black gay and lesbian church, Faith Temple Christian Church. (Moorland-Spingarn Research Center, Howard University).

minister rejected him and cut him off from family, children, and church." In 1969 they were separated and in 1971 they divorced, but he remained active in local affairs, serving as chairperson of a textbook selection committee for the Kansas City public schools.[5] In the intervening years, not unlike Brother Grant-Michael Fitzgerald, Tinney turned increasingly to religion in the midst of his sexual awakening. He enrolled in a course offered by the Oral Roberts Ministry and received a certificate after he had completed a track on Christian living, "Following Jesus of Nazareth." (Years later Tinney clipped and saved a report that indicated that a son of Oral Roberts was gay and had committed suicide.) By the end of the decade, Tinney enrolled in the Nazarene Theological Seminary in Kansas City. He may have chosen Nazarene for its nearby location, its reputation as racially progressive, and its continuing evangelical outreach in the state. In 1968 the school had staged a major rally at Kansas City Municipal Stadium that attracted an audience of about 27,500. The Nazarene church encouraged outreach to black members as well as all-black congregations, endeavored to appeal to youth, and taught how to meld spiritual fulfillment with intellectual pursuits. Although the leadership was in flux, the church managed to avoid controversial issues, such as sexual liberalism, abortion, and gay rights, that increasingly divided other congregations. In an interview, one church official described the Pentecostal church as based on "perfect love" but sought to correct the impression that this meant speaking in tongues: "The Nazarene church, with its Holiness basis of sanctification and perfect love shouldn't be misconstrued as endorsing the controversial ritual of speaking in tongues as a necessary sign of the Holy Spirit."[6]

Tinney was likely drawn to the church's public support for racial integration, to the claim "it never had racial problems," and to the fact that the Nazarene school in Chicago had elected a black student president. The school offered a range of courses in theology, education, and social sciences, from World Evangelization, Ministerial Practicum, and Gospel of Luke to Dynamics of Leadership, Christian Pastorate, and Wesley's Theology. Though few of the course offerings appear to have explored themes of race, several did touch on the origins of Pentecostalism, such as the Homiletical Study of Holiness, a subject that would occupy Tinney over the course of his career. After he matriculated, Tinney worked in the Department of Publications of the church and then spent a year in Urban Ministries in Chicago from 1972 to 1973. Urban Ministries gained a wide following among African American grassroots activists, but Tinney's papers provide no other evidence about his role in this group, or the impact of it on his own political viewpoint.[7] Beyond the church, Tinney's passions were teaching, writing, and reforming. In the 1970s, he served as an assistant editor of the *Kansas City Call* (an African American weekly newspaper) as well as a special reporter. He also served as managing editor of a bimonthly magazine based in New York, edited two religious publications, and helped to found *Spirit: A Journal of Issues Incident to Black Pentecostalism*.[8]

Even though he had lost his wife and children, Tinney did not publicly come out as gay. But in his capacity as a journalist, he took note of various efforts to stimulate a dialogue on sexuality among Pentecostal leaders and students. In 1974, he wrote an article, "Ministering in a Gay Church," that reported on LaPaula Turner, a black clergywoman who served at the recently formed gay congregation the Metropolitan Community Church (MCC). He noted that Turner was once married, later came out as gay, and planned to be "'married.'" As a woman, however, Turner felt that some gay men doubted her religious authority because they believed that "women had no place as a minister" and reported that questions of homosexuality were even more fraught. She also believed, reported Tinney, that too many black gay Christians would "accept the discrimination against them in their own churches as a form of punishment for being gay." Tinney's reporting demonstrated a level of empathy and openness, but even at the height of gay liberation, it seems he would not make a similar move.[9]

After reporting, editing, and teaching in Kansas for six years, Tinney moved to Washington, D.C., to become interim editor of the *Washington Afro-American* and then won a permanent appointment from the publisher to edit the long-standing black newspaper. Soon he was also hired as a speechwriter and strategist for the black congressman John Conyers (Democrat from Michigan) and Samuel Jackson (one-time undersecretary at Housing and Urban Development under President Jimmy Carter and considered the highest-ranking Pentecostal in government). Into the 1970s in D.C., Tinney remained active in civic affairs: he sang in the Star of Bethlehem Church of God in Christ Youth Choir, edited a local interracial journal, and volunteered at the Lorton Prison. Living a double life—remaining in the closet while pursuing social justice—Tinney rose to a place of considerable prominence in Washington's black political circles.[10]

In 1972 Tinney applied to the graduate program of the Department of Political Science at Howard University. Like Fitzgerald and Beam, Tinney selected a course of study that permitted or facilitated a certain level of personal insight (educational sociology) as well as a social critique of power and inequality (political science). Arguably appearing to be white, Tinney may have decided to study at the premier black university in the nation to fulfill his desire for a kind of racial recognition. He excelled in his graduate course work almost from the first semester, earning a GPA of 4.00 for several semesters and an overall 3.79 for course work in black studies, theory and politics, statistics and research methods, and African and black politics. His master's thesis examined the racial tensions and transition of the Kansas City high school where he had taught, and this research was accepted for the conferral of the degree in 1974. He then pursued doctoral work in the Department of Political Science.[11]

Awarded a research assistantship and then a research fellowship, Tinney moved swiftly through the doctoral program. By 1977 he had passed his comprehensive exams in black politics, political theory, international relations, and comparative African government; continued with his research on religion and politics; and within two years completed his dissertation, "A Theoretical and Historical Comparison of Black Political and Religious Movements." Already excelling in the department, Tinney had gained a national reputation as a popular lecturer and expert at conferences and in the press. He had impressed the faculty and gained a recommendation from them for a Danforth Foundation Fellowship. Throughout graduate school, Tinney remained in the closet. His publications did not address gay issues, nor did much of his journalism. Tinney had lived quietly with two successive Pentecostal lovers—the first was likely the man he left his wife for. But neither his personal papers nor his published writings elaborate on the nature of his romantic relationships. In 1976, his career burgeoned with an appointment to a lecturer position in Howard University's prestigious School of Communications, "pending completion and award of the doctoral degree by this fall."[12]

Tinney was a prolific writer, authoring hundreds of articles in sixty periodicals, as well as brochures, tracts, annual reports, and fliers. His larger scholarly objective was to legitimate the study of Pentecostalism and correct its reputation as a faith of the poor and illiterate that was stigmatized by its public association with speaking in tongues and faith healing.[13] Once appointed to Howard, he became even more ambitious and productive. He helped to organize and host a number of conferences that promoted both journalism and scholarship on the church. The conferences alone, described as a "Herculean task" that Tinney accomplished almost "single-handed," signaled his national prominence. Beyond his service to the department, including the coordination of a certification program, Tinney offered courses in communication, such as Fundamentals of Journalism, and some based on his specialization in the field, such as History of the Black/White Press. In 1976 he delivered papers titled "The Blackness of Pentecostalism," "Sociological Transition of the Church of God in Christ," and "History of Holiness and Pentecostal Movements" and became a leading expert on what was becoming the fastest-growing denomination in the world. At the time, some six million Pentecostals worshipped in the United States and some thirty million worldwide.

Tinney published a wealth of research that demonstrated that the denomination's founder was William J. Seymour, an African American man in Los Angeles, and later published both articles and a monograph on his role in and contributions to the Pentecostal church. The following year he began delivering papers on the African American press, and by the late 1970s he focused his energy and research on peer-reviewed scholarship. Tinney produced a number of bibliographies, articles, and book chapters and prepared a book manuscript, "Afro-American Holiness and Pentecostal Churches," to be completed before his expected tenure review commencing in 1982. He had already published his research on faith in the African diaspora and then submitted his revised dissertation for consideration for publication by Howard University Press.[14]

In form and spirit, black Pentecostalism resonated with a potential black gay search for personal expression and rich community life, but in terms of doctrine the fundamentalist literalism was perhaps even less conducive to Tinney's gay desire than the Catholic doctrine was for Fitzgerald. James Baldwin's meditation on Pentecostalism, adolescence, and desire in *Go Tell It on the Mountain* has been read from many vantage points—as a veiled coming-out story to a refusal of gayness—and over the years the author himself offered varied interpretations to the public. In a perceptive literary analysis of the coming-of-age novel, one critic observes that Baldwin's "sensuous depiction of a single moment of religious ecstasy suggests that even as the conversion rituals of church holiness culture reveal the very flesh and blood of black life, they also reveal how tenuous the church's grip is on the potentially wayward sexual desires that it both fears and depends on." Most critics acknowledge Baldwin's steady criticism of the church in subsequent writings, most notably in the socially influential *The Fire Next Time* (1963). Yet what remained resonant of black gayness throughout Baldwin's writings was the perpetual oscillation not only across the color line but also between secular and religious points of view or orientations.[15]

Historians trace the larger Pentecostal movement, stressing biblical literalism and ecstatic worship, back to the Methodist conversion of slaves and ex-slaves in the nineteenth-century southern church, often referred to as the invisible church. The institutional network of churches expanded in response to the terror of the 1890s, when southern African Americans endured segregation, disenfranchisement, and lynching, and the largest, the Church of God in Christ, incorporated in Memphis in 1897. In the early years, Pentecostals divided over the Trinity, with some believing in the holiness only of a single Jesus figure, while others disagreed over the conduct of service, specifically whether individual testimony may precede the sermon. During the Great Migration to the urban North, storefront churches, sometimes mislabeled cults, provided the settings of ritual life, and by the 1920s, black Pentecostalism became an urban, working-class religion that called for a strict connection between faith and practice. In a 1982 ethnography of three Pentecostal churches in Boston, Arthur E. Paris described how the church provided prayer meetings and social services, but the call-and-response between minister and congregation was at the heart of their worship. Sermons often stressed uplift, perseverance, and edification, while the "congregation is both audience and actor." Similar to Catholic worshippers, Pentecostals emphasized biblical education classes, and many memorized long passages of scripture to apply literally to everyday situations. Unlike the solemnity of Catholic ritual, however, Pentecostal services oscillated between traditional prayer and group shouts; song service began early and permitted boisterous hand-clapping and bodily gesticulation. According to Paris, some sought relief from illness or spiritual suffering, but "seeking relief is not embarrassing, as coming forward during the altar call would be."[16]

Tinney was invested in explicating the black origins of Pentecostalism as well as its radical, even nationalist, implications, but he also would have to grapple with its prohibition of homosexuality. Although only men served as pastors and deacons, women were assigned significant roles that stressed maternal care and organizational authority. Both men and women were expected to remain celibate before marriage, but some scholarship suggests that women paid a higher price for breaking these and other rules of comportment. Yet scholars also indicate that urban storefront churches created in the era of migration loosened gender expectations and that therefore the politics of respectability relaxed to the extent that church mothers felt a greater sense of autonomy and authority.[17]

Why Tinney was so drawn to religion remains a matter of speculation, in much the way that it is difficult to pinpoint the motivations of Fitzgerald. Tinney, the prolific religious studies scholar, rarely commented on his own faith or its role in his life. For both men, their religious callings interacted or in some sense facilitated the process of coming out and probably somehow managed their desire, offering them the support for personal reckoning or assuaging guilt. Fitzgerald came out soon after joining the Salvatorians, but Tinney remained closeted to many in the worlds of journalism and the university, as well as to those in his church, for many years. And while the Catholic church had promoted outreach to the laity, and the most liberal, especially the Salvatorians, encouraged members to pursue their own objectives, Tinney sought to navigate the worlds of a conservative religion and an equally conformist profession at a time when neither had shown tolerance for gay identities or ideas. Both institutions did promote ideals of individual freedom and the mission of black liberation, and somewhere in this tension between institutional prohibition and principles of self-expression he found a way toward the recognition of his black gayness.[18]

Faith under Fire

Up until 1979, James Tinney had not pursued serious research on gay issues or history. The turning point was not homophobia but racism, and the conversion was catalyzed not by his experience of the black church but from his conflicts within gay activism. In 1979 a national steering committee completed organizing the first National March on Washington for Lesbian and Gay Rights to be convened on the National Mall that summer, but black gay activists criticized the planners for failing to produce an inclusive program. In response, the recently formed National Coalition of Black Gays organized a major event, the First National Conference of Third World Lesbians and Gays, on the Howard University campus that featured panels on racism and sexism in the Third World, black gays in the prison system, and people of mixed blood, something that would be of particular interest to Tinney. He later wrote that the historic gathering "demonstrated a new sense of political activism" in the face of white-dominated media and particularly the omission of an announcement for the conference, and the event culminated in an all-black march down Georgia Avenue for gay rights. Tinney was out, proud, and mobilized.[19]

According to news reports, an audience of close to one thousand turned out to listen to Audre Lorde at the keynote address on Saturday night. She stated, "I have waited all my life to see this occasion. Who would have ever dreamed 20 or 30 years ago that black lesbians and gay men would finally get it together?" Lorde went on, "Howard University will never be the same. This city will never be the same. We will never more fear racism, sexism, classism, or homophobia in the black community." The mobilization at Howard permanently altered black gay history, and Tinney would never be the same. He joined a caucus of black men who returned to meet at the Harambee House (an affiliate of the Harambee school where nearly a decade before Fitzgerald was forced to resign). They planned to organize a "Committee on Black Gay Men" that would meet the following year at Morehouse College, the historically black school in Atlanta.[20]

The 1979 National March on Washington for Lesbian and Gay Rights and the black lesbian and gay breakaway conference prompted Tinney and a group of students to organize a gay and lesbian organization at Howard—Lambda Student Alliance (LSA)—which faced considerable opposition on campus. Tinney had already helped form a social group for Pentecostals on campus in an effort to overcome the stereotypes associated with ecstatic religion. In the fall of 1979 the LSA at Howard chose officers, convened meetings, and invited Tinney to speak and tender advice. To gain members, those involved circulated fliers and told friends but did not seek a lot of publicity for fear of disruption from outsiders, according to the strategically placed announcement in the *Washington Blade*. They also sponsored a conference on black gay issues, but Tinney reminded the group that the only official requirement to do so was the approval of a single faculty member and that therefore the event did not signal the support of the administration or progress in the larger university community. Apparently due to lack of advertising, Tinney reported that "hardly any university students or faculty (except those with contacts in the Gay community) were even aware that a Black Gay conference was held."[21]

Yet the fallout from the March on Washington for gay rights signaled a crucial shift in the course of black gay activism. In the aftermath, a student in communications at Howard, Sidney Brinkley, helped to found the first black gay publication, *Blacklight* (which continues to be published), while Tinney expanded his research to cover gay issues and sexual politics. By the end of 1979, the gay student group at Howard convened its second meeting, relying on word-of-mouth to gather membership, and half of the students attending were women. Tinney served as a guest speaker a year later, and he gained more publicity with his advocacy on gay issues.[22]

In 1981, Howard's LSA was the first gay organization to gain recognition at a historically black college or university, but it had been a difficult process. Although the group had secured ten signatures and submitted bylaws to the school, the student government officers refused to sign the LSA petition. According to Tinney, the former president of the student association was a Pentecostal, and his successor was a Muslim man who had stated for the record his hope that the university would reject the group's application for funding. The controversy revealed as well the level of hostility to homosexuality on campus, and a published survey indicated that many felt "this is not the kind of issue we [in the black community] want to deal with." The Howard group had fought for recognition for two years, but the university refused to make any public statement. With the application now stalled, two outside attorneys approached Howard's legal counsel, after they had won a favorable ruling from a local judge on a similar rejection of a gay group at the Catholic Georgetown University. The university administration eventually granted the LSA's request but continued to deny that the president had made the decision or that they had been influenced by the threat of litigation.[23]

It is difficult to know if his colleagues at Howard would have appointed Tinney had they known then of his sexual identity, but resistance to the LSA had proven not only catalytic but also indicative of campus climate. Tinney could not turn back—he had chosen to come out publicly before he had earned tenure, the often politicized, unpredictable, and arduous administrative process of individual review before a faculty member is granted permanent lifetime employment. This political choice was a very courageous act, but soon Tinney experienced turbulence in the first round of the tenure process. Already, after coming out, Tinney had been dismissed by the Pentecostal chaplain as the faculty advisor, and some correspondence from administrators and faculty in his department suggested that his prospects for tenure were unfavorable, not only because of unspoken hostility to his homosexuality but also because of an uneven teaching record. Either from habit or distraction, Tinney proved to be an unreliable colleague and teacher at times. In 1979, his chair warned him about missed classes and requested a memo of explanation "in light of the disorder and dissatisfaction that they caused." Tinney had not been available for at least four days and wrote that he had escorted his students on a trip to the Smithsonian museum. This seemed to satisfy the chair, but she lamented that his leave without prior notice prevented her from protecting his otherwise "generally good record" from "rumors." In the following years, he seemed to disregard his chair's warning and exposed himself to what appeared to be legitimate criticism for failing to meet his duties. In the spring semester of 1981, Tinney missed the first day with both of his scheduled classes, History of the Black/White Press and Fundamentals II, and received a memo from his chair, along with a handwritten list of the names of the students who had waited for him to arrive.[24]

The following school year in the fall of 1981, now under a different departmental chair with whom he would routinely conflict, Tinney received another memo about teaching, this one including sterner wording: "Violation of University Policies." Tinney had apparently missed four school days and a total of sixteen classes, which constituted a significant professional lapse. In another teaching incident, a student filed a grievance against Tinney that alleged he had reviewed her papers unfairly, neglected to keep an appointment, and made a comment about her sexuality. In response, Tinney distributed a survey to the members of the course to poll their opinions on the accuracy of the charges of harassment, abuse and personal insult, and he was exonerated by 15 no to 2 yes and 4 unsure on the question of harassment; by 17 to 2 to 2 on the question of verbal abuse; and by 13 to 2 to 6 on the question of a personal insult about sexuality. Over the years, he would receive low merit rankings for teaching from his department, and perhaps some of this had to do with the impression that Tinney put teaching second to research or was unreliable to a fault. Yet Tinney also won recognition for his dedication to his students. At the end of the year, the School of Communications Student Council nominated Tinney for the Danforth Associate Program, noting his excellence in the field of journalism. The nomination also pointed out that he had gained the "respect" of students and was an energetic and engaged teacher: "Each semester, Dr. Tinney opens his home to classes, exposing students to his extensive research files and vast library focusing on aspects of Black American Society."[25]

In October 1981 the university administration issued a letter of tenure denial and informed Tinney of his dismissal from Howard. The same month, the president of the Student Council wrote to Tinney to tell him that the council had decided to sponsor the "First Annual School of Communications Student Council Roast" and that from nominations and votes he had been chosen from his department. The president billed the event as the largest fund-raiser ever, urging him to accept the honor. In any case, in part because of the student recognition and likely because of his pursuit of legal action in retaining an attorney, Tinney's tenure decision was soon reversed: "The final favorable action came only after the student council selected him as the only member of his department to be 'roasted' and given an award for 'outstanding student support and excellence in teaching.'" Because of continued student involvement—and a phenomenal record of scholarship—Tinney somehow saved his career at Howard.[26]

The fact was that Tinney deserved tenure. In the two or three years leading up to his tenure decision, Tinney appeared frequently in the *Dean's Newsletter* with reports of his publications, conference presentations, radio interviews, and service. Combined with organizing the annual conferences, his research and community outreach distinguished Tinney as a national leader in the field of Pentecostal studies. Coming out as gay was daring, but the riskiness only propelled his frenetic schedule forward and agitated his extraordinarily productive mind. By the end of 1981, in light of students' appreciation and likely because of his threat to pursue litigation, Tinney's department had reversed itself and recommended him for tenure, which was soon approved by the dean and the president. The following year, Tinney sought recommendations and applied for a position at the University of the District of Columbia, probably because of the discord and difficulty in his department, but what became of this effort to leave Howard remains unclear, other than that he never did resign.[27]

Like Grant-Michael Fitzgerald, Tinney long grappled with the contradictions and conflicts between his faith and desire, and his search for reform also paralleled ongoing efforts by a number of organizations to persuade religious leaders of the humanity and salvation of gay men. Fitzgerald had studied, organized, and lobbied as effectively as possible, at a moment of liberal change, but had lost that fight on every front. By the 1970s, his religious community had become more cautious, as directives issued from above called for a repudiation of the Gay Ministry Task Force and sharp distancing from the appearance of moral permissiveness. Into the 1970s, however, more liberal denominations had opened their churches and ministries to gay men and lesbians and refused to apply biblical injunctions too literally or punitively. Yet as evangelicals, Pentecostals promoted a literal reading of the Bible, a belief in revelation through the body and the individual spirit, and the ritual of talking in tongues as the spirit of Christ passed into their bodies. Because of the apparent depth of the orthodoxy, Tinney spent an enormous amount of energy in researching and writing on the problem of how to reconcile religion with homosexuality.

In 1980, Tinney presented a long, detailed, and rigorous paper, "The Separation of 'Being' and 'Doing': The Last Evangelical Refuge against Homosexuality," which examined what he conceived as a set of historical stages of rejection of the homosexual. Tinney described a gradual moral evolution dating from Aquinas that designated homosexuality as "one of the worst, if not the worst, sin possible"—it was unpardonable, akin to demon possession. By the 1960s, however, modern scholars, according to Tinney, linked homosexuality to mental disturbances—a "psychopathology that warrants medical intervention." As Fitzgerald had found, the subsequent revision of the American Psychiatric Association designation of homosexuality as a mental illness motivated some theologians to treat sexual orientation as beyond the control of the individual and therefore a condition that ought not to be subject to punitive actions by the clergy. The increasing influence of psychology and the emphasis on mentality opened up a distinction between identity and behavior that continued to inform popular understandings of gayness. In religious conversations, this was understood as the distinction between "doing" and "being," which allowed for individuals to admit their same-sex desires but not act on them, to remain celibate, and therefore to remain valid in the eyes of God. For Tinney, this reflected an important advance in stages, from the worst sin to illness to condition and action. Eventually, he believed, religious thinkers would consider the "condition not blameworthy."[28]

This formulation prompted a number of theologians to modify the orthodox position of homosexuality as the worst sin and accept gays who "repented" their sexual urges, but almost none of these authors accepted the notion of a Christian practicing homosexuality. Because Christians believed in a natural order created by God, they understood sexuality exclusively as a reproductive act in the context of marriage. Tinney suggested that the traditional separation between "doing" and "being," as well as "raw sexism," lay "at the heart of Evangelical homophobia" and called for more research and recognition of the connections between gay, feminist, and religious struggles.

Perceptively, it would seem, Tinney argued that "one of the most unexplored areas of research is that relating to the similarities and ties between racial oppression and Gay oppression, between the ontologies of Black (and Hispanic, First American, and Oriental) and Gay identities."[29]

In challenging religious injunctions and calling for reform, Tinney had to think through the nature of race and sexuality in new ways. He compared religious views of blacks as sinful with those of gays as criminals against nature to understand the extent to which God and the church played a "similarly restraining role" for both minority groups. Unlike secular writers and activists who championed gay liberation, Tinney had to explain an etiology of homosexuality that would compel religious authorities to forgive and include gay men and lesbians. The first tack was again to present the case of the celibate gay or lesbian worshipper seeking salvation. But if homosexuality, broadly defined, included fantasy, same-sex emotional intimacy, and gay social networks, how could one measure abstinence—how could one entirely refrain from homosexuality? Citing some of the same authorities as Fitzgerald, Tinney argued against the practice of celibacy for the laity because of its negative emotional effects.[30] With the increasing prominence of his public speaking, Tinney was featured alongside Brother Grant-Michael Fitzgerald in a special issue of *Insight: A Gay Christian Quarterly* on the subject of being black, Christian, and gay, revealing a new level of attention to a struggle that Fitzgerald had been waging since the early 1970s.[31]

In lecturing and writing and particularly at religious conventions, Tinney deployed ever-more intricate and well-reasoned philosophical arguments in support of religious reform, pivoting from questions of sexual identity to fine theological points. In 1980, the White House invited Tinney to address a meeting between representatives of religious organizations and the staff of President Carter. In this instance, Tinney first claimed the mantle of Pentecostalism, perhaps to secure a kind of public legitimacy, and situated himself as "representative" of many Pentecostals. In what may be considered something of a bald-faced lie, Tinney proclaimed, "I want to forever silence those who think that holiness and Spirit-filled living are in any way inconsistent with homosexuality," arguing that thousands of members had learned to accommodate homosexuality. Given that Tinney's presentation took up fewer than two pages, it would seem his time was limited, and reductive statements and convenient misstatements would have to suffice. Tinney concluded with a plea for lesbian and gay appointments to the government, inclusion in the Civil Rights and Voting Rights acts, and immigration reform for homosexuals.[32]

As he sought to win converts in religious circles to a more inclusive conception of worship, Tinney also looked to forge a shared sense of black manhood in much the same way as Joseph Beam. In his essay "I Love My Black Brothers," he referred to a range of masculine types—church femmes, drag queens, and hustlers—that were the object of his inclusive affection. His only objection was to the men whose bias against homosexuals fostered social intolerance. In rejecting black nationalism, or "some other lofty-sounding 'ism,'" Tinney called for "gay humanism and gay realism."[33]

By the beginning of the 1980s, a prolific writer and popular speaker, Tinney had earned a national reputation as a black gay intellectual. Like a generation of black religious thinkers, he worked on the front lines of social change but did so at the impossible intersection of evangelicalism, race, and gay politics, and his words and deeds marked an important departure in black gay history. In 1981, Tinney was invited to address the First International Convention of Black and White Men Together, convened in San Francisco. Tinney's speech, titled "Problem Areas in Inter-racial Relations in the Lesbian/Gay Community," set out to sketch new political strategies for enacting progressive racial and sexual change. He began by questioning the efficacy of personal politics and rejected the notion that individual or personal change improved racial or larger inequalities, highlighting racism throughout societal institutions. As he surveyed categories and concepts, he asserted that cultural differences derived from race and not class, that black lesbians worked at the cutting edge of change, and that black separatism sprang from a reaction against white bias. "The truth is that most white gay environs and organizations are still not safe places for Third World people," he asserted.[34]

Perhaps his most challenging words concerned his rendering of the "sordid history of religion." Tinney explained that African Americans remained invested in the church but that organized religion served to perpetuate inequality and social control. At the heart of his message was an exploration of the contradictory role of the church for black gay men: as a site of sexual oppression—something that most gay men understood—but also as a foundation of racial community, which many had not considered. Tinney did not seek to address black gay men exclusively, speaking instead of groups in broad sweeps of history. Even as he self-identified as black, and as "one of us," his sexual politics remained inclusive. In other words, he took on the role of racial mediator rather than an identity at the intersection, like Beam and younger black activists. He acknowledged the innovation of black feminists but did not then go on to apply their insights through a more searching critique of Pentecostalism.[35]

In the years since coming out and earning tenure, Tinney presented more papers on homosexuality and religion but also started to address what he considered to be the imminent threat of the religious New Right and its consequences for both black and gay political progress. As the Republican Party gained more power, liberal political groups coalesced to formulate a strategy and called for monitoring discussions of religion in the press. In major religious conventions, Tinney distinguished the so-called born again movement from the origins of Pentecostalism, claiming that the New Right evangelicals practiced racism, sexism, and homophobia.[36]

As Tinney continued to focus and speak on the subject of gay and lesbian Pentecostals, however, he encountered more and more resistance. When he was invited to lecture at Ohio State University, several members of the gospel choir shouted him down, stating that the Bible declared homosexuality to be a sin and forcing him to stop until they had finished and their group exited. Next, the leading Pentecostal publication issued an editorial calling for the removal of this "wicked man from among yourselves" and characterized his organization's attempts to tie "liberation theology (a class struggle for political rights) and full rights for homosexuals" to be a shock. Yet not long before, the same journal had invited Tinney to edit a special issue on black Pentecostalism. In the midst of this attack, Tinney's press release stressed the extent of his public speaking to a broad range of religious institutions and his role in mobilizing against the New Right, but the intersection of religion and homosexuality was becoming more contentious and explosive. By 1981 an influential black Pentecostal pastor who had guided the pioneering Chicago Woodlawn Organization, which had successfully ministered to local gangs, resigned from the editorial board of *Spirit* in protest of Tinney's openly gay positions, declaring himself to be "appalled" because Tinney had gone "far beyond the concept of help and understanding" by refusing to classify homosexuality as a sin. He went on to suggest that Tinney had gotten "caught up" in a "contemporary wave of sexual permissiveness," while in turn Tinney criticized him for "homophobia and [a] parochial outlook," but most Pentecostals probably sided with the opposition.[37]

After addressing the American Conference of Lesbian and Gay Christians, Tinney in 1982 announced his plans to conduct a D.C.-area revival for gays and lesbians to affirm their faith and salvation in the church. In response, to his apparent surprise, the Church of God in Christ moved to excommunicate Tinney. Bishop Samuel Kelsey, a pastor in Washington, D.C., publicly declared that Tinney "cannot be both Christian and gay," according to a report, and rejected his plans for the revival. He also noted that Tinney could be readmitted to the church should he denounce the sin of homosexuality. For many, the bishop's decision was unexpected because Tinney had come out years before. But the idea for a gay and lesbian citywide revival had gained considerable attention, supposedly bringing reproach and embarrassment to the church. In a published report quoting Tinney, he observed that "the revival led to it." He also conjectured that beyond the publicity, the revival signaled that he was not an isolated figure but rather a leader of a growing movement. The event had now become as important to Tinney as to his opponents—a sign of his independence and renewal of his own spiritual confidence. He had not ministered in more than twelve years, since his divorce, when he felt he could no longer do so, and had instead pursued his career in journalism. For Tinney, the revival provided a forum through which to address the homophobia of the church and what he characterized as "a hunger in the Lesbian and Gay community." Described as a real success, the revival reportedly attracted fifty worshippers to All Souls Unitarian Church for a Saturday service that also featured the Harlem head of the MCC, the Reverend Renee McCoy.[38]

In protest against his excommunication, Tinney formed the Pentecostal Coalition for Human Rights, which reportedly attracted many members, while local supporters circulated posters and fliers that advertised upcoming demonstrations on his behalf. During the controversy, Tinney reportedly explained to the bishop and trustees of the church that Pentecostals "have always been known for having disproportionately-high numbers of overtly gay musicians and members." For the church, however, Tinney's sexual identification combined with promotion of gay religious worship crossed the line, revealing the fact that Tinney appeared to "have no shame," according to the bishop. The contrast between Tinney's contributions to the church and his sudden removal remained striking. The religious press noted that excommunication was seldom practiced, identifying Tinney as the "leading scholar on Black Pentecostalism" who had published a book about "the very bishop that expelled him." Only the previous year, Tinney had given a keynote address at the Society for the Study of Black Religion, a group that had membership by invitation only. Despite its initial refusal to do so, Tinney had succeeded in pressing a local gospel radio station to air commercials for the black gay revival by threatening it with the local ordinance that prohibited discrimination on the basis of sexual orientation.[39]

In response to his excommunication, Tinney also organized and carried out the formation of Faith Temple, which he described as a "Third World" lesbian/gay Christian church, which held its first worship service in September 1982. According to reports, only twelve were present, but all experienced a "warm feeling of the presence of the Holy Spirit." Faith Temple shared facilities with Calvary United Methodist Church and planned to surpass the latter's membership of fifty in the near future. In addition to services, the new denomination served as a launch for protest against Tinney's excommunication, offering breakfast before the eleven o'clock picket line formation at the Temple Church of God in Christ.[40] It was reported that Tinney and sixteen others picketed outside the church during Sunday worship services, billed as the "first ever conducted against a local church by lesbians/gays." The demonstration sparked numerous verbal exchanges, and the church authorities summoned the police and urged them to make arrests. According to one report, an opponent "spoke in tongues" against the gay group in the name of Jesus, and "pandemonium reigned several times during the protest." In the confrontation, a candidate running to unseat Representative Walter Fauntroy attacked the protesters for bringing gay rights into the black church; however, all but two of the protesters for Tinney were also black. They carried signs asserting the wrongfulness of the action: "Stop Religious Hypocrisy" and "Jesus Loves Me, Why Don't You?" Tinney was photographed holding a sign that read "The Holy Spirit Dwells in Lesbians and Gays Too." In one account, the bishop had announced that Tinney would be welcomed back into the church if "he 'repents' his homosexuality," but of course Tinney had no intention to do so.[41]

Not long after his excommunication, Tinney was ousted from the Society for Pentecostal Studies during its twelfth annual meetings. The group included more than four hundred members drawn from theological and academic ranks, and Tinney had belonged since its founding in 1970. But Tinney was also seen by many as part of the liberal breakaway faction seeking to reform doctrinal commitments in order to make the church more inclusive. When he set up his table for his Pentecostal Coalition for Human Rights at the meeting, "a full scale debate broke out" followed by a head-on confrontation. At that point, the dean of Fuller Theological Seminary approached Tinney to inform him of a school policy forbidding the discussion of homosexuality (a policy implemented in response to the formation of a gay-straight student alliance on campus). After Tinney disassembled the table, he continued to distribute literature to the conference attendees without incident. But authorities in the society convened a secret meeting, voted to return Tinney's membership renewal fee, and informed him that he was trespassing on the campus. A plenary membership meeting later voted overwhelmingly to uphold the decision, and Dr. James Forbes, a professor at Union Theological Seminary, was the lone dissenter in the group that approved Tinney's ousting.[42]

Only ten months after the excommunication, the Church of God in Christ invited Tinney back to address an educational conference, and he accepted the speaking engagement. The church did not move to restore his membership, and yet their move showed some softening. More than one hundred deans and faculty participated in the conference, which went off without a great deal of controversy, though it was noted that the authority who excommunicated Tinney, Bishop Kelsey, did not attend the convention. Several hecklers interrupted him even though Tinney did not talk about homosexuality; rather, he spoke about the larger history of the Pentecostal church. Afterward, he observed that the invitation "does reveal that there are many persons in the church who think that sexual orientation is less important than the skills and knowledge that a person has to share." To a certain extent, the controversy that Tinney aroused appears out of proportion to any threat he posed and perhaps reflected the particularly conservative stance of religious leaders. Yet across the nation, it was reported that white gay churches, such as the MCC, faced public approbation as well. According to an article in *Newsweek* in 1982, in the prior fourteen years, seventeen churches of the MCC denomination were "put to the torch," with a recent case of arson in Atlanta, and many more had been vandalized.[43]

At Howard, despite the eventual triumph of gaining recognition for the gay student group and earning tenure, Tinney's presence became more contentious. In the institutional culture at Howard, like at most universities, petty jealousies and rivalries swirled around the departments. Tinney had barely survived the review process, and now issues such as release time, teaching duties, and merit reviews reflected more closely the potential biases of his colleagues. By 1983, Tinney had become an increasingly popular speaker and sought-after writer, likely overshadowing a number of his colleagues. In August, the department chair informed Tinney of his teaching duties, adding that he was assigned an additional course, which was a considerable burden that went unexplained. Then Tinney requested to swap course sections with another faculty member, so that he would not have to teach five days a week, and about a week later he requested a graduate assistant to help with his research on the black press, but these requests were not granted. In September, Tinney complained. He wrote a long a memo to the chair of his department to express his "concern about what I perceive to be a growing pattern of my being treated differently than other member [*sic*] of this department." His reasons included the assignment of the fourth class, despite the fact that over the previous seven years, he had regularly taught only three classes. He also noted that his request to exchange class schedules was refused, pointing out that "this is the first time I have ever been assigned a Tuesday-Thursday class in addition to my Monday-Wednesday-Friday classes." This was also the first time he was assigned to teach at 8:10 A.M., despite the fact that he suffered from insomnia. "I am a senior professor, but am not accorded the same consideration as junior professors in our department," Tinney complained. "Imagine, then, my feelings of 'insult-added-to-injury' when in our Aug. 18 faculty meeting, I am told by you that I am the only professor in the entire department who is being forced to teach four classes." He went on to describe the preferential treatment given to the junior faculty who were given credit for pregnancy, community work, and research. "My record will show that I have published more articles in both refereed and nonrefereed publications than any other member of this department," he declared. Given his outstanding achievements, Tinney found his treatment "to be almost unbelievable."[44]

Tenure had given Tinney security, but as an associate professor he reported to chairs and deans, abided by continuing departmental review, and had to negotiate personal rivalries. About a year after the tenure review, Tinney was invited to speak at Yale University, a remarkable and prestigious accomplishment that must have thrilled him. It was a chance to speak on race, religion, and gay issues at a place where his ideas could have an impact and influence leading scholars. Shortly before the event was scheduled, Tinney's chair denied his request to leave campus on that Friday—although Tinney had submitted the paperwork three days before his expected departure—because of a regularly scheduled faculty meeting. The same day that he heard from the chair, Tinney shot off a long memo, explaining that he had received the chair's memo too late to cancel the engagement and that he would leave for New Haven the next day. But Tinney was not exactly modest in tone or message: "I feel certain that my colleagues would better understand my not being here than Yale would understand a cancellation. My name has already been placed on literature distributed over a wide region relative to this speaking engagement and Yale called me to confirm my presence as late as this past weekend."[45]

The cultural capital of the invitation would be thrown back at the seemingly jealous chair. "I sincerely hope that this action on your part (denying me the right to speak at another university) is not the result of improper motive or arbitrary and capricious decision-making," Tinney stated. Here perhaps he pushed the envelope a bit too far—after all, he was only recently tenured, an associate professor, speaking to his superior who was approved by the university administration. He concluded with the information that he would be lecturing on homosexuality and the church, and with the observation that his engagement "lends credibility to the department and Howard University as a whole." He sent copies of the memo to the Executive Committee of the Department of Journalism and to his dean. Tinney had also pointed out that requesting excuses from meetings was usually considered perfunctory and rarely required even a reply. The chair's action therefore appeared to confirm Tinney's claims to an emergent pattern of differential treatment that was personally troubling and potentially damaging to his career. Nonetheless, he went to the trouble of securing a proxy for the faculty meeting he would miss, left town for New Haven, and went on with his luncheon address and lecture sponsored by the divinity school's Women's Center, Center for Human Rights, and Gay-Straight Coalition. According to a press release there, Tinney spoke before a "full assembly of students and faculty," lectured on the subject of homosexuality and Pentecostalism, and explored options for finding greater tolerance in the church. Finally, it repeated what Tinney must have told the audience: "Ironically, Howard University refused to grant Tinney official permission to leave campus (despite the fact he teaches no classes on that day) to speak at Yale. The unprecedented denial was received by Tinney in writing on the eve of his departure for New Haven."[46]

Upon his return, Tinney received a memo from the chair agreeing to a meeting to discuss the matter of the absence. Ten days later, Tinney retained an attorney, Susan Silber, for representation in an "employment dispute at Howard University." According to the contract, Tinney agreed to pay a refundable retainer of $500, with additional installments scheduled for ten days later and then every two weeks. There the matter apparently ended, however, leaving Tinney frustrated and angered but no extant records indicating litigation or even disciplining from above for his decision to leave campus.

The following year, in another piece of correspondence that he saved, Tinney was informed that he would not receive an increase in salary, in part because of a shortfall in funding and in part because of his low percentile ranking. The memo indicated that faculty had to achieve a 5 out of 10 in the three categories of merit—research, teaching, and service—in order to qualify. Tinney's averages for 1983 and 1984 were marked "very unimpressive": 1 for teaching, 9 for research, and 1 for service, which earned him a merit rating of 0 for teaching, 3 for research, and 0 for service.[47] Tinney did not save any records regarding his teaching or mention how it was evaluated, but it is worth remembering that he had started out as an educator, teaching at a Kansas City high school, and that he was a popular speaker; there is a case to be made that he remained an effective performer in the classroom. As for service, much of what Tinney published involved public outreach, not only academic research. He addressed major social problems and sought to disseminate his scholarship well beyond the university. In 1984 Tinney won the second place Cassles Memorial Award presented by the Religion Newswriters Association for "excellence in the reporting of news of religion in secular newspapers."[48]

Perhaps Tinney himself took comfort in his outside accomplishments and community recognition as he turned away from the hostility of his colleagues and toward his church, lecturing and writing. He continued to write on William Seymour and found that one of the most characteristic aspects of Pentecostalism, speaking in tongues, was becoming more widespread, was considered "unique and superior" to other forms of religious expression, and received more and more congregant approval. Seymour had been born in slavery in Louisiana and founded the church in his early fifties. Tinney dismissed the stereotypes of Seymour as "untidy" and "poorly dressed" and described an extant photograph in which he wore his hair natural and had a beard with connected sideburns. This was also Tinney's own choice for hairstyle, perhaps as an homage or a gesture of tradition or heritage. He also described Seymour's conflicts and struggles, at one point mentioning that he had left his pastorate when authorities restricted the ritual of speaking in tongues. In his new church, Seymour preached to congregations in which members felt the Spirit in their bodies and voices, became healed by the touch of a minister or another designated figure, and even regained their sight after a period of blindness.[49]

In 1982, Tinney and a number of other black gay and lesbian Christian leaders issued what he described as a "virtual 'manifesto'" that attacked the homophobia of the black church. According to the report, the group demanded the right to speak of itself in the name of black church, citing the increasing number of black gay churches in major cities. "Black lesbians and gay men are the exiles," Rev. Renee McCoy declared, "the people who need the good news." Their criticism of the church presented an ultimatum—either become inclusive or refrain from preaching the gospel—and also pointed to the negative views propagated by a Howard University professor of psychiatry. Again, Tinney intersected with Brother Grant-Michael Fitzgerald, who was quoted criticizing his own church as "'racist, sexist, and homophobic.'"[50] Into the 1980s, between his academic research and an increasing numbers of invitations to speak and present his ideas, Tinney concentrated on formulating a kind of Christian ethics, oscillating between the reform of the black church and translating religious principles for gay and lesbian laity. From the small beginnings of the MCC and other gay and lesbian religious organizations, by the 1980s more than twenty-five denominational caucuses ranging from Mormons to Pentecostals had demonstrated greater tolerance toward gays and lesbians. Finally, a number of black gay and lesbian congregations were following Tinney's example and establishing black gay churches, including Rev. Renee McCoy's MCC in Harlem.[51]

Tinney had helped to transform the gay and lesbian religious landscape. In 1981, he had presented an important sermon to the MCC of Philadelphia, "'What Doth Hinder Me?': The Conversion of a Black Homosexual as Recorded by St. Luke," in which he claimed that the world's oppressed—women, people of color, and gays—were the most deserving of redemption. Rather than stress procreation, Tinney embraced a charismatic notion of the experience of the Holy Spirit and what he termed "the ecstasy of sexual climax as symbolic" of a union with God, toward the achievement of a reunion of body and spirit in "perfected sexuality." In this quest, Tinney argued for no distinction between heterosexual and homosexual, because "all stand equally in need of forgiveness based upon faith in Jesus Christ apart from any works." Although he had stressed the need to develop an ethical response to Christian exclusion, he also advanced a concept of a gay Christian "love ethic" that grappled with the "lusts of the flesh" by emphasizing a positive view, following biblical teachings, rather than a negative disavowal of the sexual other. By now, with the advances of gay liberation, a number of black religious leaders endorsed Tinney's eschatology, while the other leading black gay minister, Reverend McCoy, publicly declared the black church to be "homophobic."[52]

Tinney's passing was reported in a number of major newspapers, including the *Washington Post*, which listed AIDS as the cause of death. In this moment, too, Tinney would have refused to hide or opt for a convenient euphemism. At the time, he was survived by his mother, daughters, and two sisters, but it remains unclear if he had much communication with his family. His Faith Temple church carried on, and his legacy to scholarship on the black Pentecostal church remains legendary.

Chapter Eight

Mobilizations and Memorials

In leading interpretations of the post–civil rights era, historians have cast the 1980s as a period of conservative retrenchment and progressive loss, spinning out narratives of social movement declension. Within gay and lesbian historiography as well, the AIDS crisis overshadows other LGBT activist initiatives, and even the few works that address black gay issues, notably Cathy Cohen's influential *Boundaries of Blackness*, chart a "breakdown of black politics" in which the public sphere failed to address the health crisis, while in *Infectious Ideas* Jennifer Brier elaborates on local failures to enact intersectional outreach to bridge black and gay neighborhoods.[1]

As we have seen, conservative tradition and political backlash often overpowered individual efforts by black gay activists: Grant-Michael Fitzgerald retreated to Europe and then to the South; James Baldwin more or less remained in exile, except for teaching a few courses at Amherst College; James Tinney was forced to the margins of key African American institutions; and Joseph Beam worked to forge a shared brotherhood on a frustratingly small scale. Despite their best concerted efforts that greatly improved upon a legacy of pathology and defamation, these activists had failed to gain recognition of black gay lives from without or construct an enduring black gay community from within.

Near the end of his life, Bayard Rustin speculated that it is "easier to overcome racial prejudice than it is sexual prejudice" and congratulated those in the gay community on their effective response to the AIDS crisis. But he cautioned that they "must be concerned with everybody who has AIDS, whether they're gay or not."[2] In practice, black activists found this to be more prescient than Rustin probably realized, for neglect and misunderstanding among white gays and the unique circumstance of black people with AIDS necessitated a multidimensional or intersectional approach.

Researchers and activists alike understood AIDS as racially inflected by the mid-1980s, and many realized that addressing the health crisis ought not to detract from ongoing efforts to sustain community and improve individual self-esteem. Black communities remained extremely vulnerable to the ramifications of AIDS, with higher percentages of impact in every category of measurement. Of the 385 reported Philadelphia cases in 1986, 187 (48.6 percent) were black, 174 (45.2 percent) white, 23 (6 percent) Hispanic, and 1 (.3 percent) Asian. Of the 5 Philadelphia pediatric cases, 4 (80 percent) were black and 1 (20 percent) was Hispanic. In some of the reports, only 40 percent of black men identified as gay, compared with 98 percent of infected white men, supposedly indicating a higher percentage of intravenous drug use among black men. Yet given the increasing distance between black and white neighborhoods, and insufficient efforts to reach out to black gay men, the statistical variance may have overlooked the number of black men who engaged in same-sex behavior but did not publicly identify as gay. According to one report, although blacks represented the largest percentage of AIDS cases in the city, there were few "black buddies" to help HIV-infected men of color with errands, medical appointments, and other everyday activities.[3]

Because the delivery of health services skewed along race lines, black gay men mobilized throughout black communities and at city hall. In turn, black political organizations, such as the Philadelphia Black Leadership Council, sponsored food drives and fund-raisers for people with AIDS, and black-led community centers, such as Burning Bush, provided shelter, meals, and recreation space for the disabled and ill. Although some white activists argued that homophobia was color blind, questions of health, drugs, and policy remained interconnected with race and resources. At one event, for example, organizers announced a fund named for the first black gay man to publicly announce his diagnosis of AIDS as well as plans for a new minority-based building or center to, in the words of one speaker, "give something back to the community." It was reported that along with Blacks Educating Blacks about Sexual Health Issues and members of IMPACT (Interpreting Minority Perspectives for Action), key organizers planned on meeting with city council members, state representatives, the local chapter of the National Urban League, and church leaders to facilitate plans for further outreach. Yet within these minority-oriented groups, conflicts over personality and prerogatives too undermined progress, with personal disputes erupting onto the front pages of the press, including a number of dismissals and resignations suggesting the ongoing volatility.[4]

About fifty demonstrators picketed outside the headquarters of the Philadelphia AIDS Task Force (PATF) to protest the "continuing pattern of racism," alleging that the firing of the task force's minority outreach coordinator stemmed from bias. In time, some of the criticism of racial insensitivity was resolved, according to reports by spokesmen, but then new reports indicated recurrent flare-ups. At one point, the head of the PATF publicly denied charges of refusing to hire a minority person to conduct outreach, and amid the fallout was the charge that white gay racism inhibited effective outreach to the black community. Tempers ran high—charges of malfeasance issued from both sides—when in one letter to the editor, a critic of white gay AIDS organizations declared, "I have sadly come to realize that the gay community in Philadelphia in reality is the white gay community. . . . I cannot and will not be a part of that community."[5]

AIDS activists organized forums to explain the extent to which racism existed in the gay community, specifically regarding funding for outreach to minorities, and to explore the impact of "racism in the bars." Into the 1980s, black activists charged that mainstream AIDS organizations had failed to recruit people of color to help care for HIV-positive black men, prompting a meeting between the head of AIDS services and members of IMPACT.[6] One of the founders of the group Philadelphia Black Gays, James Roberts, delivered a major address at a local conference on the health crisis, pointing out, again, the extent to which larger questions of race became inseparable from managing the response to the disease. In his speech, Roberts discussed the problem of misrepresentation of black gay issues not only in the mainstream media but also in the gay press. He cited the larger backlash against civil rights, conservative trends in the Supreme Court, increasing visibility of extremist groups such as the Ku Klux Klan, and the fact that "the decline of activism on the part of black people since its zenith in the early 1970's has lulled many white Americans—including white gay and lesbian Americans—into believing either that black people have 'made it' or that they are 'content with their less-than-equal lot.'" But the fact is that Roberts saw little difference between the rightward backlash and the negligent gay community, citing a widespread indifference to white racism. In particular, he recalled his experience as assistant editor at *Au Courant* and pointed out that he found little substantive coverage of black issues, except for the random "ornamental" mention in the entertainment section or perhaps a sensational crime story. Because of misrepresentation and underreporting, it was impossible for the community to respond to the crisis or to address the fundamental question of "why black people with AIDS often do not have proper access to medical assistance, food stamps, [or] supplemental social security income," Roberts charged.[7]

The pressure of AIDS mobilized new networks of communication around identity and institution-building among black gay men. At a workshop on masculinity and health, for example, Joseph Beam reported on the work of Julius Johnson, a San Francisco psychologist, who differentiated between "black-identified black gay men and gay-identified black gay men."[8] In 1986 Clifford Rawlins, a therapist and community activist, formed a support group for black gay men, Adodi (a Portuguese word derived from Yoruba, meaning "homosexual man") intended to supplement other black male institutions, such as fraternities or church groups, in a way that affirmed gay identity—"for black gay men to deal with their own issues." Other local groups that had never or rarely addressed gay issues now sought to increase awareness. An associate of the Philadelphia Urban League spoke at a forum on racism in the lesbian and gay community, sponsored by Innerpride, the local organizing collective associated with the National Coalition of Black Lesbians and Gays at the Friends Center in Philadelphia. Here again James Roberts, also president of Innerpride, instructed local organizers to mobilize their membership to vote in upcoming elections as a means to respond to the crisis and warned against blind support of a political party because politicians would become unresponsive to communities that they took for granted. National black gay and lesbian organizations continued to focus on community building, political lobbying, and publishing *Black/Out*, which was still edited by Beam, for the purpose of informing "members of our community to hear our news, with the emphasis on 'ours.'"[9]

The AIDS crisis had intensified black gay separatist impulses even as it moved black gay men toward a broader black brotherhood to care for those whose connections to the Center City gay bar scene remained more conflicted or tenuous. While focusing attention on black community building, however, local gay organizing was not always uncontested or unified. Len Bost, a member of Black and White Men Together and a cochair of the Mayor's Commission on Sexual Minorities, complained that a recent forum on race and the health crisis was personally insulting insofar as the BWMT's well-known efforts on behalf of antiracism went unrecognized, including a forum the group had held at the Smart Place, a popular bar with an interracial clientele, some three years before. Also unheralded were the many "brochures, posters and seminars" that BWMT had promoted "within the black community."[10]

An important exception to the diversion of activist energies into monitoring AIDS research and treatment was the expansion of the BWMT. As indicated in chapter 6, Beam's relationship to the group was soon strained and he decided not to return to the meetings, in part because of his dislike of the anthology *Black Men/White Men*, produced by the group's founder, Mike Smith. He was not alone, and the BWMT remained both controversial and sometimes even polarizing.[11]

Yet the Philadelphia-BWMT remained active on a number of fronts of anti-racism work that suggests not only the seriousness of its purpose but also the political and social complexities of the 1980s.[12] The group started in 1981, with the first meeting held at the Smart Place; the steering committee convened at the dining room of Equus, another racially mixed destination. By 1982, Philadelphia-BWMT distributed a newsletter, hosted a well-attended dance party at the Gay Community Center, and organized public forums on race issues. From the beginning, the group formed along an emergent network connecting New York, Philadelphia, and Boston, with frequent visits of the local group to the larger chapter in Manhattan for instruction, sharing of information, and socializing. BWMT's critique of racism challenged the optimism of the gay revolution by complicating the notion that sexuality was always liberating and by exposing embedded practices of everyday racism. By the same token, founder Mike Smith had always refused to equate achieving sociability across the color line with societal change or racial equality: "As if making love to one will somehow eradicate racism!" In acknowledging the prejudice facing interracial couples and groups, however, he spoke openly of their stigma and of the "curiosity seekers" whose desire for interracial relations was defined by the larger culture of racialized pornography that saturated gay culture with objectified images of black potency, hypersexuality, and dominance.[13]

Yet members of the Philadelphia-BWMT realized that black gays were suspicious of their group's intentions for these very reasons. Even before the chapter was started, Beam and a number of black gay men had participated in Philadelphia Black Gays and other black gay groups, such as Just Us—Black Men's and Women's Social Group, founded in the early 1970s, and Mox-Nix, a black social group started in the late 1960s. Like the group that James Tinney helped to organize at Howard, Philadelphia Black Gays originated in the 1979 Third World Gay/Lesbian Conference in Washington. In 1981, the Philadelphia-BWMT invited members of Philadelphia Black Gays to address one of its general meetings and attempted to explain to them their organization's history, goals, and activities. Although Philadelphia Black Gays did not keep a transcript, members recalled a sense of confusion. Was BWMT a social group or advocate for black-white sexual relations, or was it (as some suspected) providing ready access to black men for wealthier and

Bayard Rustin (*center*) and BWMT members Russell Webb and Michael Lisowski. In the 1980s, chapters of the gay interracial organization Black and White Men Together formed in major cities and provided safe social spaces as well as advocating for racial justice. The National Association of Black and White Men Together honored Bayard Rustin with their first Lifetime Achievement Award in 1985. (Courtesy of D. A. Leonard).

often otherwise segregated white men? After the meeting with Philadelphia Black Gays, however, the Philadelphia-BWMT noted that "although the two groups exist for different reasons, through continued communication they can build trust so that the two groups will be able to work together on issues of common concern."[14]

In addition to providing a social outlet, the Philadelphia-BWMT's primary objective was to address and reform patterns of racism directed against black gay men and black and white couples. In an important essay on "breaking the taboo" against interracial relationships, the group reported that on the streets of Philadelphia gay individuals could walk in comfort, and so too could gay couples, but "to really wake up your fellow pedestrians and motorists, just step out on the town as an interracial same-sex couple. Usually it's just a stare or two, but muttered comments and catcalls from speeding cars are not uncommon." In breaking "two taboos," such a couple confronted the realities of "a racist society, and its effects invade the awareness of perpetrators and victims alike." Yet the essay concluded on a note of optimism to assert that "a foolish, vile taboo is beginning to die in America" and that a nation priding itself on unity and diversity would change. These were the main ideas that the BWMT disseminated in its printed literature, at its meetings, and in public forums.[15]

The Philadelphia-BWMT also carried on the tradition of investigating classified advertisements in the gay press for racial bias. Beginning in 1981, members of the group called for a meeting with the editor of the *Philadelphia Gay News*, Mark Segal, to discuss what they referred to as gay discrimination but reported that he missed their first planned appointment. Segal requested another chance to meet with the members, many of whom hoped he would "finally resolve the issue of racist help wanted ads," referring to ones that specified "whites only." By this time, the publication of such advertisements constituted a violation of federal law, but for the members of BWMT they served as an important reminder of the gay community's history of racism. In either case, after some lag and deflection, claiming that he was short-handed and overburdened, Segal agreed to correct the policy and remove the offensive ads.[16]

The chapter also criticized racial bias in personal or sexual classified advertisements. As members put it, "There's no question that many of the white persons who advertise the ritualistic 'GWM/GWF seek same' reject people of color simply out of routine," and here they sought to intervene in the perpetuation of stereotypes and sexual objectification. In their deliberations over racism, they rejected the increasingly vocalized concept of reverse racism and declared that "color-on-white racism is virtually nonexistent" in reference to black gay men's preferences or actions in predominantly white gay communities. "Prejudice without power is a little like shouting at your television set," they pointed out. Though the BWMT was established as a black-white organization, across the nation chapters readily expanded to include Chicano/Mexican, Native American, and Asian gay men, and by the mid-1980s the organization renamed itself Men of All Colors Together.[17]

In educating diverse communities on racism, the BWMT confronted the endemic problem of discrimination in gay community institutions. As the numbers of gay bars and steam rooms multiplied in Center City and West Philadelphia, including increasing numbers of black gay bars into the 1980s, a range of establishments continued to target particular groups, tastes, and fetishes. Separating race out and refusing to admit black patrons proved to be pervasive among white proprietors. In preparation for its campaign to stop the practice, the Philadelphia-BWMT observed and later participated in the activities of the New York chapter of the BWMT, whose membership organized demonstrations against racial profiling in gay bars. The New York group went undercover to test various door policies by dispatching groups of white members, black members, and interracial couples. According to a detailed report, a group of four whites as well as an interracial couple were admitted to one particular bar without incident, but four black patrons, all of age, were kept waiting at the door, and two were not permitted entry when a staff member claimed that they lacked sufficient identification, even after they had presented their passports. The New York chapter filed a complaint of discrimination against the establishment, and a judge reportedly compared its campaign against racial bias to the civil rights activities of the NAACP.[18]

"Racism is alive and well in Philadelphia," declared Don Ransom, cochair of the Philadelphia-BWMT in the early 1980s. Ransom reported an incident where he and two black friends, ages fifty-eight and sixty-two, were required to present identification to gain entry into a local gay bar while young white gay men walked right through without incident. In response, Philadelphia-BWMT developed a bar discrimination survey and assigned participating members to teams or pairs that would test the door policies throughout the city. In turn, the Coalition on Lesbian and Gay Policies of the BWMT announced the completion of its research into the "hiring and admission policies of Philadelphia's lesbian and gay bars," to be released in a published document that "represents two year's worth of surveys and observations of lesbian and gay bars throughout the region." The document featured a summary of the coalition's investigation into some twenty establishments as well as a set of recommendations for uniform admission and hiring policies.[19]

In response to these patterns of exclusion from and the segregation of gay bars and clubs, increasing numbers of black men turned away. It was reported that only two black bars were supporting a donation drive sponsored by the PATF, and one of the most popular black bars, Allegro II, chose not to participate in the campaign. Some black gay patrons donated money but showed little interest in attending the white bars hosting the events. Into the 1980s, the number of predominantly black gay bars increased, expanding Philadelphia nightlife and redefining black gay identity. In a gay newspaper column, "The Black Scene" by Brett Masseaux, the reporter promised to review at least two black gay clubs each week, offering a thorough evaluation that characterized style of dress, decorum, and overall enjoyment. Of the several clubs described, the Terminal was characterized as "a nice place to go" but did not have much "class," although it served high-class liquor and offered "a jukebox full of good music." Masseaux also noted the apparently notorious Ritz. Widely considered to be among the most popular of the gay bars, despite the heavy cigarette smoke, the Ritz had the sort of reputation that made its patrons deny they visited it and yet "everyone from every walk of life, every social circle and level of sophistication" eventually showed up there.[20]

The proprietors of several local black gay bars complained of racially biased police harassment and false citations for noise and disturbance of the peace. When one of the most popular black gay bars moved to a new location, it was forced to close amid charges of racial bias and noise complaints. The owner retorted, "My kids are flawless," and added that when Woody's (a popular white bar) "lets out onto 13th Street, no one says a word. Why do I get cops and aggravation?" After the city officials and other observers became involved, the debate unfolded into one of racism versus simple business competition. The dominant ethic of gay metropolitan culture was defined by capitalist accumulation and a culture of abundance—the liberationist ideology that more bars and clubs yielded more sexual freedom and satisfaction—but reporting on and seeking to reform bar racism shifted the terrain. Now, black gay men and their supporters protested against established patterns of exclusion, one of the few if only groups in the community targeting the gay bar as a site of sustained activism.[21]

Memorials

After the publication of *In the Life* in 1986, Joseph Beam's ambition to attain the stature of Audre Lorde or Barbara Smith was seemingly within reach, and after Lorde read the anthology while in transit to Boston, she exclaimed that "I can't tell you how much it means to me that all of you exist." That year Beam received invitations to speak at several conferences, such as the Pennsylvania Ink Celebration; appeared at bookstores and community performance spaces; and presented his writings at activist meetings, such as the first Northeastern Lesbian, Gay, and Bisexual People of Color Conference. The release of the anthology had lifted his visibility, and he reported that his "schedule for the first couple of months of the year is filling up with Black History Month events, etc." As he prepared for what he referred to as "Part II"—another anthology of writings by black gay men—he took special pleasure in bringing *In the Life* to college and university campus groups. In 1986, for example, he spoke at Cornell University and the following year at the Gay, Bisexual, and Lesbian Alliance of Amherst College, the Gay Men's Alliance of Hampshire College, and Brown University. The increasing number of gay and lesbian bookstores provided yet another forum, with Beam launching his tour at Giovanni's Room Bookstore, a triumphant return, and

Joseph Beam at BWMT. At the 1987 BWMT annual convention in Milwaukee, Joseph Beam agreed to speak at the Banquet. Although Beam had once attended meetings of Philadelphia-BWMT, by this time he had turned away from interracial activism. In his speech, he criticized the group and set off a storm of controversy. (Courtesy of D. A. Leonard).

speaking at Lambda Rising bookstore in Baltimore and the West Philadelphia Regional Library (in the same lineup of speakers as Don Belton, a black gay novelist, whose *Almost Midnight* was recently published). In some cases, Beam received modest honorariums for an appearance, while others were uncompensated.[22]

In the Life was also widely reviewed in the gay press, to almost unanimous praise, with editors ranking it among their top picks and placing it on their best ten lists. Hailing the book as "exciting" and "new," reviewers noted the variety and range of voices that Beam presented to his readers, and a feminist press predicted the collection "will have a cross-over market among lesbians of color and white women of politics, just as This Bridge has found a strong readership among gay men of consciousness," referring to the feminist classic *This Bridge Called My Back* that had inspired Beam. His work also drew personal letters of praise and gratitude. A formerly married writer informed Beam that his was "the type of book that I as a Black gay man have been looking for."[23]

Increasing visibility and positive reviews helped Beam to realize some of his dreams, but the fame fueled rather than satisfied his ambitions. When his friend Essex Hemphill, a poet, won a fellowship from the National Endowment for the Arts, Beam planned to follow him, but the NEA rejected Beam's own application. Barbara Smith visited Paris in the summer of 1987, sending him a postcard of the Arc de Triomphe, and he dreamed of European travel as well. When he wrote to London-based artist Isaac Julien to announce that he planned to attend the International Radical and Third World Book Fair and speak there, he also had to report of his fatigue and economic instability, both of which interfered with some of his publicity dates and made international travel in the near future unlikely. The fact was that many of his public appearances paid little or nothing, and by 1987, after the novelty of basking in the limelight had worn off, he reported that he canceled a public engagement in order to work "five or six meals a week at the restaurant." Alyson Publications continued to send royalty checks of $150 or so, his mother sent him extra funds to help with his rental, and his editorial work on *Black/Out* paid irregularly, but he remained far from the status of a self-supporting writer.[24]

Beam had constructed essay after essay on the formation of black gay identity, but he also intended to reach across divisions of sexual orientation. Yet few bisexual or straight men had contributed to his project, and none of the major black publications, such as *Jet* or *Ebony*, reviewed *In the Life*. Beam may have presented at universities but not at historically black colleges and universities; he may have lectured at conferences but not at those convened by black organizations. Neither the NAACP nor the National Urban League recognized Beam in any way. He had written of a shared black masculinity and heavily critiqued white gay mores but actually found little recognition in predominantly straight black audiences. Over the months following publication, Beam gradually lost touch with the contributors to the anthology and even some of his close friends, and the number of his letters decreased and his writing slowed. A couple of authors complained to Beam about the payment of royalties, charging that he had "not lived up to your end of the deal" and that "there is no question that the book is making money." Meanwhile, Barbara Smith wrote to Beam in concern, after not hearing from him for "so long"; she noted, "You haven't returned my phone calls." When he finally replied months later, she wrote back gratefully, confirming his sentiments: "I would echo your statement in your letter, I'm alive, but not doing very well." Though Smith complained of unending work and lists of tasks, perhaps Beam had referred to his worsening health.[25]

Beam died several days before his thirty-fourth birthday, pronounced dead on December 27, 1988, at 5:35 P.M. Aware of the significance of history and the potential he had to change it, Beam may have pondered his legacy before his passing. The consummate archivist, he preserved everything he received and carbon copies of everything he sent in his Spruce Street studio. Did he imagine that his possessions would be collected, archived, and cited—that he would become a historical figure? Not only was history his favorite subject in high school, but studying history informed all of his writings on gay identity. In either case, Beam's notes and correspondence, Xeroxes and diaries, were destined for cataloging in some library, and so in March 1989, Beam's mother, Dorothy Beam, wrote to Rita Addessa, the head of the Philadelphia Lesbian and Gay Task Force, to announce that the "Schomburg Library has requested Joe's papers," referring to the major repository for African American materials, located in the Harlem branch of the New York Public Library. "I plan to get them ready in about 6 months: I need help," Dorothy Beam exclaimed.[26]

As his mother collected his remains for posterity, the memorialization of Beam began with the publication of his obituaries—each with shared details as well as disparate versions of his passing. The facts of the death announcement for Beam relied on a summary of the findings of the Philadelphia Medical Examiner, compiled in the file labeled "Beam, Joseph, 6253–88," which indicated his full name, address, race, and marital status but listed the incorrect age of thirty-five. The medical examiner determined that the immediate cause of death was acquired immunodeficiency syndrome, according to a summary report signed by a medical doctor, after the coroner's examination completed on Beam's birthday, December 28, 1988. At the time, at six feet and one and a half inches, Beam weighed only 150 pounds. The official rendering of the circumstances of his passing remains as persuasive as any, based in part on information from the rental superintendent who discovered him. Beam, "the decedent," was "found dead lying on the bathroom floor by the apartment house manager, Mark Crossly," and was "last seen alive Wednesday (12–21–88)"; he "did not show up for work Friday." When the superintendent opened the door with a passkey, he smelled odor and then broke the door chain, discovering Beam and characterizing his apartment as not in excellent shape but in "its usual state."[27]

Almost exactly a year before, James Baldwin had died—of natural causes, not of AIDS—and his passing proved instructive on the politics of remembering black gay lives. Beam's close friend Barbara Smith published a powerful essay on Baldwin's funeral in which the nation's finest black writers—among them Maya Angelou, Amiri Baraka, and Toni Morrison—neglected to mention Baldwin's gayness in their eulogies. Smith created the metaphor of burying the dead twice, which nicely captured the double life that Baldwin had presented, both transcending and committing to gay black men. "Although Baldwin's funeral completely reinforced our Blackness, it tragically rendered his and our homosexuality completely invisible," she wrote. Compounding the loss of Baldwin was a deafening silence about his homosexuality because gays and lesbians lost "the challenging impact that telling the whole truth at Baldwin's funeral could have had . . . and nobody knew his full name."[28]

The death of Beam illustrated the historical transformation in race and sexuality wrought by activists over the past quarter century, for his funeral was a landmark in black gay recognition and the building of a community of belonging. The eulogies and personal testimonies crafted a memory of tragic loss and loneliness, with acquaintances reporting that Beam had disappeared and had collapsed while alone and that "friends said . . . that he had been in ill health and had been extremely depressed."[29] Here was also the seeding of a rumor that later informed the myth—told to me in interviews and debated in the press—that Beam committed suicide, but many obituaries rushed to his defend his integrity, refusing to speak ill of the dead. From as far away as London, it was reported that "there were no traces of drugs or alcohol in the body," as well as the story that he "withdrew from his circle of friends and wasn't returning calls." Another newspaper reported that he "had been depressed for several months" and, quoting his mother, "the more he ate, the thinner he got." His mother explained, "He told me that I worry too much. When he came here once, he just looked so drawn and I said to my husband, 'Sunny, Joe is carrying the weight of the world on his shoulders.'"[30]

The consummate local activist and organic intellectual, Beam had in reality attained global recognition, even though he had never traveled outside the United States, had little international correspondence in his papers, and probably never even realized his reach. Beam's mother reportedly received condolences from Australia, Canada, England, Israel, and Mexico, while a gay community center in London sent flowers arranged in the shape of a heart. In death, the closet opened and the silences were broken: Beam's alma mater, Franklin College, where Beam had struggled to cope with his sexuality, published a long obituary that featured photos of Beam in high school and his student identification card, reporting that his mother was "overwhelmed by hundreds of sympathy cards, letters of condolences and phone calls." Though Beam had criticized the city's black newspaper for ignoring gay issues, the *Philadelphia Tribune* ran two obituaries, identifying him as a black gay writer and quoting several of the speakers at his memorial service.[31]

The lessons to be taken away were those that Beam had lived by: "Now that he is gone, we are made painfully aware of how important it is for all of us to speak for ourselves."[32] His unexplained disappearance had caused a genuine shock, while the discovery of his death exposed a paradox: how could someone as dedicated to the formation of community have remained so isolated, removed, and secretive about his HIV status?[33] Perhaps Beam would have approved of the testimonials, at least to the extent that they served to enact a kind of collective identification and through their recollection helped to create a sense of black gay identity, folding disparate experiences and remembrances into the collective ritual. The memorial was also invested in the politics of coming out—in visibility and the declaration of the self as transformative. Yet to be remembered as alone and isolated may have illustrated black gay marginalization or shamed the community into embracing each other, and yet in a sense this remembrance also publicly eternalized Beam's personal suffering.

Beam's close friend, the poet Essex Hemphill, captured the sentiment of the moment in a beautiful poem, "When My Brother Fell (For Joseph Beam)."

It is difficult
To stop marching, Joseph
Impossible to stop our assault.
The Tributes and testimonies
In your honor
Flare up like torches.
Every night
A light blazes for you
In one of our hearts.[34]

At the memorial service on January 5, 1989, in West Philadelphia, reportedly hundreds of relatives, friends, and well-wishers attended, identified by the press as "members of the gay and lesbian community, local friends and activists from Washington to Los Angeles," coming "to pay tribute and to mourn his loss." Barbara Smith and Becky Birtha, both black lesbian feminists, and Renee McCoy, the executive director of the National Coalition of Black Lesbians and Gays, delivered tributes; it was also noted that Beam's friend and contributor to the anthology Assotto Saint attempted to speak but was "too moved, too angry to continue." Saint later died of AIDS in New York, and so perhaps his distress at the service reflected his confrontation with his own fate as he coped with the loss of Beam.[35]

In the Beam correspondence, after a particularly long day of reading and copying, I found a set of letters to and from doris davenport, a black poet, which struck me as humorous at first. She began with an enthusiastic salutation,

"Hey Joseph, how are you?," and then reported that she had lost her job at a factory because of tardiness. Although an artistic soul, she had to earn a living in wage labor but apparently was not very punctual. But she then changed the subject and asked Beam if he had enjoyed "talking to my Jonathan," a close friend for whom she apparently cared a great deal. She once mentioned to Beam that she would take him as a lover if he were a woman. She sent fliers that advertised Beam's anthology to Jonathan, and in a second hastily composed letter, she again mentioned Jonathan to Beam. She told Beam that she read to "Walton" from the anthology, describing him as "a wonderful friend of mine, a gay, feminist, and black man who teaches at the University of Iowa."[36] Suddenly, in a familiar burst of emotion in the archive, I realized that she had attempted to connect Beam with Jonathan Walton, a black gay scholar who had taught about African American subjects in the Department of History more than a decade before I arrived. Walton was a popular teacher and had died suddenly of complications from AIDS in 1987, the year I started graduate school. Though davenport gave Walton's contact information to Beam, I never found evidence that the two ever communicated.

If Beam died alone, it was probably his choice to do so, for he had friends and family within reach but he chose not to reach out. Perhaps this decision or predicament resulted from the times, from the context of silence and misrecognition that he worked to break through. Beam's greatest mentor, Audre Lorde, wrote a poem for the publication that Beam had edited, *Black/Out*, which she titled "Dear Joe," that figured the process of black gay mourning as one of anger and rage.

> How many other dark young men at 33
> left a public life becoming legends
> the mysterious connection
> between who we murder and who we mourn?

Sustaining an uncharacteristic bitterness, Lorde wrote unrelentingly of "wrong prejudice lazy," referring not only to black straights but also the pathology of black gay culture itself that allowed for Beam's death in isolation, "in the side pews." In evoking the street culture that Beam had written into history, Lorde concluded with an image evocative of the anger that Beam himself had wrestled with:

> a drag-queen with burgundy long-johns
> and a dental dam in his mouth
> is buying a straight-razor.[37]

Because his communities had not accepted one another, Joseph Beam remained at bay. In his moving testimony, James Roberts wrote that "most black gay men that I know never heard of you. Why is that? Because we live in a separatist society," he concluded, and this explained why Beam was "best known to people who frequent gay and lesbian bookstores or who read the gay/lesbian press. As you know, relatively few of them are black." Like Bayard Rustin and James Baldwin, Grant-Michael Fitzgerald and Beam, James Tinney and other cultural activists and writers, black gay men's struggle for recognition failed more often than succeeded, proceeded along shared but too often divergent paths, and never fully achieved for them a beloved community.[38]

Epilogue

Carrying On

Into the 1990s, medical scientists and epidemiologists continued to analyze the causes and consequences of racially disparate HIV infection patterns in which black men tested positive for the virus at twice the rate of white men, and by 2000, black men continued to double the white rate, while critics blamed health care providers and activists for failing to disseminate information on safer sex beyond the white gay community. Indeed, one explanation for the racial disparity was that dominant conceptions of black masculinity inhibited involvement in gay institutions or networks and that therefore black men were simply less informed about safer sex practices. Rev. Renee McCoy, a longtime activist and pioneering founder of a black LGBT church, has argued that because of homophobia and conservative religious values in black communities, "many turn blind eyes and deaf ears to targeted prevention messages focused on labels such as 'gay' or 'down low'" and that many were willing to put risk and sexual gratification ahead of their own health. Another contemporary source of the disparate infection numbers was the escalating rate of incarceration of black men. Social scientists have established a high correlation between incarceration and rising infection rates for African American men and women. But even for black men involved in gay communities, the annual infection rates were considerably higher, which some observers attributed to a lack of self-esteem. In the face of an epidemic, a new generation of black gay activists rediscovered the importance of recognition: to "work to overcome internalized homophobia, and develop self-love and a positive self-image," as one journalist put it.[1]

The search for venues of black gay self-expression and for positive images—now seen by many as a matter of life and death—was thwarted by skewed representations of AIDS in mainstream black publications into the late twentieth century. To return to some of the sources with which this book began, consider the reporting on AIDS in *Jet* magazine. In the 1990s, the widely circulated weekly continued to run stories on a variety of subjects related to homosexuality, many of them more serious and less defamatory than fifty years before. Yet even as black gay communities formed in major cities, virtually none of the news in the magazine acknowledged these organizations or the publications that Joseph Beam's generation had created. Some of the reporting recalled *Jet*'s original days of spreading sex education; it disseminated information on the HIV disease and dispelled the myth that oral sex or "deep kissing" caused transmission.[2] Yet the vast amount of the coverage of AIDS rarely even identified black gay men and instead carried features on AIDS and Africa, African American women, and athletic and religious figures.[3]

From the beginning of the epidemic, black gayness was often implied in numerous reports and stories, but black gay men remained largely hidden from view. The fact that the major black news story on AIDS concerned Magic Johnson, the heterosexual star basketball player who in 1991 publicly disclosed his HIV status, spoke volumes. Soon after coming out as HIV positive, Johnson retired from athletics at a time when some players and coaches feared contracting the virus from contact with him, and he began making public appearances and hosting fund-raisers. He published a best-selling autobiography with plans for its production into a television miniseries and marshaled his considerable entrepreneurial talents to build a "multimillion-dollar empire" while disseminating information about AIDS worldwide. For many Americans—and certainly many African Americans—Johnson was the public face of the disease. He also became the face of recovery and, before the end of the decade, reported that he was benefiting from "powerful" drugs that had reduced the virus to "undetectable" levels.[4] In addition to Johnson, the announcement that the black tennis player Arthur Ashe was suffering from AIDS-related illness introduced yet another example of highly publicized heterosexual infection.[5]

Even reports about HIV in nuclear families sidestepped how the disease had been transmitted in the first place, avoiding a discussion of African American bisexuality.[6] In a long feature on AIDS activist Rae Lewis-Thornton, details of her organizing against and recovery from the disease were presented but not how she was infected or what had become of her partner, leaving the reader to speculate. In another story of black female infection, a popular writer published a memoir on her experience with the disease, "Faith under Fire," in which she encouraged men to "be who you are," and yet the terms "bisexual" and "gay " remained unmentionable.[7] After Max Robinson, the first black television news anchor, passed away from the disease, some reports speculated on his "promiscuous lifestyle" but never confirmed his bisexuality or homosexuality. With the exception of three obituaries (of Sylvester, the entertainer; of Willi Ninja, the star of a documentary on black gay lives; and of Willi Smith, the fashion designer), at the height of the AIDS crisis black gay men remained invisible in the most widely circulated publication in black America.[8]

As a result many activists believed that saving black gay lives required speaking out, and again black gay journalism and artistic projects became crucial to the group's progress. By the 1990s the National Coalition of Black Gays' quarterly journal, *Black/Out*, had established a political presence in Washington and beyond, while new publications in metropolitan areas—the journal *Blacklines* in Chicago and *BLK* in Los Angeles—presented variety of writers objecting to social discrimination, highlighting the need for community, and reimagining the meanings of identity; at the same time, a national gay magazine, the *Advocate*, ran features on black gay life on a regular basis. The possibilities for correcting negative stereotypes, restoring self-worth, and building AIDS support networks increased exponentially.

This scattered movement for affirmation often legitimated itself with references to black gay history. *BLK* constructed a timeline for its readers, "Major Events in Black Gay History since Stonewall," which began with the Stonewall Riots but also listed such highlights as "1974: Sierra Domino, nation's largest studio of black gay erotica established in San Francisco"; "1979: Baldwin's *Just Above My Head* included black gay lovers, affirmatively portrayed"; "[1983:] James Baldwin, America's greatest living male author, comes out at BWMT/ N.Y. event"; and "1985: Bayard Rustin breaks silence on his gayness when he addresses NABWMT convention." As we have seen, Rustin's long career was marked by almost anything but silence on the question of his sexuality, but at a moment of abiding political faith in speaking out and being seen, Rustin's speech seemed to signal a historic turning point.[9]

Routinely journalists and activists celebrated the gay achievements of Rustin and other civil rights pioneers. In "Remembering Our Past," one writer claimed both Lorraine Hansberry and James Baldwin as leaders in the "war against racism, sexism, and homophobia/heterosexism," though with a popular gloss that erased the complexities of both their activism and marginalization. At one point, for example, the piece asserted that "by 1957, Baldwin's works were well known . . . [and] critically successful" and he had "established himself as a significant American writer," when in fact Baldwin faced enormous hostility after the publication of novels dealing with homosexual themes and even more controversy at the height of black power. As

for Hansberry, drawing on her 1957 letters to the *Ladder*, *Blacklines* concluded that she "was privately coming out" in order to construct a genealogy that secured a sense of lesbian identity legitimated by history. Rustin was
honored in an Atlanta rally sponsored by Unity Fellowship Church, *Venus*
magazine, and the Men of Second Sunday Discussion Group, and later the
Greater Chicago Committee presented a Bayard Rustin Award to black lesbian activists and AIDS organizations. Another popular monthly published
a picture of Rustin, along with the historical notation "Organizer of the 1963
March on Washington," in a public notice urging black gay readers to vote
in the 1998 elections. Journalists invoking black gay history—with photos of
Rustin, Baldwin, and Hansberry and sometimes the poet Langston Hughes—
sought to use the past to create pride for the present and to connect an often-
romanticized version of the civil rights movement with the contemporary
struggles for gay equality.[10]

Meanwhile, it was noted that for the first time, "two Black lesbian and
gay activists helped lead the official national commemoration of the Martin
Luther King, Jr. National Holiday," bringing the story full circle from one of
historical invisibility in 1963 to inclusive celebration less than forty years later.
After this ceremony in Atlanta, the two aforementioned activists, Keith Boykin and Dr. Sylvia Ruhe, also appeared at Morehouse College, the historically
black school, to discuss homophobia and the black church, and at another
event Boykin challenged the homophobia of an emergent New Right Christian
coalition. However, in 2002 at Morehouse College, a black male student was
assaulted after reportedly "looking at" another male student in a communal
shower. The disturbing report indicated that the sophomore was "expelled
after beating another student with a baseball bat," and that the "consensus
of Morehouse's student body is that 'a lot of people believe that he deserved
to get beaten up if he was looking in the shower stall, but everyone thinks
the bat was a little extreme.'" It was also noted that a fraternity and gay club
had planned to stage a public forum on homophobia, but after the incident
they were forced to cancel the event by the administration. An ad hoc group
later described an atmosphere of "rampant homophobia and misogyny on
campus." The climate that James Tinney confronted at schools like Howard
still proved remarkably resistant to reform on the issue of homosexuality,
but not all historically black colleges and universities had the same reputation. A leading women's studies professor at Spelman, Beverly Guy-Sheftall,
reported that she understood her college to be welcoming to LGBT students,
while she acknowledged that the treatment of gays varied widely at the 105
historically black institutions of higher learning. Perhaps only when teachers

and administrators reach out to students and other campus leaders—and incorporate an appreciation of black gay achievements into both student life and instructional curriculum—will the climate for black gay men and women continue to improve.[11]

More recently, journalists have spoken out about the level of violence that black gay men confront on a daily basis. Writing on the intersection of "black in a gay space," one essayist reflected on how New York police officers routinely harassed him and his friends without cause and then recounted the murder of a black gay fifteen-year-old, a personal acquaintance. Although a national movement to protest violence against young black men and to value black lives has gained tremendous momentum in the second decade of the twenty-first century, little or no mention is made of black gay men and the particularities of homophobic violence.

Yet at the same time, in 2013 Jason Collins grabbed national news headlines by becoming the first openly gay or out athlete in a major league sport, recruited to play in the National Basketball Association. That this first for gay history happened to involve a black man reminds us of the extent to which black gay men have always been at the forefront of public visibility and national awareness, dating back to Baldwin's gay novels and Rustin's embattled activism. Finally, while acknowledging the progress represented by Collins's celebrated gay visibility, on-the-ground writers and activists wondered about acceptance for the less-than-respectable transgender and working-class folks. One writer noted, "There is no single way to be black and gay in America, but it is clear that there are too few spaces for most black gay men to exist in their entirety as well."[12]

Progress has seemed undeniable: the stereotypical opposition between normal, respectable black masculinity and effeminized homosexual deviance that dominated midcentury newsprint and scholarship is fast becoming a relic of the past. The men pictured in *Jet* magazine who adopted the styles of female impersonation to identify as gay in the 1950s left a powerful legacy for the marginalized men of color who perform in highly stylized drag balls, in what is known as "ballroom culture," in major cities across the nation. In the late 1980s, documentary filmmaker Jennie Livingston followed the lives and performances of black and Puerto Rican gay youth who competed for titles in ballroom events by donning costumes, dancing, and "vogueing." Not totally unlike *Portrait of Jason*, the documentary, *Paris Is Burning*, released in 1990, gained unexpected public attention after making the rounds on the independent film circuits. It too tended toward a kind of objectification that presented underground gay deviance for popular consumption without listening for the voices from the margin, titillating the audience with a kind of sexual pathology that seemed to render black gay men legible only as the subjects of a study on the disadvantaged and marginalized rather than as fabulous performers in their own right.

Contemporary activists and performers now mobilize around issues concerning transgender identity. In 2014, a black transgender entertainer, Laverne Cox, appeared on the cover of *Time* magazine, the first transgender male-to-female to do so. Cox was born and raised in the South and recalled that she and her brother were always expected to uphold traditional masculinity: "In black communities, all the black men are going to jail or they're gay—this is what I heard growing up." To openly defy gender conventions was dangerous and costly, leading to an early suicide attempt, family estrangement, and bullying, but by high school she had identified as female and flouted all the norms, and after college she began living as a woman and then underwent the surgical transition to female. In 2008 Cox was the first African American transgender woman to appear on a reality television show, the first producer and star of her own show, and in 2014 she starred in a popular television series dealing with women and lesbian relations in prison. As a result of her activism, Cox felt that she had arrived at a "tipping point" where it was "no longer acceptable for trans lives to be stigmatized, ridiculed, criminalized, and disregarded." At the third annual Black Trans Advocacy Conference, another trans activist explored the dangers of public visibility in transitioning, not only due to homophobia but also because of the perils of black manhood. A female-to-male subject, the writer also reflected on attempting to forge a new perspective on women of color, calling for greater "intersectional awareness" as "trans people around the globe are breaking ground in multiple fields." The popular television series *RuPaul's Drag Race* features a weekly contest hosted by the black drag queen RuPaul to discover the most talented female impersonation performer.[13]

Perhaps the most striking continuity in black gay history has been the struggle to find acceptance for gay men in the church. In the years after the death of both Grant-Michael Fitzgerald and James Tinney, Rev. Carl Bean founded United Fellowship Church in Los Angeles to provide AIDS counseling and pastoral outreach. According to Bean, years before he had created a Bible school "on Monday nights in a black lesbian's home"; but eventually the group grew so large that it could no longer meet in the living room, so he went on to found a black gay church. When his critics asked him about biblical injunctions against homosexuality, Bean replied that all theological teachings were selective and some were no longer observed. As a result of his work, Bean became a highly visible leader whom the media turned to for expert advice on issues related to black gay men, and in turn the project of building a black gay church advanced rapidly. His counseling and care organization increased to eight employees who served a primarily Hispanic and black clientele, estimated at around seven hundred people, through "visits, money grants, performing funerals, support groups, and buddies," with a budget of $700,000. By 1990, both Bean and McCoy led the United Fellowship Movement, "the first national ministry of black lesbian and gay Christians" that had effectively "brought their straight families to share with them a positive and healthy experience of gay life in a format that was at once familiar and safe."[14]

Just as Carl Bean laid the foundation for a national black gay church, some black conservatives mobilized against gay rights. Some championed the conversion movement in which ex-gay men employed faith and religious teachings to convert the willing to a heterosexual orientation, just as they had in the days of Brother Fitzgerald. According to a 2007 story, a black lesbian and supporter of gay equality recently announced that after consulting with her pastor about the conflict between her sexuality and faith, she would renounce lesbianism. But even so, she reported that local black churches had not "welcomed her with open arms." In Milwaukee, black ministers refused to admit openly gay men in the "Black Church Week Prayer for the Healing of AIDS," though they did eventually relent after black gay protest. Another man recalled that after he had confided in his pastor about his homosexuality, the next week she publicly exposed him to the congregation, leading to an exorcism-like ritual to purge the homosexual demon from him. As the congregation poured burning oil over his head, the young man reported that he realized what was happening and quickly exited, never to return.[15]

Despite these and other examples of homophobia, gay men not only attended church but also supported the right to same-sex marriage, and more and more couples chose to form a lasting union before God. In Cleveland, after meeting in a Bible study group, two African American men fell in love and three years later decided to marry, but after their church "got wind" of the ceremony, they were summoned by an elder and "kicked out of the choir." They left the church and mounted a boycott on World AIDS Day, but apparently no other congregants followed their protest. For the vast majority of African Americans, religion remained highly important (in a national poll, 83 percent regarded it as "important in their lives"), and activists argued that in response to rising HIV infections, African American ministers had a duty to reach out and save black gay men. Some prominent black ministers did so, including Dr. Jeremiah Wright (President Barack Obama's former minister) of Trinity United Church of Christ, who reportedly offered his ministry to all. Yet discrimination persisted. Men and women had confided in their ministers only to be outed, and in others, transgender men and women were forced to leave their churches.[16]

The marriage equality movement has raised complicated questions about the connection between identity and religion as well as about the legacy of the civil rights movement for gay rights. Within individual states debating and voting on whether the government ought to permit unions of same-sex couples, some observers have concluded that black voters tend to reject gay marriage. With national attention riveted in 2008 on the back-and-forth battle in California over the Proposition 8 ballot measure to ban gay marriage in the state, some reports indicated that although 51 percent of white voters rejected the measure, a clear majority of blacks voted in favor of the ban, despite the fact that many African American leaders and organizations urged a no vote. Suddenly, the unimaginable political victory—the election of the first African American president in 2008—coincided with the defeat of the right to same-sex marriage, which now symbolized the next stage of the fight for gay equality. Without marriage equality back in the 1960s, referring to the end of the long history of prohibition of interracial marriage, one journalist observed that President Obama might never have been born. More than one commentator attributed black support for the proposition to the conservative forces of the black church, while some gay journalists compared the cause of gay marriage to the African American civil rights movement, arguing that "if any other group of people in America had their fundamental rights subjected to popular vote, there would be universal outrage in this country." Yet which group exactly did the author refer to, given his concluding remarks that "for us, as for African Americans who lived through the 60s, many apparent failures will, in retrospect, clearly be progress." Who was meant by the reference to "us"—where were black gay commentaries?[17]

News commentators and organizational spokesmen alike frequently stumbled over issues of homophobia in their rendering of civil rights history and black activism, in part because of a lack of historical evidence. When Alveda King, the niece of Martin Luther King, called gay rights an affront to the civil rights movement and popular gospel singers sang homophobic lyrics, there seemed to be little distinction between conservative and liberal views. But straight black activists also joined national gay rights movements, while more black legislators publicly endorsed gay rights measures—and real change was imminent. By the middle of the first decade of the twenty-first century, major civil rights figures, such as Julian Bond, the ex-head of the NAACP, declared that fighting AIDS meant addressing deeply ingrained patterns of homophobia—"one of the major obstacles to black Americans coming to grips with this disease."[18] By 2012, the NAACP announced its support for the legalization of same-sex marriage and identified marriage as a civil right that deserved protection under the Fourteenth Amendment. Not long after, President Obama also announced the reversal of his position on the marriage equality movement.[19]

Meanwhile, a recent poll in Maryland revealed that 55 percent of black voters supported an amendment that legalized same-sex marriage, and a powerful documentary, *The New Black*, chronicled the successful cross-race mobilization for the referendum. In nearby D.C., though a gay marriage bill sailed through the city council, a local poll found that only 37 percent of black residents supported same-sex marriage, compared with 83 percent of white respondents. It is worth noting that many black gay men support the marriage equality movement but have not necessarily been at the forefront of the major national organizations, such as the Human Rights Campaign or the National Gay and Lesbian Task Force, that spearheaded the cause.[20]

Throughout this succession of political crises that have defined our times—from the rise of the New Right to the spread and decline of the AIDS epidemic to the recent constitutional validation of gay marriage—the contours of black gay history have continued to shape and in turn responded to enduring questions of identity and identification. By the 1990s, the tensions underlying Joseph Beam's often painful negotiation between gay and black identities generated yet another intersectional dialogue, this time having to do with a sort of ordering of the individual. In a long essay on "Black Gay v. Gay Black," L. Lloyd Jordan welcomed readers to the "debate of the 90s" supposedly raging among activists about how to prioritize their personal loyalties. One point of contention was racial desire—whether one slept with white or black men—which publicly revealed painful internal conflicts that sometimes led to accusations of racial denial or of wishing to be white: "Black gays believe that gay blacks hate their own race as reflected in the pursuit of white (or non-black) lovers." Drawing on recent social science research produced by black gay academics, the essay suggested that prior to the mid-1970s, most black gay men may have engaged in gay sex but primarily felt black. "Another type of black gay man is also closeted, but has or wants a gay social life," Jordan noted, while the smallest numbers were the Afrocentric activists, and here the essay identified Joseph Beam, stressing his later phase of black community-building. The burgeoning concern with black self-esteem and psychology recognized the real damage done to black affect by homophobia while opening the door to armchair psychology and personal taunts. At one point, the author observed that although the pioneering organization the National Coalition of Black Lesbians and Gays was led by an all-black board, all of the members were involved in interracial relationships.

While debates raged over the reputed racial loyalties of black gay men involved in interracial relationships, a cohort of more marginalized black men from predominantly black neighborhoods and networks surfaced in the press and in AIDS activism. According to a study by a San Francisco-based social scientist, a significant percentage of men classified by pollsters as black-identified respondents (compared with 90 percent of gay-identified men) stated that they were not active in the black community, but these figures were contested and the data incomplete, and letters to the editor revealed yet more dimensions of the debate. Columbia University graduate student William Hawkeswood objected to the "peculiar logic" of the social science research in San Francisco that presented variations of identity as a problem of abiding conflict rather than highlighting new organizations, such as Men of All Colors Together and Gay Men of African Descent, that sought to support black-identified gay men. If conflicts over identity and desire stimulated fierce dialogues, the more significant development was the recognition of persistent black gay institutions, specifically "AIDS agencies, support groups, churches, and cultural organizations" that for several decades now formed the bedrock of community life.[21]

Another legacy of Beam and Tinney in particular was the emergence of black gay and lesbian academic networks. In Chicago, for example, it was reported that black queer scholars headed departments or institutes at the University of Illinois, DePaul University, Northwestern, and the University of Chicago. In St. Paul, Minnesota, Don Belton taught courses on creative writing and recently published an anthology of essays titled *Speak My Name: Black Men on Masculinity and the American Dream*, which features both academic and literary essays including gay subjects, while at a book signing Belton addressed the topic of racial and sexual passing. In 2008 the performance studies scholar E. Patrick Johnson released his oral history, *Sweet Tea: Black Gay Men of the South*, to much acclaim and later went on to perform a selection of the interviews in a much-touted one-man show.[22]

Across gay neighborhoods in major cities, the emergent strategy of mobilizing black gay voices led to the rise of fanzines or small journals, literary workshops, and writing programs dedicated to giving expression to marginalized voices. One of Beam's closest friends and allies, the black lesbian feminist Barbara Smith, observed that black gay writing diverged from black lesbian analysis, in part because of the latter's longtime connection to feminist politics, but also hoped for a future of collaboration between men and women: "I think it's important, too, for us to respect each other as black lesbians and gay men, not just in a literary context, but in general." But in some ways the prospects for such an alliance were dimming, as black gay academics, novelists, and journalists continued to die in the AIDS epidemic. A generation of black gay literature was lost. At the same time, surviving writers continued to face marginalization by the white gay establishment. In a newly convened annual conference, OutWrite, it was announced that Alyson Publications, the leading gay publisher, would sponsor a writing contest named after Joseph Beam. But when Sasha Alyson contacted Dorothy Beam, she declined to authorize the award, in part because of strained relations with the press, and so the chair of the committee, Jeffrey Escoffier, agreed to oversee the competition. Due to a delayed start, the committee received only seven books for consideration, and then Essex Hemphill and other black gay writers learned that none of these were authors of color. Not surprisingly they were outraged and soon protested, sparking yet another round of identity politics controversy. Hemphill urged that the competition designate a black winner, while Alyson countered that "in Joe Beam's case, he was black and gay . . . but he was also a pioneer, a writer and an editor." In the end, Hemphill and others leveled a charge of racism, given the fact that a number of works by black gay and lesbian writers were overlooked, and again it seemed that gay institutions had refused to address their own biases.[23]

By the beginning of the twenty-first century, the rise of black queer discourse accompanied the revelation of the so-called down low (or DL). For instance, the transgender performer Kevin Aviance gained international fame with his music and dance routines through an expanding circuit of nightclubs or discos. Dressed in revealing bikinis and necklaces, and sporting a shaved head, Aviance transgressed and blurred the boundaries not only of sexuality but of gender and race, attracting a large following among queers of color around the world. At the same time, something like the opposite trend was also gaining momentum. In feature-length exposé, "Troopin' on the Low," the question of young black men who "pride themselves on being 'unlockable'" was introduced to readers in the context of the AIDS crisis. In this rather critical examination, men on the DL were described as fooling "themselves into thinking they are outside the gay community," when in fact they were seen by many as dangerous because of their "sky-high rates of HIV infection." Understood as bisexual, DL men were supposedly the victims of black homophobia, lack of mainstream images, and their own fears of effeminacy and public identification. For the author of the essay, there was a "terrible irony in the lives of DL boys": "They will inherit the role of pariah they had hoped to avoid as they develop opportunistic infections associated with AIDS" and will then have to contend with the "same homophobia they have perpetrated from their families and homies." The discourse of the DL sparked lively and informative debates, to be sure, but one negative, potentially damaging position equated black bisexuality, the DL, and unsafe sex practices in a sensationalist way that demonized black gay men more generally. The phenomenon of the DL stimulated a powerful discussion of the ethics of sexual discretion and responsibility but also revealed the effects of a long-term black gay alienation from the white gay mainstream that Beam and others had first explored almost a quarter century before.[24]

In an effort to counteract a range of negative images, black writers penned informative defenses of bisexuality, while a black director produced a gay DVD series, *The Closet*, that featured black bisexual men in a positive light. The success of the black gay novelist E. Lynn Harris signaled the new possibilities for black gay literary identification. Harris's novels feature bisexual black men who move within black institutions, such as the family and church, or even play professional athletics. "My audience is definitely African-American, both gay and straight," declared Harris. Appealing to his growing readership, Harris held book signings in both Afrocentric and LGBT bookstores.[25] At many levels of society, in cities and rural areas, among politicians and black activists, the question remained daunting: Why were black men so much more likely to contract HIV than white men? Across the board, the answer involved sensitive issues of internalized objectification and self-worth.[26]

If Beam and his contributors to *In the Life* pioneered a new community voice, cultural activists struggling for black gay visibility confronted the repressive forces of the New Right, diving headlong into the culture wars. The pioneering black gay documentarian Marlon Riggs had earned an Emmy Award for his important film *Ethnic Notions* (1987) and had recently completed a new work on black gay culture titled *Tongues Untied* (1989). The film presented poetry, dramatic performances, and live action, blended together to evoke a shared sense of black masculinity. In fact, the opening scene featured Beam's anthem-like phrase, "Black men loving black men is the revolutionary act of the 1980s." Some of the most striking scenes served to reverse the objectification evident in pornography and photography by featuring gentle and sensitive black men showing positive affection for one another, rather than rehearsing the stereotypical aggressive black male ravishing a passive white bottom. Instead of hulkish, black bodies conjured up by the white gaze, the film presented graceful and vulnerable performances. There were few traces of *Portrait of Jason*'s Jason Holliday or its obsession with hustling whites, self-destruction, and pathology. But while *Tongues Untied* garnered awards in Berlin, Los Angeles, and New York, it stirred controversy in mainstream America. By 1991 the Public Broadcasting Service had offered the film to its local affiliates, but a number of stations refused to show it because of supposedly lewd content. "Fears that donors to the station would find the film offensive was the most commonly cited reason off the record for shelving the broadcast," it was reported. Yet the film did not contain sexually explicit material. While San Francisco, New York, and Los Angeles stations went forward without complaint, Philadelphia and other top markets refused to air the film. Others chose to delay the broadcast until later in the evening, some as late as 11:30, while cities with significant black populations, from Detroit to Milwaukee to Atlanta, reported viewer complaints. Atlanta, for example, found that opinion ran about 50 percent for and 50 percent against, while Milwaukee's station general manager found the work to be "offensive" and "'just too graphic.'" But supporters of the program also stepped forward, declaring that "viewers who think they simply can't deal with the sight of two shirtless men rolling around in bed in slow motion, well, perhaps they should consider this an instructive dose of reality."[27]

In an interview about the controversy, Marlon Riggs distinguished himself as the heir apparent of Joseph Beam. For Riggs, the production of black gay films served to counter the forces of stigma and objectification, for he understood his work to present black gay men with "a visible and visual representation of their lives." "You don't really live and you're not really somebody until you're somehow reflected on the screen," he stated, which was all the more urgent because of black straight bias in film. In reference to the popular black director Spike Lee, Riggs observed in 1999 that "he's a very young and homophobic man and I hope that he will rise and measure up." He also reported that audiences expressed anxiety to him about the new emphasis on black brotherhood, in part because they imagined Riggs to be criticizing black-white relationships. But Riggs explained his adaptation of Beam's phrasing by referencing the larger urban crisis that had inspired it. "In relationships between black men in this country in the context of so much violence, internalized anger, repressed emotions, [and] detachment . . . us learning to love one another . . . would be such a radical break from our entire history in this country that it would in fact, not just be a revolutionary act, but the revolutionary act for black men in America." In 2004, nearly twenty years after Beam had penned his key essay on black brotherhood, independent film producers released *Brother to Brother*, which portrayed the anxieties of a confused black gay artist with flashbacks referencing gay Harlem Renaissance writers, such as Richard Bruce Nugent and Langston Hughes, earning a prestigious Sundance Film Festival Award.[28] In 2008 it was announced that a DVD version of Riggs's *Tongues Untied* was to be released "for a new generation to witness," after fans had been scrounging for years for copies of the film (which reportedly went for hundreds of dollars).[29]

For Riggs, then, the point was not only to affirm black brotherhood across sexualities but also to preserve black gay history. "It's worthwhile to take the risk to document our lives and to tell our stories and, essentially, to come out," he said. Later in the interview, Riggs was asked about the black gay versus gay black controversy, to which he replied that one of the main purposes of his film was to address the falseness of such a choice. He described the debate as "dangerous" because it contributed to the further "marginalization of our sexuality." Riggs concluded that "our sexuality has been treated . . . as not having a history—that is, our community has no history because what we do and what we value in terms of our sexuality has not been affirmed by the majority culture."[30] The legacy of the men and women featured in this book remains an abiding desire for this history: for self-definition and self-expression, for the support of family and community, for the sustenance of faith and love.

Notes

Abbreviations

Introduction

1. *BWMT Newsletter New York* 2, no. 7 (1982): 1, BWMT Ephemera Collection, WW; James S. Tinney, "James Baldwin 'Comes Out' at Gay Forum," *Blacklight* 3, no. 5 (1982): 1.

2. "BWMT Celebrates Fifth Anniversary, March 7–13, 1986," *Philadelphia Gay News*; "Ad Hoc Planning Report," January 19, 1986, BWMT Ephemera Collection, WW; "BWMT—PHILA, 5th," BWMT Ephemera Collection, WW.

3. D'Emilio, *Sexual Politics*; Bérubé, *Coming Out under Fire*; Chauncey, *Gay New York*; Stein, *City of Sisterly and Brotherly Loves*; Houlbrook, *Queer London*; N. Boyd, *Wide-Open Town*; White, *Pre-Gay L.A.*; Avicolli, *Smash the Church*; Faderman and Timmons, *Gay L.A.*; Howard, *Men Like That*; Hoag, *Same-Sex Affairs*; Marcus, *Making Gay History*; Beemyn, *Creating a Place for Ourselves*; Stryker and Van Buskirk, *Gay by the Bay*.

4. Kunzel, *Criminal Intimacy*; Canaday, *The Straight State*; Stein, *Sexual Injustice*; Sides, *Erotic City*; Marcus, *Making Gay History*; Stein, *Rethinking the Gay and Lesbian*

Movement; Rupp, *Desired Past*; White, *Pre-Gay L.A.*; Armstrong, *Forging Gay Identities*; Faderman and Timmons, *Gay L.A.*

5. Mumford, *Interzones*; Ngo, *Imperial Blues*; Molesworth, *And Bid Him Sing*; Wilson, *Bulldaggers, Pansies, and Chocolate Babies*; Christa, *Gay Voices of the Harlem Renaissance*; Wirth, *Gay Rebel of the Harlem Renaissance*; Van Notten, *Wallace Thurman's Harlem Renaissance*; Tillery, *Claude McKay*.

6. Hine, "Rape and the Inner Lives of Black Women," 43–44; Mitchell, *Righteous Propagation*; Summers, *Manliness and Its Discontents*; "LGBT African-Americans and African-American Same-Sex Couples," 2012, Williams Institute, Los Angeles, Calif.

7. Pharr, *Homophobia*; Harper, "Racism and Homophobia as Reflections of Their Perpetrators," 64–65; Fone, *Homophobia*.

8. Gilman, *Difference and Pathology*, 25; Fanon, *Black Skin, White Masks*, 180, 112.

9. Ross, "Beyond the Closet as Raceless Paradigm," 176; King, *On the Down Low*; Boykin, *Sex, Lies, and Denial in Black America*; McCune, *Sexual Discretion*, 9.

10. Hawkeswood, *One of the Children*, 185.

11. Duberman, *Hold Tight Gently*; Feldstein, *How It Feels to Be Free*; J. Jones, *Dreadful Deceit*.

12. On queer theory, see Bravmann, *Queer Fictions of the Past*; Sedgwick, *Epistemology of the Closet*; Halperin, *How to Be Gay*; and Doan, *Disturbing Practices*, 27–57.

13. Keita, *Race and the Writing of History*, 8.

14. Benhabib, *Claims of Culture*, 51.

Chapter One

1. Baldwin, "Sweet Lorraine," reprinted in Hansberry, *To Be Young, Gifted and Black*, xii; "'Raisin in the Sun' Opens at the Walnut," *Philadelphia Bulletin*, January 27, 1959, Lorraine Hansberry File, FBI (hereafter Hansberry FBI File); James Baldwin, "Is *A Raisin in the Sun* a Lemon in the Dark?" in Kenan, *James Baldwin*, 29–33.

2. Baldwin, *The Fire Next Time*, 77; Schlesinger, *Robert Kennedy and His Times*, 331; Welch, "Spokesman of the Oppressed?"

3. Auchincloss and Lynch, "Disturber of the Peace: James Baldwin—An Interview (1969)," in Standley and Pratt, *Conversations with James Baldwin*, 77; on injuries to Smith, see Weatherby, *James Baldwin*, 220; "Robert Kennedy Consults Negroes Here about North," *New York Times*, May 25, 1963, 1; "Common Burden: Baldwin Points Duty of Negro and White," *New York Times*, May 3, 1964, X1.

4. Quoted in Weatherby, *James Baldwin*, 223. Weatherby relied on Schlesinger's accounts; see Schlesinger, *Thousand Days*, 962–63.

5. Weatherby, *James Baldwin*, 222; James Baldwin File, FBI, 815, 1072 (hereafter Baldwin FBI File); Schlesinger, *Robert Kennedy and His Times*, 332, 335.

6. "RFK in Fight of His Life—and Knows It," *New York Journal American*, May 28, 1963; "Robert Kennedy Fails to Sway Negroes at Secret Talks Here," *New York Times*, May 26, 1963, 1; "Rising Negro Militancy," in Baldwin FBI File, n.d., 1028; "Administration in Cold Sweat over Rising Negro Militancy," *Militant*, 1, Baldwin FBI File, 1026–28; Weatherby, *James Baldwin*, 226, 228–30; Baldwin, "Lorraine Hansberry at the Summit."

7. Robert F. Kennedy to John F. Kennedy, May 25, 1963, Meetings: Tape 89 (JFK-POF-MTG-089-002), John F. Kennedy Presidential Library and Museum, Boston, Mass.; at the meeting were Henry Morganthau (television producer, for Baldwin's subsequent

appearance), Jerome Smith, Harry Belafonte, Lena Horne, James Baldwin, Lorraine Hansberry, David Baldwin, Edward Fales, Thais Aubrey, Kenneth Clark, Clarence B. Jones, Robert P. Mills, Rip Torn, and Edwin C. Berry. See also Clarence Jones to the editor, *New York Times*, June 7, 1963, Special Correspondence, 1961–1964, Assistant Attorney General Files, 1958–1965, Burke Marshall Personal Papers (BMPP-008-009), John F. Kennedy Presidential Library and Museum, Boston, Mass.

8. O'Reilly, *Racial Matters*, 102.

9. Lorraine Hansberry, "Myself in Notes," 1953, file Personal, box A, Restricted Materials, LHP; Gore, *Radicalism at the Crossroads*, 64–65, 51–55.

10. Memo, n.d., p. 2, Hansberry FBI File; memo, March 29, 1959, ibid.

11. Memo, September 1956, ibid.; memo, January 2, 1959, ibid.; "Counterpoint to 'A Raisin in the Sun,'" *New York Post*, July 1, 1959, in ibid.

12. Cruse, *Crisis of the Black Intellectual*, 281–83.

13. L. Jones, "The Revolutionary Theatre," in *Selected Plays and Prose of Amiri Baraka / LeRoi Jones*, 131–36; Elam, "Cultural Capital and the Presence of Africa," 685; Keppel, *Work of Democracy*, 189–90; McDuffie, *Sojourning Freedom*; Gore, *Radicalism at the Crossroads*; Davies, *Left of Karl Marx*.

14. Higashida, *Black Internationalist Feminism*, 57–81; Washington, "Alice Childress, Lorraine Hansberry, and Claudia Jones," 193–94; Wilkins, "Beyond Bandung."

15. From LHN to the *Ladder*, *Ladder*, May 1957, 27–29; on its background, see Katz, *Gay American History*, 425; letter signed "L. H. N." (Lorraine Hansberry Nemiroff, her married name). Barbara Grier (Gene Damon, pseud.) identifies Hansberry as the author of this and the following letter in her column "Lesbiana," *Ladder*, February–March 1970. See also Lipari, "Rhetoric of Intersectionality," 233; Higashida, "To Be(come) Young, Gay, and Black." Sometimes referred to as the first published out black lesbian, Anita Cornwell later wrote to the *Ladder* in 1971; Cornwell, "Open Letter to a Black Sister," *Ladder*, October–November 1971, 33–36.

16. "L.N.H. to the Ladder," *Ladder*, September 1957, 30. According to an article about her epistolary coming out, Hansberry also wrote a letter to *One*, the homophile journal, but never sent it.

17. Standley and Pratt, *Conversations with James Baldwin*, 156; LNH, personal diary, December 2, 1963, 28, Restricted Materials, LHP; Stockton, *Queer Child*.

18. Liberman, "Measure Them Right"; LNH, personal diary, December 18, 1963, 80, LHP; Nemiroff, *To Be Young, Gifted, and Black*, xvi.

19. LNH, personal diary, November 21, 1963, 25; December 17, 1963, 75–76; December 13, 1963, 35; L.H.N. to Molly Cooke, n.d., p. 3, all in Restricted Materials, LHP.

20. Lorraine Hansberry to My Dear, December 25, 1955, Restricted Materials, LHP; Wilkerson, "Dark Vision of Lorraine Hansberry"; Higashida, *Black Internationalist Feminism*, 68–69; Gore, *Radicalism at the Crossroads*, 141. Nemiroff remarried in 1968 and passed away in 1974. His wife, Jewell Handy Gresham, became executor and died in 2005. See "Robert Nemiroff, 61, Champion of Lorraine Hansberry's Works," *New York Times*, July 19, 1991; Carter, *Commitment and Complexity*, 2–24; and Gresham interview.

21. LNH, personal diary, December 18, 1963, 80; July 5, 1964, 111; July 29, 1964, 124, Restricted Materials, LHP.

22. Fred Harvey Harrington to Robert Nemiroff, February 11, 1965, file 3, box 68; Commission on Religion and Race National Council of Churches to Robert Nemiroff, January 15, 1965, file 3, box 68; Elizabeth Sutherland to Robert Nemiroff, May 3, 1965, file 4, box

68; Jerome Smith to Mr. Nemiroff, January 8, 1965, file 4, box 68; Whitney Young to Robert Nemiroff, n.d., file 4, box 68; Roy Wilkins to Robert Nemiroff, January 14, 1965, file 4, box 68; John Lewis to Robert Nemiroff, January 12, 1965, file 4, box 68; Martin Luther King Jr. to Robert Nemiroff, January 13, 1965, file 4, box 68, all in LHP.

23. "600 Attend Hansberry Rites: Paul Robeson Delivers Eulogy," *New York Times*, January 17, 1965, 88.

24. Hansberry, *A Raisin in the Sun: The Unfilmed Original Screenplay*, ix–xxii.

25. Martin and Lyon, *Lesbian/Woman*; Grier and Damon, *Lesbiana*, 185; Higashida, *Black Internationalist Feminism*; Lipari, "Rhetoric of Intersectionality."

26. Rich, "Problem with Lorraine Hansberry"; Nestle, *Restricted Country*, 100–102; Baldwin, "Sweet Lorraine," in Hansberry, *To Be Young, Gifted, and Black*, xiv–xv.

27. Leeming, *James Baldwin*, 37–55; Weatherby, *James Baldwin*, 6–88; "Disturbing the Peace: James Baldwin," *Mademoiselle*, May 1963, 174–75, 199–204, 205–6; repeated in Baldwin FBI File, 1017–18.

28. Baldwin, MacInnes, and Mossman. "Race, Hate, Sex & Color," 55; Kalamu ya Salaam, "James Baldwin: Looking toward the Eighties," in Standley and Pratt, *Conversations with James Baldwin*, 184; "The Black Scholar Interviews James Baldwin," *Black Scholar* 5 (December 1973–January 1974), 33–42; Standley and Pratt, *Conversations with James Baldwin*, 142–58, 197–98; Baraka, "Jimmy!," 132–33.

29. Baldwin FBI File, 1009, 348; "James Arthur Baldwin," memo, October 19, 1963, ibid.

30. Ibid., n.d., 387; n.d., 1255; 1258; 1617.

31. Ibid., memo, November 10, 1963, part 2; memo from DeLoach, July 20, 1964, part 3; "James Arthur Baldwin," 1018.

32. Leeming, *James Baldwin*, 228; Baldwin FBI File, 208.

33. Baldwin FBI File, 1225, 104; Reider, *Word of the Lord Is upon Me*, 92.

34. Rev. D. Edward Wells, "Book of the Week," *Pittsburgh Courier*, May 23, 1953, 8; Gertrude Martin, "Book Review," *Chicago Defender*, June 13, 1953, 6; John K. Hutchens, "Book Review," *New York Herald Tribune*, May 18, 1953, 13; Orville Prescott, "Books of the Times," *New York Times*, May 19, 1953, 27; Donald Barr, "Guilt Was Everywhere: Go Tell It on the Mountain," *New York Times*, May 17, 1953, BR5; Paul Sampson, "Cage of Negro Writing Sprung: Protest Element Minimized," *Washington Post*, May 17, 1953, B6.

35. Roi Ottley, "The Negro Seeks a Way Out," *Chicago Daily Tribune*, July 12, 1953, B7.

36. Bobia, *Critical Reception of James Baldwin in France*, 20–22; "A Sophisticated Fare for Trained Appetites," *Washington Post*, October 14, 1956, E7; Jacqueline Lewin, "*Giovanni's Room* by James Baldwin," *Daily Boston Globe*, November 18, 1956, A31; Granville Hicks, "Tormented Triangle," *New York Times*, October 14, 1956, BR3.

37. J. Saunders Redding, "Book Review," *Afro-American*, May 16, 1953, 22C; J. Saunders Redding, "Book Review: *Giovanni's Room*," *Afro-American*, November 17, 1956, 2; J. Saunders Redding, "Baldwin Novel Nightmarish," *New York Herald Tribune*, January 27, 1957, E9. For comparing Giovanni to Richard Wright's Bigger Thomas, see Porter, *Stealing the Fire*, 142–46, and Porter, "James Baldwin and the Problem of Vocation."

38. Adams, "Giovanni's Room," 133; John Hall, "James Baldwin Interviewed" (1970), in Standley and Pratt, *Conversations with James Baldwin*, 77.

39. Etta Moten, "Book Review," *Atlanta Daily World*, June 3, 1962, 2; Marion Starkey, "A Harlem Othello: But Shakespeare Method Missing from Baldwin Big, Brutal Novel," *Boston Globe*, July 1, 1962, A52; L. Jamison, "Pulse of New York's Public," *New York Amsterdam News*, September 29, 1962, 10; Mario Puzo, "His Cardboard Lovers," *New York Times*, June

23, 1968, BR5; Eliot Fremont-Smith, "Books of the Times," *New York Times*, May 31, 1968, 27; Paul Goodman, "Not Enough of a World to Grow In," *New York Times*, June 24, 1962, 219; Faith Berry, "About Paul Goodman," *New York Amsterdam News*, November 3, 1962, 10; Lawrence Neal, "The Black Writers' Role," *Liberator*, April 1966, 10–11, 18.

40. Baldwin FBI File, 1300–1301; *Times-Picayune* (New Orleans), June 21, 1963, ibid., 1625; "Book Censorship by a Flatfoot," *Cleveland Call and Post*, August 31, 1963, 3; "Call Baldwin Book Obscene," *Cleveland Call and Post*, July 6, 1963, 4C; Nora Campbell, "He Still Lied," *New York Amsterdam News*, July 16, 1960, 10; Wolfgang Binder, "James Baldwin, an Interview" (1980), in Standley and Pratt, *Conversations with James Baldwin*, 206.

41. Goldstein, "Go the Way Your Blood Beats," 175, 177.

42. Sarotte, *Like a Brother, Like a Lover*, 102–3; May, "Ambivalent Narratives, Fragmented Selves"; for reviews of *Tell Me How Long the Train's Been Gone*, see Michael Joseph, "Fat Cat on the Mat," *Times Literary Supplement*, July 4, 1968, 697; and Straub, "Happy Ends"; also see "James Baldwin—An Honest Writer," *Cleveland Call and Post*, November 11, 1961, 6C; and Bradbury, "Race and Sex."

43. *Philadelphia Weekly Gayzette*, November, 22–29, 1974, 12.

44. Bayard Rustin to Algernon D. Black, August 20, 1963, reel 10; Benedict H. Hanson, August 19, 1963, reel 10, both in BRP.

45. "Wide Disapproval Found For March," n.d., reel 10, BRP; "Crude Tactics Won't Help the Negro," *New York Herald Tribune*, June 21, 1963, reel 10, BRP.

46. Ella Baker to Bayard Rustin and Stanley Levinson, July 16, 1958, reel 3, BRP.

47. William Robert Miller to Bayard Rustin, May 19, 1968, reel 3, BRP; typescript, n.d., 102–3, reel 3, BRP; Hamilton, *Adam Clayton Powell, Jr.*, 337. For the emphasis on Rustin's anxiety, not King's, see Haygood, *King of the Cats*, 265.

48. James Baldwin, "The Dangerous Road Before Martin Luther King," *Harper's*, February 1961, 42.

49. Hon. Adam C. Powell, "My Black Position Paper," *Congressional Record*, n.d., reel 4, BRP; "Confidential," n.d., reel 4, BRP. Fairclough does not mention homosexuality in his narration of the threat and subsequent resignation, characterizing it instead as "red-baiting." See Fairclough, *To Redeem the Soul of America*, 73; "Negro Rally Aide Rebuts Senator," *New York Times*, August 16, 1963, 10; "Rustin and Tom Kahn to A. Philip Randolph," August 16, 1963, in Long, *I Must Resist*, 266–68; and W. Jones, *March on Washington*, 170.

50. D'Emilio, *Lost Prophet*, 348; D'Emilio interview; Weatherby, *James Baldwin*, 233; "Now That the March Is Over," *Chicago Sun-Times*, August 29, 1963, reel 7, BRP.

51. "Rally to Mourn 6 Slain Negroes," *New York Times*, September 19, 1963; James Baldwin, "Statement by James Baldwin," September 16, 1963, 1–3, reel 1, BRP; "Memo to New York Area Participants in the March on Washington," reel 1, BRP; memo to Members and Friends of the League, October 2, 1963, reel 7, BRP; "The Civil Rights Revolution," n.d., reel 7, BRP; personal diary, September 16, 1963, 6, fall–September 1963, LHP.

52. Fairclough, *To Redeem the Soul of America*, 203.

53. Carbado and Weise, *Time on Two Crosses*, 116–29.

54. Memo, September 23, 1965, reel 3; "Rustin Speech Raises Oath Issue," n.d., reel 3; Bayard Rustin to Donald A. Deppe, September 23, 1965, reel 3; "Rustin's Scheduled Speeches in Maryland Stir Controversy," *Washington Post*, September 24, 1965, reel 3, all in BRP.

55. John Benner, "Invitation Stands: Rustin Will Speak," *Diamondback*, September 27, 1965, reel 3; "Two Politicians Blast Rustin's Rights Talk," *Diamondback*, September 23,

1965, reel 3; Donald A. Deppe to Bayard Rustin, September 24, 1965, reel 3; "Rustin Speech Raises Oath Issue," n.d., reel 3; from Arthur J. Adkins to Bayard Rustin, September 28, 1965, reel 3, all in BRP.

56. Betta Growell, "Convicted Sex Pervert and Civil Rights Leader to Be Police Lecturer," *Maryland Monitor*, September 16, 1965, reel 3, BRP; "Rustin's Talks Closed to Public and Press," *Washington Post*, October 9, 1965; "Police Applaud Rustin; Security Was Tight," *Washington News*, October 13, 1965, reel 3, BRP.

57. "U.M. Chided for Inviting Rustin Talk," *Baltimore Sun*, October 14, 1965, reel 3; "Rustin Urges Police to Seek Civilian Aid," newspaper clipping, reel 3; "Canceled FBI Talk at U.M., Hoover Says," n.d., *Baltimore Sun*, reel 3; "Rustin Cleared for Talks at U. of Maryland," *Washington Post*, September 23, 1965, reel 3, all in BRP; "Memphis Strike Seen as U.S. Test," *New York Times*, April 7, 1968, 65.

58. "Bayard Rustin: Contradictions of a Legendary Leader," *Washington Post*, August 21, 1983, reel 3; memo, n.d., reel 3; Bayard Rustin, "Civil Rights: 20 Years Later," *Newsweek*, August 29, 1983, 11, reel 3, all in BRP.

59. "To March on Washington," August 28, 1963, file 10, box 57; Walter E. Fauntroy Papers, Special Collections Research Center, Gelman Library, George Washington University, Washington, D.C.

60. "Audre Lorde's Speech during the Anniversary March on Washington," *Gay Community News*, September 10, 1983; "Morning Rally," file 38, box 30, Fauntroy Papers.

61. "Jobs, Peace and Freedom: A Dream Shared," *Gay Community News*, September 10, 1983.

62. De Veaux, *Warrior Poet*, 80–81, 326–27.

Chapter Two

1. Moon, "Outlaw Sex"; Goffman, *Asylums*, 147; Goffman, *Encounters*, 116–17.

2. Phillips, *War!*, 95, 110–11; Bérubé, *Coming Out under Fire*, 58–59, 79; D'Emilio, "Homosexual Menace," 226–40; Johnson, *Lavender Scare*.

3. Green, *Selling the Race*, 91, 154, 210; Meyerowitz, "Women, Cheesecake and Borderline Material"; M. Williams, "'Meet the Real Lena Horne,'" On typical photographs of black women, see the following in *Jet*: "Modern Living," December 3, 1953, 40–43; "Are More Co-eds Becoming Unwed Mothers?," January 14, 1954, 18–19; "Beach Negligee," April 29, 1954, 15; and "Intoxicating Takella," March 4, 1954, 35–36.

4. D'Emilio, "Homosexual Menace," 230–36; Petigny, *Permissive Society*, 250–58; Weiss, *To Have and to Hold*, 116–39; "Miss. Firm Plans to Film Story of Emmett Till Murder," *Jet*, vol. 9, no. 13 (1955), 6–7; Thornton, "Murder of Emmett Till."

5. Conerly, "Swishing and Swaggering," 387.

6. Daniel, *Black Journals of the United States*, 157–60, 213. See the following in *Jet*: "The Truth About Stag Parties," June 12, 1952, 24–25; "What Men Don't Know about Sex," May 22, 1952, 26–27; "Are Men More Romantic Than Women?," December 11, 1952, 20–23; "Why Husbands Beat Their Wives," September 11, 1952, 20–21; "Sexiness Is New Trend," November 20, 1952, 38–39. On Africa, see "Love in Africa," *Jet*, July 31, 1952, 16–17, and "Black Supermen," *Jet*, August 21, 1952, 16–17.

7. See the following in *Jet*: "Where Is Third Man in Till Lynching?," September 29, 1955, 8–9; "Another Till Case Except for Police Action," vol. 9, no. 1 (1955), 14–15; "Sheriff Unable to Find Clues," vol. 9, no. 1 (1955), 8–9; on Till, see "From the Notebook," vol. 9, no. 1 (1955),

11; "Fear Negro Slain for Using White Toilet on Tenn. Train," vol. 9, no. 9 (1955), 6; "White Man Threatened Child Because She Is Colored," July 9, 1959, 16–17; "Dixie Integration Opposed by 46 Groups," vol. 9, no 12 (1955), 7.

8. See the following in *Jet*: "Jail Atlanta White Woman Caught with Negro," 22; "Negro Sits beside White Girl, GI's Draw Fines," December 10, 1953, 4–5; "FBI Seizes Bopster, White Wife in Extortion Try," August 18, 1955, 49; "Mixed Marriages Pose Few Problems for Couples," May 11, 1967, 11; on antimiscegenation in Wisconsin, see "Owner of Mixed Resort Gets Threats on Life," May 15, 1952, 9.

9. "Sentence White Girl Who Stole Negro Lover," *Jet*, August 21, 1952, 31.

10. "Maid, 18, White Man Imprisoned for Lewd Act," *Jet*, vol. 10, no. 16 (1956?), 20.

11. "The Sex Lottery Racket," *Jet*, August 6, 1953, 20–21; "The Lowdown of Sex Parties," *Jet*, April 1, 1954, 56–57.

12. See the following in *Jet*: "Jailed Blonde, Negro Boy Friend," June 12, 1952, 29; "5 Va. Negroes Jailed for Interracial Sex Orgies," March 11, 1954, 21; for typical photos, see "Modern Living," December 3, 1953, 40–43; Louie Robinson, "Are More Co-eds Becoming Unwed Mothers?," January 14, 1954, 18–19; and "Intoxicating Takella," March 4, 1954, 34–35.

13. See the following in *Jet*: "Brides Sometimes Return to Homes," January 17, 1952, 20; "White Prisoner Enters Negro Cell, Attacks Woman," January 8, 1953, 39; "Denies Interracial Sex, La. White Man Sues," May 21, 1959, 16; "Fired after Mixed Marriage," July 26, 1956, 17; "Some End in Blood and Tears," January 17, 1952, 22–23; "White Woman Marries Negro, Loses Her Child," April 10, 1952, 22; "Widow of White GI Refused Money for His Death," July 22, 1967, 46; "Mixed Couple's Case May End All Housing Bias," November 16, 1967, 22; "8 La. Couples Nabbed for Mixed Marriages," March 24, 1955, 20; "Appiah Quits Nkrumah's Party on Gold Coast" and "White Man Marries Negro, Loses Racial Identity," February 24, 1955, 12; "Mixed Couple Says N.Y. Cops Persecuted Them," March 3, 1955, 24; "Dismiss Vice Charges against Mixed Couple," April 7, 1955, 20; "5 Prostitutes, Ages 11–12, Sent to SC Institution," November 14, 1957, 45; "Woman in Robinson's Death Hates Sex with Men," June 15, 1967, 2; "Mixed Marriages Cause Youth to Slay Bully," July 10, 1952, 27; Francis H. Mitchell, "Birmingham Castration Victim," January 2, 1958, 20.

14. See the following in *Jet*: "South Dakota Repeals Mixed Marriage Ban," February 21, 1957, 24; "Nebraska Kills Mixed Marriage Legislation," March 21, 1957, 26; "N. Dakota Lifts Ban on Interracial Marriage," March 10, 1955, 20; "Maryland Repeals Law Banning Mixed Marriage," March 23, 1967, 3; "Bill to Repeal Mixed-Marriage Ban Introduced," March 9, 1967, 22–23; "Does Mixed Marriage Hurt Race Relations?," July 3, 1952, 20–21; "New Law Allows GIs to Legalize 'Brown Babies,'" July 17, 1952, 17; "What Happened to the War Brides?," January 17, 1952, 18–19; "Mixed Marriage Booms in Ethiopia," January 3, 1952, 68; "White Women in Negro Society," June 5, 1952, 48–49; "Sorority Pledges White Member," June 5, 1952, 52; "Why More White Men Are Marrying Negro Women," December 3, 1953, 18–21.

15. See the following in *Jet*: "Intermarriage Will Be Common," September 18, 1952, 6–7; "Does Mixed Marriage Produce Better Babies?," March 19, 1953, 20–23; "Are Mixed Marriages Increasing?," June 9, 1953, 24–25; "Why More White Men Are Marrying Negro Women," December 3, 1953, 18–21; "Ex-Dancer, Wife Abroad on $5000 Business Deal," June 24, 1954, 26.

16. Hamilton, *Adam Clayton Powell, Jr.*, 184–85; "Detroit League Starts Sex Education Program," *Jet*, December 1, 1966, 7; "Masturbation, Sex outside Marriage Not Condemned," *Jet*, December 8, 1966, 45; Rev. Adam Clayton Powell, "Sex in the Church," *Ebony*, December 1951, 27–34.

17. Powell, "Sex in the Church," 27–34; Frazier, *Black Bourgeoisie,* 231.

18. "Why 'Passing' Is Passing Out," *Jet,* July 17, 1952, 12–16; "Have Negroes Stopped Passing?" and "Most Passing Is for Economic Improvement," *Jet,* September 13, 1956, 10–12; "The Man Who Lived 30 Years as a Woman," *Ebony,* October 1951, 8, 23–25.

19. "Gay Affair Names 'Queen,'" *Jet,* November 15, 1951, 63–64.

20. Ibid.; "Male or Female?," *Jet,* December 13, 1951, 35.

21. "1 in 1,000 Born without True Sex," *Jet,* January 22, 1953, 50; "Male Dancer Sex Changed, Marries Musician," *Jet,* July 13, 1967, 58.

22. Meyerowitz, *How Sex Changed,* 39. See the following in *Jet*: "Male or Female?," December 13, 1951, 35; "Man Can Impersonate Woman, Says Ohio Court," March 21, 1957, 25; "Ex-Warden Says Most Crimes are Due to Sexual Shortcoming," May 26, 1966, 50–51; "Teen-Age Shoplifting, Sex Club Leaders Sentenced," December 18, 1952, 59; "Jail Female Impersonators and Boy Friends," February 14, 1952, 25; "The Truth about Female Impersonation," October 2, 1952, 26–31.

23. See the following in *Jet*: "Negro Figures in Probe of Czech Sex Parties," June 12, 1952, 6–7; "Teacher Fired after Male Kissing Party," February 3, 1955, 21; "Texas Female Impersonator Charged with Murder," August 8, 1957, 46; "Ohio Homosexual Killed in Male Lovers' Quarrel," April 2, 1959, 44; "Dissatisfied with Sex Act, Man Kills 'Boy Friend,'" January 15, 1953, 20.

24. See the following in *Jet*: "'Prophet' Jones Buys $550,000 Theater Building," November 20, 1952, 42; "Prophet Buys $1,000 Pen Set," January 29, 1953, 28; "Prophet Jones Predicts War at Chicken Dinner," December 9, 1954, 26; "Men Who Dislike Sex," March 4, 1954, 22–23.

25. "Prophet Jones Predicts War at Chicken Dinner"; "Accuses Prophet Jones of Race Slur on Radio," *Jet,* February 3, 1955, 14.

26. See the following in *Jet*: "Prophet Exposed after Police Agent Digs into 'Secret' Past," March 8, 1956, 22–24; "The Private Life of Prophet Jones," March 11, 1954, 67; "Prophet Jones Morals Case Hearing Scheduled," July 12, 1956, 48. Retzloff, "'Seer or Queer?,'" 287.

27. "Words of the Week," *Jet,* August 9, 1956, 30.

28. "Gladys Bentley Marries Calif. Cook," *Jet,* September 18, 1952, 19; "Can Science Eliminate the Third Sex?," *Jet,* January 22, 1953, 46–49.

29. Kinsey, Pomeroy, and, Martin, *Sexual Behavior in the Human Male,* 625–31; Kinsey, Pomeroy, Martin, and Gebhard, *Sexual Behavior in the Human Female,* 4–5; "Kinsey Report," *Jet,* July 16, 1953, 11.

30. Kinsey, Pomeroy, Martin, and Gebhard, *Sexual Behavior in the Human Female,* 457; "Can Sex Cause Heart Trouble?," *Jet,* June 19, 1952, 20–23; Robert Johnson, "Are Women Changing Our Sex Morals?," *Jet,* August 27, 1953, 26–28.

31. "The Laws of Love," *Jet,* April 29, 1954, 28–30; "Why Lesbians Marry," *Jet,* January 1, 1953, 20–23.

32. Johnson, "Are Women Changing Our Sex Morals?"; "What Widows Do about Love," *Jet,* April 8, 1954, 28–30.

33. Drucker, "Keying Desire"; Griffith, "Religious Encounters of Alfred C. Kinsey"; Capshew et al., "Kinsey's Biographer"; "Dr. Alfred C. Kinsey Delivers Fourth Annual Founders Lecture," *Hilltop,* December 1, 1948, 3; Gebhard and Johnson, *Kinsey Data,* 428–29, 436–37, 522–23.

34. Chiang, "Effecting Science, Affecting Medicine"; Terrence Kissack, "Alfred Kinsey and Homosexuality in the 1950s"; Allyn, "Private Acts/Public Policy"; Markell Morantz, "Scientist as Sex Crusader."

35. See the following in *Coronet*: Peggy Craig, "What Have 'Sex Experts' Done to Children?," January 1955, 111–15; John Kurd Lagemann, "How Women Hurt Men," December 1959, 158; Carol Hughes, "My Prisoners Are Women," May 1955, 36–40; L. W. Robinson, "The Real Differences between Men and Women," May 1959, 154–58; Rugo A. Bourdeau, "Myths That Imperil Married Love," December 1958, 172–73; Phyllis Goldman, "20 Questions Most Asked about Sex," September 1958, 132.

36. Jesse DeVore, "Article on Homosexuals Drew Fire," *New York Amsterdam News*, October 12, 1957, 28; "Let's Be Honest about Homosexuals," *Our World*, August 1954, 48–49; Meyerowitz, "'How Common Culture Shapes the Separate Lives'"; Houlbrook, *Queer London*, 146–48; Canaday, *Straight State*; Chauncey, *Gay New York*.

37. "Committee on the State of the Family," 1–3, folder 8, box 66, part 1, Daniel Patrick Moynihan Papers, Library of Congress, Washington, D.C.

38. Rainwater and Yancey, *Moynihan Report and the Politics of Controversy*, 88.

39. Kermit Mehlinger, "The Sexual Revolution," *Ebony*, August 1966, 57–58; Clark, *Dark Ghetto*, 107.

40. Frazier, *Negro Family in the United States*, 343–57; Kardiner and Ovesey, *Mark of Oppression*, 185–86, 210–11, 186, 312, 315.

41. "Pettigrew," December 28, 1964, folder 8; "Notes by DPN, Assistant Secretary of Labor" (n.d.), folder 9; "Memorandum for Mr. Daniel Patrick Moynihan," folder 8; "Selected Quotations from "To Be Equal" by Whitney Young," folder 9; "Ginsberg," January 13, 1965, folder 9, all in box 66, part 1, Daniel Patrick Moynihan Papers, Library of Congress, Washington, D.C.

42. Jean M. White, "Report Finds Negro's Family Life Crumbling," *Washington Post*, August 23, 1965; "Causes and Cures," *Newsweek*, August 30, 1965, folder 9, box 66, part 1, Daniel Patrick Moynihan Papers, Library of Congress, Washington, D.C.; "New Crisis: The Negro Family," *Newsweek*, August 9, 1965, 32–35; "Moynihan Report," *New Republic*, September 11, 1965, 8–9; Rainwater and Yancey, *Moynihan Report and the Politics of the Controversy*, 35; "Family Report Sparks Debate," *Washington Post*, November 17, 1965; "The Moynihan Report: Comment on Addenda to Earlier Analysis," *Christian Century*, February 9, 1966, 180–83; John Herbest, "Moynihan Hopeful U.S. Will Adopt a Policy of Promoting Family Stability," *New York Times*, December 12, 1965; "The Moynihan Report," *Christian Century*, December 15, 1965, 1531–32; "Moynihan of the Moynihan Report," *New York Times*, July 31, 1966; "A Mother Can't Do a Man's Job," *Newsweek*, August 22, 1966, 41.

43. Stack, *All Our Kin*, 44; Ferguson, *Aberrations in Black*, 124–25; Scott, *Contempt and Pity*, 125, 150–56; for a similar critique, see Clarke, "Failure to Transform," 200; V. Smith, "Discourses of Family in Black Documentary"; Spillers, "Mama's Baby, Papa's Maybe"; McDowell, "Reading Family Matters"; Lubiano, "Black Ladies, Welfare Queens, and State Minstrels," 323–63; Briggs, *Reproducing Empire*, 170–91.

44. Swan, "Methodological Critique of the Moynihan Report"; Staples, "Male-Female Variations," 11–20.

45. Staples, "Sexuality of Black Women"; Staples, "Male-Female Variations"; Staples, "Black Sexuality"; Staples, "Human Sexuality."

46. Staples, "Myth of Black Matriarchy" (quote on 15); Staples, "Myth of the Impotent Black Male" (quote on 5); Staples, *Black Family*, 79. On Momism, see Van Den Oever, *Mama's Boy*, 6–7, and Plant, *Mom*.

47. "A Response to Clemmont Vontress," *Black Scholar* 3 (November 1971): 42–43; Vontress, "A Response to Robert Staples," *Black Scholar* 3 (November 1971): 46–49; Staples,

"Myth of the Impotent Black Male," 5–6, 9; Sizemore, "Sexism and the Black Male," 7; Staples, "Masculinity and Race," 176; Staples, "Race, Liberalism-Conservativism and Premarital Sexual Permissiveness"; Mae C. King, "The Politics of Sexual Stereotypes," *Black Scholar* 5 (March–April 1973): 13–22.

48. See the following in *Jet*: "Chicago Detective Arrests 17-Year-Old 'Madam,'" November 21, 1963, 24; "White Man and Negro Wife to Remain in Arkansas," November 29, 1963, 33; "Masturbation, Sex outside Marriage Not Condemned"; "Wants Sex Change," March 16, 1967, 59; "Frye: I Want to Be a Man; But It Is Hard," September 9, 1965, 18; "People Are Talking About," February 17, 1966, 42; "People Are Talking About," November 4, 1964, 43; "People Are Talking About," May 14, 1964, 45; "Commons Okays Ease in Britain's Homosexual Law," July 2, 1964, 15; "Sex Dominates White Thought in Miss.," July 23, 1963, 54; "Negroes Often Lynched for Crimes of Guilty Whites," July 23, 1964, 6–8; "White Woman Says African Is Child's Father," October 6, 1964; "Sex, the Kruschev's Fall Dominate News in Washington," October 29, 1964, 6–7; "People Are Talking About," December 15, 1966, 44; "People Are Talking About," March 30, 1967, 42.

49. See the following in *Jet*: Larry Still, "What Is a Negro? Court Case May Come Up with the Answer," December 17, 1964, 14–17; "Maryland Allows Negroes to Marry Whites," February 23, 1967, 23; "Bill to Repeal Mixed-Marriage Ban Introduced," March 9, 1967, 22; "Defeat of Mixed Marriage Bill in Md. Brings Tears," March 24, 1966; "Maryland Repeals Law Banning Mixed Marriage," March 23, 1967, 3; "Mixed Marriage No Problem for British Cleric, Wife," September 15, 1965, 45; "Taking Child from Parents Is Called Cruel Punishment," October 14, 1965, 16–17; "Child Was Born to an Interracial Couple," October 14, 1965, 18–19; "Mixed Couple Suffers Ordeal, Job Losses in Custody Battle," April 7, 1966, 46–47; "People Are Talking About," December 31, 1964, 42; "Judge Spouts Off on Social Mixing of Races," December 1, 1966, 14; "White Wife Charges Man Made Her a Prostitute," January 14, 1964, 51; "White Man Seeks to Wed Negro in L.A. Sues," March 23, 1967, 17; "Negro Men Deliver Damaging Blows at Sex-Filled FLA. Trial," February 3, 1966, 48–49; "People Are Talking About," April 21, 1967, 42; "Homosexual Acts May Be Beneficial, Priests Agree," December 28, 1967, 26; "British Clergy Favors Legalizing Homosexuality," May 27, 1965, 42; "People Are Talking About," November 16, 1967, 6; "Women Protest Sex Act; Cause Actress to Lose Role," November 9, 1967, 24–25.

50. See the following in *Jet*: "Sex Fears Spur Hysteria of Whites, Bennett Tells Probers," November 23, 1967, 4–5; "White Man's Sex Beliefs Called 'Irrational,'" May 20, 1965, 47; "Negroes Studied during Sex Act Reveal Their True Sexual Traits," May 19, 1966, 46–48; "Shouts of 'We'll Kill Whites,' 'Burn' to 'This Is War' Heard," September 2, 1965, 4–5.

51. Radner and Luckett, *Swinging Singles*.

52. Alvin Poussaint, "Blacks and the Sexual Revolution," *Ebony*, October 1971, 112–13.

53. Ibid., 113.

54. Ibid., 118; Alvin Poussaint, "Sex and the Black Male," *Ebony*, August 1972, 120; Leslie, "Slow To Fade?"

Chapter Three

1. Hendin, *Black Suicide*, 70.

2. Ibid., 49, 69, 52–53.

3. Kristeva, *Powers of Horror*, 15–17, 53–55; Hartman, *Scenes of Subjection*, 58–59; Thomas, *Masculinity, Psychoanalysis, Straight Queer Theory*, 64–67.

4. Introduction by Wendy Clarke, *Portrait of Jason*, August 7, 2005, file 1, box 6, SCP; Lauren Rabinowitz, "Interview with Shirley Clarke," 20, in author's possession; "About the Making of *Portrait of Jason*," *Village Voice*, August 24, 1967, file 1, box 6, SCP.

5. Jennifer Doyle, *Sex Objects*, 62.

6. Introduction by Wendy Clarke, *Portrait of Jason*, August 7, 2005, file 1, box 6, SCP.

7. "About Shirley Clarke," http://nwfilmforum.org/downloads/0000/0567/portraitofjason.pdf; "About Jason," file 1, box 6, SCP; Rabinovitz, *Points of Resistance*, 94–99, 110–15.

8. See the following in SCP: Robert Brustein, "Theater: Junkies and Jazz," *New Republic,* September 28, 1959, file 11, box 3; Elliot Norton, "Drama 'The Connection' Real Blockbuster in N.Y.," *Boston Daily Record*, May 11, 1960, file 11, box 3; Arthur Gelb, "News and Gossip Gathered on the Rialto: Bank with Theatrical Ideas, a New Actress, and a Beatnik Audience—Swinging," *New York Times*, December 27, 1959, p. XI, file 11, box 3; Brooks Atkinson, "Jack Gelber's Harrowing Drama about Social Life among the Junkies," *New York Times*, February 7, 1960, file 11, box 3; Don Heckman, "'The Connection'—A Review," *Jazz Monthly*, April 1960, p. 29, file 11, box 3; negative reviews include A. H. Weiler, "Observations on the Passing Picture Scene," *New York Times*, February 21, 1960, file 11, box 3; "Of Local Origin," *New York Times*, February 13, 1962, folder 2, box 4; "Choice of Words," *New York Times*, February 11, 1962, file 2, box 4; "How to Get a Free Hand in American Film-Making," *Times*, June 17, 1961, file 3, box 4; G. G. Patterson, "Current Film Notes," *Toronto Film Society*, February 24, 1967, file 3, box 4; and "Reviews," *Reporter*, November 8, 1961, file 3, box 4.

9. See the following in SCP: Don Heckman, "The Connection—A Review," *Jazz Monthly*, April 1960, p. 29, file 2, box 4; Henry Hewes, "Broadway Postscripts: Miracle on Fourteenth Street," *Saturday Review*, September 2, 1959, p. 26, file 2, box 4; "Junkies and Jazz," *Time*, September 28, 1959, 4.

10. Seiver, *Soul Searching*, 67–68. See the following in SCP: Donald Ritchie, "Letter From Cannes," *Nation*, June 17, 1961, pp. 526–27, file 2, box 4; Bayard Rustin to Wiseman Film Productions, December 3, 1963, folder 5, box 4; "Notes of SC," n.d., file 6, box 4; "Review of *Portrait of Jason*," *Datebook*, May 12, 1968, file 1, box 6; Gibson A. Danes to Shirley Clarke, May 14, 1964, file 5, box 4; "About the Making of *Portrait of Jason*," *Village Voice*, August 24, 1967, file 1, box 6.

11. See the following in SCP: Vincent Canby, "Portrait of Jason," *New York Times*, September 30, 1967, file 1, box 6; Arthur Knight, "Cinema Verite and Film Truth," *Saturday Review*, September 9, 1967, 41, file 1, box 6; John L. Wasserman, "'Portrait of Jason' Is Funny and Shattering," *San Francisco Chronicle*, November 6, 1969, file 1, box 6; G. M., "Portrait of Jason's Portrait," *Cavalier*, January 1968, file 1, box 6; "Two Imperfect Portraits: Jason Holiday and Bob Dylan," *Cinema*, n.d., file 1, box 6.

12. Rabinovitz, *Points of Resistance*, 133–34; "About Shirley Clarke," http://nwfilmforum.org/downloads/0000/0567/portraitofjason.pdf; "About Jason," file 1, box 6, SCP.

13. See the following in SCP: "Reviews," *New York Post*, October 3, 1967, file 1, box 6; *Downtown*, October 17, 1967, file 1, box 6; *Newsweek*, November 6, 1967, file 1, box 6; *Campus Forum*, University of Minnesota, November 22, 1966, file 1, box 6; *London Festival Choice*, 1967, p. 18, file 1, box 6; "Anything Goes: Taboos in Twilight," *Newsweek*, November 6, 1967, p. 74, file 1, box 6; Arthur Knight, "Cinema Verite and Film Truth," *Saturday Review*, September 9, 1967, p, 41, file 1, box 6; John L. Wasserman, "'Portrait of Jason' Is Funny and Shattering," *San Francisco Chronicle*, November 6, 1969, file 1, box 6; Robert Hatch, "Films," *Nation*, October 30, 1967, file 1, box 6; "An Unbridled Hustler Sits for a Portrait," May 6, 1968, file 1, box 6; *Newsweek*, November 11, 1967, file 1, box 6.

14. See the following in SCP: Joseph Morgensten, "Film Review," *Newsweek*, October 9, 1967, 106, file 1, box 6; J. M., "Jason's Voyage," *Newsweek*, November 6, 1967, file 1, box 6; "NBC-TV *Today Show*," *Film Facts*, n.d., file 1, box 6.

15. See the following in SCP: William Wolf, "The Cameraman, Sociologist, Psychiatrist, and Peeping Tom," *New Films*, September 30, 1967, 61; "Two Imperfect Portraits: Jason Holiday and Bob Dylan," *Cinema*, n.d., file 1, box 6; Ray Olson, "Scorching 'Portrait of Jason' Strips Homosexuals of Pretenses," *Campus Forum*, University of Minnesota, November 22, 1967, file 1, box 6; *Nation*, October 30, 1967, file 1, box 6; Richard Roud, "Portrait of Jason," *London Festival Choice*, 1967, file 1, box 6.

16. "Some Comments on the Film," n.d., file 1, box 6, SCP; "Movies," *Newsweek*, November 6, 1967; Shirley Clarke, *Portrait of Jason* (1967).

17. "Party," June 9, 1967, file 1, box 6, SCP; "Review," *New Yorker*, n.d., file 1, box 6, SCP. On request for a reduced rate to screen the film in post-riot Detroit, see Andrew Gorski to Shirley Clarke, March 8, 1968, file 6, box 5, SCP; Rabinovitz, "Interview with Shirley Clarke," 21–22, in author's possession; M. Adams, "Unusual 'Jason' at Kenmore Cinema," *Boston Globe*, September 3, 1968, file 1, box 6, SCP; Robert Hatch, "Films," *Nation*, October 30, 1967, file 1, box 6, SCP.

18. Rabinovitz, "Interview with Shirley Clarke," 19, in author's possession; Shirley Clarke, "An American Film Institute Seminar with Shirley Clarke," January 8, 1975, 34–35, file 2, box 15, SCP.

19. Morton Weiner to Shirley Clarke, June 12, 1968, folder 6, box 5; Shirley Clarke to Morton Weiner, June 13, 1968, folder 6, box 5; Shirley Clarke, "Portrait of Jason, 1968–1971," folder 10, box 14, all in SCP.

20. McIntosh, "Homosexual Role," 184.

21. http://nwfilmforum.org/downloads/0000/0567/portraitofjason.pdf.

22. Wlodarz, "Beyond the Black Macho"; Ongiri, *Spectacular Blackness*, 180–81.

23. Harris, "'I'm a Militant Queen.'"

24. Morgan, "Pages of Whiteness," 291; Howard, *Men Like That*, 200–220; Bernardi, "Interracial Joysticks," 223; Bronski, *Pulp Friction*, 1–21; Strub, "Historicizing Pulp"; Kendall, *Gay Male Pornography*, 52–65.

25. L. Williams, *Hard Core*, 30; Gunn and Harker, introduction; Bergman, "Cultural Work of Sixties Gay Pulp Fiction," 35–40; Haut, *Pulp Culture*; Champagne, "Stop Reading Film!"; Schott, "'Moonlight and Bosh and Bullshit'"; McBride, *Why I Hate Ambercrombie & Fitch*, 100–105.

26. Bernardi, "Interracial Joysticks," 221–43.

27. *Bar Room Bail*; *Swim Team Stud*; McBride, *Pride and the Power*; Harlow, *Soul Brothers*.

28. George, *Black in White*; Whitney, *Endless Spiral*, 3; Kirby, *Black Meat*, 18–19.

29. Dodson, *Black and Gay*, 8–9.

30. Ibid., 16, 38, 41, 88, 94–95, 192; Hernton, *Sex and Racism in America*.

31. Garfield, *Dark Brothers*, 19.

32. Ibid., 49, 111, 128–30.

33. *Black Sadist*, 17–20.

34. Ibid., 90–91, 101, 110–11, 156–58.

35. Linda Williams, "Skin Flicks on the Racial Border: Pornography, Exploitation, and Interracial Lust," in Williams, *Porn Studies*, 275–76, 301; Nash, *Black Body in Ecstasy*, 2–3.

36. Lambert, *Master Black*, 100; McClintock, "Maid to Order," 211.

Chapter Four

1. Marable, *Malcolm X*, 135–36; Perry, *Malcolm*, 28–29.
2. Cha-Jua, "From Malcolm X to El Haij Malik El-Shabazz"; Peniel Joseph, "Still Reinventing Malcolm," *Chronicle of Higher Education*, May 6, 2011, B6–B9; William Jelani Cobb, Book Review Forum, *Crisis*, Summer 2011, 25–26; Nayaba Arinde, "Malcolm X Grandson Decries Marable Biography on 86th Birthday," *New York Amsterdam News*, May 19–26, 2011, 3, 38; Paul Grenada, "Malcolm X Uproar Stirs Community," *New York Amsterdam News*, May 16–18, 2011, 1, 34; Toure, "Malcolm: Criminal, Minister, Humanist, Martyr," *New York Times*, June 17, 2011. A positive review appeared in the journal that Marable helped to found. Ralph, "Manning Marable and the Value of Leadership"; H. Boyd, "Malcolm and Manning."
3. Perry, *Malcolm*, 77, 83; Kelley, "Riddle of the Zoot."
4. Simmons and Riggs, "Sexuality, Television, and Death," 135.
5. Bayard Rustin, "Bayard Rustin Meets Malcolm X" (1960), in Carbado and Weise, *Time on Two Crosses*, 164–72; "Malcolm X Termed Stimulus to Action," *New York Times*, March 1, 1965, 17.
6. Bayard Rustin, "Making His Mark: The Autobiography of Malcolm X," in Carbado and Weise, *Time on Two Crosses*, 73–181.
7. Kahn and Rustin, "Ambiguous Legacy of Malcolm X"; Homer Bigart, "'Malcolm X-Ism' Feared by Rustin," *New York Times*, March 4, 1965, 15.
8. L. P. Neal, "A Reply to Bayard Rustin: The Internal Revolution," *Liberator*, July 1965, 6–7; John Leo, "Trends of the New Left Alarm Intellectuals of 'Old Left' at Conference Here," *New York Times*, May 8, 1967, 33.
9. Bayard Rustin, "The Myths of the Black Revolt," *Ebony*, August 1969, 96–104; Huey P. Newton, "The Black Panthers," *Ebony*, August 1969, 107–12; Biondi, *Black Revolution on Campus*, 133; Leonard Harris, "The Myth of Bayard Rustin," *Liberator*, October 1969, 4–7.
10. Baldwin FBI File, 989, 995, 1510–12, 1752–54.
11. Cleaver, *Soul on Ice*, 89.
12. Mel Watkins, "Black Is Marketable," *New York Times*, February 16, 1969, BRA3; Earl Caldwell, "Black Bookstores Creating New Best-Seller List," *New York Times*, August 20, 1969, 49; "'Soul on Ice' Paperback to Bow Feb 18," *Chicago Daily Defender*, February 12, 1969, 8; "Professor to Review Cleaver's 'Soul on Ice,'" *Chicago Daily Defender*, October 18, 1969, 4; "Cleaver Book Featured in Black Hand Society Forum," *Chicago Daily Defender*, February 3, 1969, 4; Grier Raggio Jr., "The Bookshelf: Complex 'Black' Voice Called Eldridge Cleaver," *Wall Street Journal*, March 13, 1969, 14.
13. "Paperback Bestsellers," *Washington Post*, May 11, 1969, 17; "Paperback Bestsellers," *Washington Post*, June 8, 1969, 317; Charles J. Hall and Marion G. Hills, "Book Review: Eldridge Cleaver," *Los Angeles Sentinel*, February 20, 1969, B5; "The New York Times Best Seller List," *New York Times*, September 1, 1968.
14. Cleaver, *Soul on Ice*, 29, 33, 83, 35, 10–12, 26–27.
15. Ibid., 107, 132–33; Medovoi, "Yippie-Panther Pipe Dream."
16. Harvey Swados, "Old Con, Black Panther; Brilliant Writer and Quintessential American," *New York Times*, September 7, 1969, SM38; Lester, "James Baldwin—Reflections of a Maverick," 224; Elgrably and Plimpton, "Art of Fiction LXXVIII," 252; Geoffrey Wolf, "Spiritual Odyssey of a Black Prisoner," *Washington Post*, March 2, 1968, A14; Grier Raggio Jr., "The Bookshelf: Complex 'Black Voice' Called Eldridge Cleaver," *Wall Street Journal*, March 13, 1969, 14.

17. Lester, "James Baldwin—Reflections of a Maverick," 224; Elgrably and Plimpton, "Art of Fiction LXXVIII," 252; Nathan Wright, "Reading For Power," *Cleveland Call and Post*, February 7, 1976, 3B; Geoffrey Wolf, "Spiritual Odyssey of a Black Prisoner," *Washington Post*, March 2, 1968, A14; Grier Raggio Jr., "The Bookshelf: Complex 'Black Voice' Called Eldridge Cleaver," *Wall Street Journal*, March 13, 1969, 14.

18. Charlayne Hunter, "To Mr. and Mrs. Yesterday," *New York Times*, March 24, 1968, BR3; Ric Roberts, "Black on Black," *New Pittsburgh Courier*, May 24, 1969, 18; Thomas Lask, "Books of the Times: Journey into the Interior," *New York Times*, March 13, 1969, 45; Truman Nelson, "From Prison—A Unique Document," *Boston Globe*, March 24, 1968, A27; George Birimisa, "Letter to the Editor," *New York Times*, March 16, 1969, D13; Earl Arnet, "Race Relations Based on Hidden Mores," *Sun*, March 30, 1973, B1; Walter J. Hicks, "Cleaver's Descent into Hell," *Sun*, July 21, 1968, D5.

19. "L. I. Students File Suit to Overturn School Book Ban," *New York Times*, January 5, 1977, 23; "7 Writers' Words Barred by Congressional Record," *New York Times*, May 11, 1975, 20; Harry Golden, "Only in America," *Chicago Defender*, June 30, 1973, 29; William Grant, "Book Banning Hits Michigan Schools," *Boston Globe*, May 12, 1974, A56; Mike Bowler, "Parents Seek Input on Books," *Baltimore Sun*, February 5, 1976, C1; Deborah Sue Yaeger, "Panel to Study Ban of 6 Books in Montgomery," *Washington Post*, November 8, 1974, C1; Deborah Sue Yeager, "County Units Back Books in Challenge," *Washington Post*, December 7, 1974, D1; Wallace Turner, "Books by Two Negroes Barred from Schools," *New York Times*, August 26, 1969, 24; "S. F. Schools Ask Court to OK Two Books," *Los Angeles Times*, September 12, 1969, 2; Max Rafferty, "Misstatement of His Position in 'Dirty Book' Case," *Los Angeles Times*, September 8, 1969, A6; "Dr. Rafferty and Book Censorship," *Los Angeles Times*, September 4, 1969, B6; Lawrence Fellows, "Campaign Seeks to Ban Books by Cleaver from Town's Schools: Resident Comments Not a Violent Town," *New York Times*, January 30, 1973, 39; Richard Margolis, "Cleaver Divides a Town: School Books Education," *New York Times*, February 11, 1973, 211.

20. "Alioto Threatens to Sue Rafferty on 'Censorship,'" *Los Angeles Times*, August 27, 1969, 3; "Alioto Criticizes Rafferty's Action in Banning 2 Books," *Los Angeles Times*, August 26, 1969, A3; Carlin L. Soule, "Cleaver, Jones Books," *Los Angeles Times*, September 9, 1969, A6; "'Read-Habilitation' Program," *Cleveland Call and Post*, August 21, 1971, 13B; "Favorite Book: Good and Wild," *Washington Post*, January 29, 1969, B4; "Cleaver Named 'Artist of Honor,'" *Baltimore Afro-American*, October 10, 1970, 13.

21. Cleaver and Gates, "Eldridge Cleaver on Ice"; "Unradical Chic," *Wall Street Journal*, March 5, 1976, 8; Bayard Rustin, "There's a Reason for Supporting Eldridge Cleaver," *Los Angeles Sentinel*, June 3, 1976, A7; "Notes on People: Group Will Aid Eldridge Cleaver," *New York Times*, February 18, 1976, 46; Bayard Rustin, "Eldridge Cleaver and the Democratic Idea" (1976), in Carbado and Weise, *Time on Two Crosses*, 202–6.

22. August Meier to Bayard Rustin, April 2, 1975, reel 1; undated and unsigned typescript, reel 1; K. Hansen, "Att. Mr. Bayard Rustin," n.d., *Louisville Defender*, typescript, reel 1, all in BRP.

23. John P. LeRoy, "Eldridge Cleaver's Missing Balls," *Gay*, May 11, 1970, 1; *Gay People's Union News*, June 1971; LeRoi Jones, "To Survive 'The Reign of the Beasts,'" *New York Times*, November 16, 1969, D1; "Christopher Street Liberation Day Announced," *Gay*, June 8, 1970, 4; Thane Hampton, "The Gay Militants: A Book of Genesis," *Gay*, May 24, 1971, 14; "Gay Bar Charged with Black/Female Bias," *Gay*, March 1, 1971, 2.

24. Duberman, *Stonewall*; Meeker, *Contacts Desired*.

25. Eisenbach, *Gay Power*, 87, 140; Gay Activists Alliance Flier, December 9, 1971, Gay Activists Alliance Ephemera Collection, WW.

26. "Ball a Panther for Peace and Freedom," *Gay*, May 19, 1970, 1; "Black Panther Party Supports Gay Liberation," *Gay*, September 14, 1970, 13; Duberman, *Stonewall*, 258–60.

27. Stein, *City of Sisterly and Brotherly Loves*, 330–40; Huey Newton, "A Letter from Huey Newton to the Revolutionary Brothers and Sisters about the Women's Liberation and Gay Liberation Movements," *Black Panther*, August 21, 1970; Bloom and Martin, *Black against Empire*, 306–7.

28. See the following in the *Black Panther*: "Miami Gay Rights Ordinance Repealed," June 18, 1977; "'New Right' Gains Political Strength," July 2, 1977, 24; "Conservative 'New Right' Gains Political Strength," July 2, 1977, 1, 24; "300,000 Demonstrate for Human Rights in S. F. Gay Freedom Day Parade," July 2, 1977, 1; "Gay Activists Vow to Fight Back," June 25, 1977, 26; "Puerto Rican Women's Leader Discusses Sterilization Abuse," May 29, 1978, 5; "Puerto Rican Workers Deformed by Poison in Birth Control Plant," May 21, 1977, 1; "Anti-prostitute Drive Fizzles in Berkeley," June 25, 1977, 2; and "Black Woman by a Black Revolutionary," September 14, 1968, 6. Additional commentary includes Kathleen Cleaver, "Racism, Fascism, and Political Murder," *Black Panther*, September 14, 1968, 8; Jay Willis, "The Sister Is a Real Panther," *Black Panther*, October 26, 1968, 4; and Seale, *Lonely Rage*, 220–22.

29. Angela Davis, "The Soledad Brothers," *Black Scholar* 3 (April–May 1971): 2–7; Billy "Hands" Robinson, "Love: A Hard-Legged Triangle," *Black Scholar* 3 (September 1971): 29.

30. Robinson, "Love: A Hard-Legged Triangle," 36; Ricardo L. Tate, "Letters to the Editor: Sex in Prisons," *Ebony*, January 1977, 17; Winston E. Moore, "How to End Sex Problems in Our Prisons," *Ebony*, November 1976, 84; Kunzel, *Criminal Intimacy*, 149–89.

31. "Fag Rag," *Fag Rag*, Summer 1972, 2. The collective assembled at 91 River Street, Cambridge, Mass., including Aaron, Allan Bérubé, Allen Young, Andy Kopkind, Bob Nalli, Bob Collins, Bob Burce, Chuck Bevitt, Charles Draper, Charley Shively, Craig Smith, Erick George, Giles Kothcer, David Harvey Blume, John Wieners, John Murray, John Mitzel, John PaPorta, Ken Beck, Larry Martin, Little John, Louis Landerson, Mauricio, Mike, Patrick Hagerty, Richard, Ron, Paul, Sylvia Sydney, Ted, Tanye, Tony, and others; "These Men behind Bars Are Looking for Letters from You!!!," *Fag Rag*, no. 26, 5.

32. "Behind Bars," *Fag Rag*, Fall 1971, 9; "We'd Make a Batch to Last a Few Days," tby freddie greenfield, *Fag Rag*, no. 42.

33. Hall, "Growing Up Gay Black and Gay," 54–55.

34. See the following in *Fag Rag*: "Letters Come to Prison" and "Prison Page," no. 25 (1978/1979), 11; Hall, "Growing Up Gay Black and Gay," 51–56; "Prison Lovers—Canteen Punks and Jail Turnouts," Winter 1974, 26; "Prisons," Fall 1973, n.p.; "I Am a Homosexual! Can You Understand?," no. 26, 4; "Gay Power Meets Straight Lib," Fall 1971, 13.

35. "Letter from Rahway," *Fag Rag*, no. 26, 4; Hall, "Growing Up Black and Gay," 55.

36. "3rd World Gay Revolution," *Fag Rag*, Fall 1971, 8.

37. "To Speak the Unspeakable," *Fag Rag*, Fall 1978.

38. "I Am a Black Faggot," *Fag Rag*, January 1973, 20; "On Human and Gay Identity," *Fag Rag*, January 1974, 13.

39. Charles Shively, "'Revolutionary' Sexism," *Fag Rag*, June 1971.

40. Stanford, *Black and Queer*, 34, 22.

Chapter Five

1. D'Emilio, "Trajectory of Homophobia and Postwar American Radicalism," 92; Echols, *Hot Stuff*; Mumford, "Trouble with Gay Rights."

2. Avella and Pekarske, *Moment of Grace*, 136–38.

3. Avella interview, May 31, 2008, 1.

4. Avella and Pekarske, *Moment of Grace*, 133.

5. Hackel and Cunningham, *Way of Love*, 158.

6. Avella interview, May 31, 2008, 2.

7. Ibid., 1–2.

8. McGreevey, *Catholicism and American Freedom*, 236–49; Curran, "Homosexuality and Moral Theology," 447; Birchard, "Metropolitan Community Church."

9. Washington, "Black Religious Crisis"; Tinney, "Black Catholics," 44–45; Plowman, "Black Revival," 42; Charles Whitman, reviews, *Christian Century*, May 15, 1974, 542–43; Tinney, "Friendship Is a Way of Life."

10. Dean Burch, "A Catholic on 'Gay' Life," *New York Times*, May 15, 1974, 45; George Williamson, "Homosexuality and Sin," *New York Times*, August 9, 1977, 3.

11. Michael Novak, "Gay Is Not Liberation," *Commonweal*, May 31, 1974, 304, 318–19. A letter to the editor dissented; see Sister Delores Kincaide, "To the Editor," *Commonweal*, November 29, 1974, 222–23.

12. Moody, "Rationing Our Rights," 147–49; Pittenger, "Homosexuality and the Christian Tradition," 178–81, quoted in Jordan, *Silence of Sodom*, 102; Georgen, *Sexual Celibate*, 8, 82, 159, 202–3; "An Exchange of Views: Celibacy and Marriage," *Commonweal*, October 12, 1973, 38–39.

13. Lars Jjornson, "Catholic Order Plans National Ministry to Gays," *Advocate*, November 7, 1973, 12; Hackel and Cunningham, *Way of Love*, 158.

14. Avella and Pekarske, *Moment of Grace*, 125–26, 130.

15. Huffman interview.

16. Hackel and Cunningham, *Way of Love*, 65–67.

17. "WITI-TV 6, Roundtable Discussion," November 17, 1974, Gay Peoples Union Records, Series 4, Audio 29, Archives Department, University of Wisconsin–Milwaukee.

18. William J. Spangler, "Philadelphia," *GPU News*, December 1972, 9.

19. Huffman interview.

20. Hackel and Cunnigham, *Way of Love*, 156–58.

21. Grant-Michael Fitzgerald résumé (ca. 1979), SDS Archives; Molenar interview.

22. Oehlke interview; Molenar interview; Avella and Pekarske, *Moment of Grace*, 108.

23. Oehlke interview.

24. Lars Jjornson, "Catholic Order Plans National Ministry to Gays," *Advocate*, November 7, 1973, 12–13; "Sanctuary House," January 11, 1974, file "Materials Relating to Homosexuality," NFPCR; Guy Charles to Rev. Reid Mayo, November 3, 1973, file "Materials Relating to Homosexuality," CFPC, NFPCR; "The Homosexual by Guy Charles," file "Materials Relating to Homosexuality," CFPC, NFPCR; *Annual Report, 1975–76, National Federation of Priests' Councils*, file "Priests/USA," NFPCR; *State of the Federation Report, National Federation of Priests' Councils 1974–1975*, file "Priests/USA," NFPCR.

25. "Catholic Priests Set Up Gay Task Force," *GPU News*, April 1974, 3; Avella and Pekarske, *Moment of Grace*, 133.

26. Lars Jjornson, "Catholic Order Plans National Ministry to Gays," *Advocate*, November 7, 1973, 12–13; Guy Charles to Reverend Reid Mayo, November 3, 1973, folder "Materials Relating to Homosexuality," CFPC, NFPCR.

27. Guy Charles to Reverend Earl Skewer, November 2, 1973, file "Materials Relating to Homosexuality," CFPC, NFPCR.

28. Minutes of the meeting, Council of Religion and Homosexuality, March 10, 13, May 23, 1972, folder 12, box 3, Eldon Murray Papers, Archives Department, University of Wisconsin-Milwaukee.

29. Ibid., June 6, September 12, November 14, 1972, March 3, 1973, October 23, 1974; "Unit on Homophobia (the Fear of Homosexuals) by Louis Stimak and Brother Grant-Michael Fitzgerald," 5, ibid.

30. "Unit on Homophobia (the Fear of Homosexuals) by Louis Stimak and Brother Grant-Michael Fitzgerald," 3; Avella and Pekarske, *Moment of Grace*, 134.

31. "A Christian, Gospel, and Ministerial Rationale for a Ministry to Homosexual Persons," SDS Archives, 3; "Dear Salvatorians," November 23, 1973, ibid.; "Unit on Homophobia (the Fear of Homosexuals) by Louis Stimak and Brother Grant-Michael Fitzgerald," 3.

32. "Ministry/U.S.A: A Model for Ministry to the Homosexual Community: A Guideline for Extending a Christian Ministry to Homosexual Persons" (n.d.), SDS Archives, 16–17, 24–26.

33. A revised preface to the report on January 24, 1974, was by George Kloster to Ramon Wagner; see Rev. Eugene C. Kennedy to Rev. Reid Mayo, March 15, 1974, file "Task Force Guide on the Homosexual," January 24, 1974, file "Materials Related to Homosexuality"; Rev. Reid C. Mayo to Charles E. Curran, January 11, 1974; Charles E. Curran to Rev. Reid C. Mayo, March 4, 1974; Charles Curran, "Toward the Church's Ministry to the Homosexual: A Theological Evaluation," March 4, 1974, all in box 14, CFPC, NFPCR.

34. Avella and Pekarske, *Moment of Grace*, 136–37.

35. John J. Egan, "Priests' Councils: Grounds for Hope," *Commonweal*, April 12, 1974, 124–25; "Stance on Homosexuality," *New York Times*, May 9, 1974, 42; Avella and Pekarske, *Moment of Grace*, 139–40; Stewart, *American Catholic Leadership*, 125.

36. "Catholic Priests Set Up Gay Task Force," 3–4.

37. Ibid.; Justice and Peace Committee Resolution, "Civil Rights of Homosexual Persons," NFPC-74-20, file 3/33, NCPCR; Ministry and Priestly Life Committee, "Developing a Theology of Homosexuality," NFPC-74-19, file 1/06, CFPC, NFPCR; "Minutes—1974 House of Delegates Convention," 10–11, file 1/06, CFPC, NFPCR; Boyce R. Hinman to Father Reed C. Mayo, May 6, 1974, file "Material Related to Homosexual," CFPC, NFPCR; Rev. Reid C. Mayo to Boyce R. Hinman, May 16, 1974, file "Material Related to Homosexual," CFPC, NFPCR.

38. "Catholic Priests Set Up Gay Task Force," 3–4; Justice and Peace Committee Resolution, "Civil Rights of Homosexual Persons," NFPC-74-20, file 3/33, NFPCR; Ministry and Priestly Life Committee, "Developing a Theology of Homosexuality," NFPC-74-19, file 1/06, CFPC, NFPCR; "Minutes—1974 House of Delegates Convention," 10–11, file 1/06, CFPC, NFPCR; Boyce R. Hinman to Father Reed C. Mayo, May 6, 1974, file "Material Related to Homosexual," CFPC, NFPCR; Reverend Reid C. Mayo to Boyce R. Hinman, May 16, 1974, file "Material Related to Homosexual," CFPC, NFPCR.

39. Avella and Pekarske, *Moment of Grace,* 139–40; "Participants in Plenary Meeting: Wisconsin Conference of Priests' Councils," October 6–7, 1974; Jerome Thompson to Delegates and Friends of NFPC in the Wisconsin Province, July 10, 1975; Rev. Jerome

Thompson to Wisconsin Conference of Priests' Councils, March 26, 1975, 4pps; "Wisconsin Conference of Priests' Councils," March 26, 1975, all in file "Milwaukee," box "Provincial Reports," NFPCR.

40. Minutes of the meeting, October 23, 1974, file 12, box 3, Eldon Murray Papers.

41. Hackel and Cunnigham, *Way of Love*, 158.

42. Avella and Pekarske, *Moment of Grace*, 240.

43. Mumford, "Trouble with Gay Rights."

44. Ibid.; Testimony of Grant-Michael Fitzgerald, Philadelphia City Council Hearings on Bill #1275, pp. 364, 381.

45. "Stormy Battle over Rights Bill," *Gay People's Union News*, March 1975, 2; *Philadelphia Daily News*, January 28, 1975, box 8, NGLTF Papers.

46. Jefferson Keith diary, Jefferson Keith Papers, privately held (in author's possession).

47. Grant-Michael Fitzgerald to Jefferson Keith, February 26, 1984; Grant-Michael Fitzgerald to Jefferson Keith, March 18, 1984; Grant-Michael Fitzgerald to Jefferson Keith, September 8, 1985, all in ibid.

48. Grant-Michael Fitzgerald to Jefferson Keith, September 8, 1985, ibid.

49. Ibid.; Mary Mosee to Jefferson Keith, June 26, 1986, ibid.; Jefferson Keith diary, August 2, 1986, ibid.

50. Jefferson Keith diary, August 2, 1986, ibid.

51. Ibid., November 22, 1986.

52. Jefferson Keith, "Eulogy," December 6, 1986, ibid.; *Philadelphia Gay News*, December 6, 1986; Jefferson Keith diary, November 22, 1986, Jefferson Keith Papers; *Milwaukee Sentinel*, December 7, 1986, 32.

53. "Grant-Michael Fitzgerald, Rest in Peace," 1986, SDS Archives.

54. Jefferson Keith diary, November 22, 1986, Jefferson Keith Papers.

55. Ibid., November 15, 1986.

Chapter Six

1. Sides, *Erotic City*, 123–40, 175–204; De Veaux, *Warrior Poet*; Springer, *Living for the Revolution*, 113–38.

2. Barbara Smith, "Toward a Black Feminist Criticism," in Hull, Scott, and Smith, *All the Women Are White*, 159; Kimberle Crenshaw, "Mapping the Margins: Intersectionality, Identity Politics, and Violence against Women of Color," in Taylor, Gillborn, and Ladson-Billings, *Foundations of Critical Race Theory in Education*, 213–46; Wing, *Critical Race Feminism*; McCall, "Complexity of Intersectionality."

3. Joseph F. Beam, notes, June 15, 1984, file 11, box 5, JFBP; Joseph F. Beam to Mom, October 25, 1974, file 1, box 4, JFBP.

4. Joseph F. Beam to Jane Motz, October 20, 1984, file 12, box 4, JFBP; Beam interview; Joseph F. Beam to Fred, November 16, 1984, file 3, box 5, JFBP; Joseph B. Beam, "Bio of Father," n.d., file 4, box 8, JFBP.

5. Joseph F. Beam, "Notebook," p. 2, file 3, box 1, JFBP; on Beam in Black Student Union, see *Almanack '74*, 47, file 4, box 1; Joseph Fairchild Beam, curriculum vita, folder 1, box 1, JFBP; Joseph F. Beam to Stanley, September 4, 1984, file 12, box 5, JFBP; composition books, February 12, 1976, file 3, box 1, JFBP; Joseph F. Beam, "Notebook," February 12, file 3, box 1, JFBP.

6. Joseph F. Beam, "Coming Out . . . ," n.d., file 4, box 1, JFBP.

7. Joseph F. Beam to Jane Motz, October 20, 1984, file 12, box 4; Joseph F. Beam to Fred, January 29, 1985, file 3, box 5; composition books, n.d., file 4, box 1; Joseph F. Beam to Steve, June 17, 1984, file 11, box 5, all in JFBP.

8. Joseph F. Beam to Steve, June 17, 1984, file 11, box 5; Joseph F. Beam, "Making Ourselves from Scratch," *Au Courant*, February 16, 1987, file 16, box 7; Joseph F. Beam to Mom and Dad, file 1, box 4; JFB writings, n.d., file 10, box 8, all in JFBP.

9. Joseph F. Beam to Colin, October 14, 1985, file 2, box 5, JFBP; Joseph F. Beam to Patrick, November 17, 1983, file 7, box 5, JFBP; Gilroy, *Postcolonial Melancholia*, 106–32; composition book, December 16, 1980, file 4, box 1, JFBP; diaries, December 16, 1980, file 4, box 1, JFBP.

10. Joseph F. Beam, Diaries, n.d., file 15, box 7; Joseph F. Beam to Max Smith, November 27, 1984, file 9, box 5; Joseph F. Beam, writings, July 18, 1983, file 5, box 4, all in JFBP.

11. Joseph F. Beam to Fred McClain, November 23, 1984, file 3, box 5, JFBP; Joseph F. Beam, "Black Gay History: Act Like You Know," n.d., file 1, box 8, JFBP; Joseph Beam, "From the Editor," *Black/Out*, Summer 1986, 2.

12. Joseph F. Beam to Steve Smith, June 26, 1984, and Joseph F. Beam to Steve Smith, June 17, 1984, file 11, box 5, JFBP.

13. Joseph F. Beam, Composition books, December 23, 1981, file 4, box 1, JFBP; Joseph F. Beam, "Painful Silence," 1–2, file 4, box 8, JFBP.

14. Joseph F. Beam, journal entry, April 29, 1984, file 8, box 5, JFBP.

15. *Philadelphia Tribune*, February 12, 1984; Joseph F. Beam, Composition books, file 3, box 1, JFBP; Munoz, "Auto-ethnographic Performance"; Joseph F. Beam, Composition books, ca. 1983, file 3, box 3, JFBP.

16. Joseph F. Beam to Steve, June 17, 1984, file 11, box 5; Joseph F. Beam, Diary, n.d., file 4, box 8; diaries, 1982, file 5, box 1; Joseph F. Beam, Composition book, n.d., file 4, box 8; Joseph F. Beam, Diary, September 28, 1980, file 5, box 1, all in JFPB.

17. Joseph F. Beam, Diary, n.d., file 4, box 8, JFBP; Joseph Beam, "Ways of Seeing," 4, file 15, box 7, JFBP.

18. "On Max Smith," n.d., file 27, box 11, JFBP.

19. Max Smith to Joseph F. Beam, August 27, 1986; Joseph F. Beam to Max Smith, August 5, 1985; Max Smith to Joseph Beam, July 31, 1985, all in file 10, box 5, JFBP.

20. Joseph F. Beam to Ombaka, August 9, 1983, file 5, box 4; Joseph F. Beam to Max Smith, August 5, 1985, file 10, box 5; Joseph F. Beam to Ombaka, May 5, 1984, file 4, box 8; Joseph F. Beam to Max Smith, August 5, 1985, file 10, box 5, all in JFBP.

21. Joseph F. Beam to Percy L. Tate (Ombaka), April 17, 1986, file 28, box 5; Joseph F. Beam to John Edgar Wideman, May 12, 1985, file 5, box 4; Joseph F. Beam, "Writings," December 1, 1983, file 17, box 8; Joseph F. Beam, Diary, April 29, 1984, file 17, box 8, all in JFBP.

22. Essex Hemphill to Joseph Beam, December 5, 1985, file 20, box 4, JFBP.

23. Hernance interview.

24. Ed H. Hernance to Joseph F. Beam, May 17, 1982, file 4, box 1, JFBP; Hernance interview; "Giovanni's Room Has New Owners," *Philadelphia Gay News*, June 1976; Joseph F. Beam to Ray, June 24, 1982, file 5, box 4, JFPB; "Edwin H. Hernance, Partner in Giovanni's Room," May 17, 1982, file 5, box 1, JFBP.

25. Joseph F. Beam to Steve, June 28, 1984, file 11, box 5; Joseph Beam, "Notes," March 7, 1986, file 5, box 5; Joseph F. Beam to Steve Smith, November 25, 1984, file 11, box 5; Joseph Beam to Max Smith, November 27, 1984, file 9, box 5, all in JFBP.

26. "Catalogue," 1986, file 10, box 4, JFBP; Barbara Smith to Joseph F. Beam, file 8, box 5, JFBP.

27. Joseph Beam, resume, file 1, box 1; May 7, 1984, to May 13, 1984, appointment books, file 1, box 1; Joseph Beam to Barbara Smith, August 8, 1984, file 8, box 5; Barbara Smith to Joseph Beam, September 11, 1987, file 8, box 5; Joseph Beam to Ken, January 31, 1984, file 5, box 4, all in JFBP.

28. Joseph F. Beam to Audre Lorde, March 14, 1984, file 2, box 5; Audre Lorde to Joseph F. Beam, n.d., file 2, box 5; Joseph F. Beam to Audre Lorde, August 14, 1984, file 2, box 5; Audre Lorde to Joseph Beam, November 16, 1986, file 2, box 5; Audre Lorde to Joseph F. Beam, June 2, 1987, file 2, box 5; Ray to Joseph Beam, May 3, 1986, file 6, box 5, all in JFBP.

29. Joseph F. Beam, "Writings," n.d., file 10, box 8, JFBP; Joseph Beam to Steve, June 28, 1984, file 11, box 5, JFBP.

30. Joseph F. Beam to Anita Cornwell, January 31, 1984, file 27, box 5; Joseph Beam, "Black Men Loving Black Men: The Revolution of the '80s," *Au Courant*, April 29, 1985, file 16, box 7; Colin M. Robinson to Joseph Beam, July 7, 1985, file 6, box 5, all in JFBP.

31. Joseph F. Beam to John McNamara, Encore Books, December 31, 1985, file 1, box 1; Joseph F. Beam to Max Smith, November 27, 1984, file 9, box 5; T. R. Witomski to Joseph F. Beam, January 8, 1987, file letters received, box 4; Lawrence Abrams to Joseph F. Beam, August 16, 1988, file letters received, box 4; Wade Epps to Joseph F. Beam, March 24, 1984, file 15, box 4, all in JFBP.

32. Max Smith to Joseph Beam, December 9, 1984, file 9, box 5, JFBP.

33. Notes on BWMT, n.d., file 2, box 5, JFBP; Joseph F. Beam, "Review," file 19, box 8, JFBP; Joseph F. Beam, review of *Black Men/White Men*, *Philadelphia Gay News*, April 12, 1984, file 16, box 7, JFBP; Brinkley, "With Friends Like These . . ."; Reginald Shepherd, "White Men's Black Men," *Gay Community News*, April 1984, 5–6.

34. Diaries, n.d., file 1, box 1; "Introduction: Leaving the Shadows Behind," n.d., file 5, box 8; memo, ca. 1985, file articles, box 1; Joseph F. Beam to Eric, February 25, 1985, file letters received, box 1, all in JFBP.

35. J. Michael Labance to Joseph F. Beam, May 31, 1986, folder letters received, box 4, JFBP; Joseph F. Beam to Barbara Smith, June 16, 1985, file 2, box 5, JFBP.

36. Joseph F. Beam to Fred, April 1, 1985, file 3, box 5; on plans to write an open letter to Baldwin, see Joseph F. Beam to Audre Lorde, April 2, 1985, file 2, box 5; Joseph Beam to Steve, June 20, 1984, file 11, box 5, all in JFBP.

37. Joseph F. Beam to James Baldwin, December 16, 1985, file 14, box 8; Joseph F. Beam to Cynthia Packard, May 2, 1986, file 14, box 8; Joseph F. Beam to Fred McClain, April 1, 1985, file 3, box 5, all in JFBP.

38. Joseph F. Beam to James Baldwin, December 16, 1985, file 14, box 8; Joseph F. Beam to Cynthia Packard, May 2, 1986, folder 14, box 8; "Go Tell It to This Country / for james baldwin," file 24, box 11; Max Smith to Joseph Beam, January 24, 1985, file 10, box 5; Sue Williams to JFB, July 18, 1985, file 3, box 4, all in JFBP.

39. Colin Robinson to Joseph Beam, July 27, 1985, file 6, box 5; Joseph F. Beam to Pearl Kiberg, July 2, 1985, file 2, box 3; "November Rent," n.d., file 2, box 3, all in JFBP.

40. Memo, June 22, 1986, file 9, box 4; Alyson Gay and Lesbian Book Catalog (December 1986), file 3, box 3; on some conflict over the flier, see Barbara Smith to Joseph F. Beam, August 14, 1986, file 8, box 5; Isaac Julien to Joseph Beam, March 22, 1987, file 1, box 5; Isaac Julien to Joseph Beam, May 27, 1987, file 1, box 5; Joseph Beam to Dear Friends, December 17, 1985, file 4, box 4; Joseph Beam to Isaac Julien, January 30, 1987, file 1, box 5, all in JFBP.

41. Joseph Beam, resume, 1986, file 1, box 1; Essex Hemphill to Joseph Beam, February 8, file 20, box 4; Joseph Beam, "Application to Gay and Lesbian Peer Counseling, 3601

Locust Walk," December 6, 1984, file 1, box 1; see inserted note in revision, Joseph Beam, resume, file 1, box 1; Joseph F. Beam to Karen Cromley, November 17, 1985, file 1, box 1; Joseph F. Beam to Lydia Wilcox, November 9, 1985, file 1, box 1; see job description, "Staff Opening List," November 1985, file 1, box 1; Joseph F. Beam to Bahia Roberts, July 26, 1985, file 4, box 1; Joseph F. Beam to Jane Motz, November 19, 1984, file 14, box 5; Joseph F. Beam to Anna Forbes, n.d., file 1, box 1; Notice for Library Assistant I Examination, the Free Library of Philadelphia, February 10, 1986, file 1, box 1; Colin M. Robinson to Willie Egyir, August 28, 1985, file 6, box 5; Joseph F. Beam to John McNamara, December 31, 1985, file, 1, box 1; Joseph F. Beam to Anna Forbes, Action AIDS, Philadelphia, file 1, box 1; Colin M. Robinson to editor, the *New York Native*, March 24, 1986, file 6, box 5, all in JFBP.

42. Joseph F. Beam to Barbara Smith, June 16, 1985, file 8, box 5; Joseph Beam, resume, 1986, file 1, box 1; "Ways of Seeing," n.d., 2–3, file 15, box 7; Joseph Beam to Patrick, December 6, 1984, file 3, box 5, all in JFBP.

43. "In the Life with Editor Joseph Beam," *Washington Blade*, February 26, 1987, file 17, box 7; Joseph F. Beam to Isaac Julien, December 29, 1986, file 1, box 5, both in JFBP.

44. Joseph Beam to Percy Tate, December 12, 1986, file 4, box 4, JFBP.

45. Joseph Beam, "Our Life, Liberty, and Happiness," n.d., file 3, box 7, JFBP.

Chapter Seven

1. "Black Lesbian, Gay Church Set Up Here," *Washington Afro-American*, September 21, 1982; Lou Chibbaro, "Fable," *Washington Blade*, September 23, 1983, 17, both in file 4, box 5, JFBP; James S. Tinney, "Why a Black Gay Church?" in Beam, *In the Life*, 70–86.

2. Lewis, "Black-White Differences in Attitudes."

3. James S. Tinney, "A Unit on Black Literature," *English Journal*, October 1969, 1028–31, box 3, JSTP.

4. James S. Tinney, "Claiming Our Identities," June 23, 1984; Tinney, "A Unit on Black Literature," 1028–31, both in box 3, JSTP.

5. Mary Lincer, "Black, Gay, and Pentecostal: Howard's James Tinney Will Probably Never Pass," *Washington Blade*, October 23, 1981, 1; "Vita," 1981, box 4, JSTP; "Introduction," n.d., box 3, JSTP.

6. "Oral Roberts, This Certificate," September 18, 1960, box 6; "Oral Roberts Joins Methodists," n.d., box 3; Mary M. Hobbs, "Nazarene Leader Confident on Meeting Challenge," *Kansas Star*, May 25, 1968, box 5; "Churches: Oral Roberts's Son," n.d., box 5, all in JSTP.

7. "Nazarene Theological Seminary, Class Schedule, Second Semester, 1967–1968," box 6; "Nazarene Theological Seminary, Tentative Class Schedule, 1968–1969," May 8, 1968, box 5, both in JSTP.

8. "Tinney Named New Editor for AFRO in Washington," *Washington Afro-American*, March 16, 1979, box 5; "Vita," 1981, box 4, both in JSTP.

9. Larry O. Brown, "Students in a Rap Session See Sex as 'a Gift from God,'" *Washington Afro-American*, March 29, 1973; "Ministering in a Gay Church," *Washington Afro-American*, August 3, 1974; "Students Urge Sexuality Confab," *Washington Afro-American*, June 15, 1974, all in JSTP.

10. "Tinney Named New Editor for AFRO in Washington," *Washington Afro-American*, December 8, 1973, 3; "James Tinney Recruited to Staff of Congressman John Conyers," *Kansas City Call*, April 25, 1975, box 4, JSTP; on Jackson, "Pentecostal in Reagan's Cabinet 'Bad News,'" *Newsletter of the Pentecostal Coalition for Human Rights*, vol. 1, no. 1, box 4, JSTP.

11. James S. Tinney, official transcript, Office of the Registrar, Howard University, box 4, JSTP.

12. "Vita," 1981, box 4; "Honoring Dr. James S. Tinney," May 13, 1978, box 6; "Former AFRO Editor Received Doctorate," n.d., box 6; Lawrence A. Still to Samuel F. Yette, March 7, 1977, box 4, all in JSTP.

13. "Vita," 1981, box 4; Janis Johnson, "Pentecostalism on Campus," *Washington Post*, May 27, 1977, box 5, both in JSTP.

14. Larry Hurtado, "Pentecostalism in Black and White: Hurtado Responds to Tinney," *Agora Magazine*, Winter 1981, 7–8, box 5; "Black Religion Writers' Workshop, July 16–20, 1979," box 4; "Black Religion Writers' Workshop, July 13–17, 1981," box 4; "Second Religion Writers' Workshop," *Academic Affairs Bulletin*, November 1980, box 5; Mildred Craig, "Positive Notes from the Black Religious Writers Conference," *Gospel News Magazine*, October–November 1979, box 5; "The Washington Scene," *Jet*, July 12, 1979, box 5; "Workshop for Religious Writers at Howard U," *Kansas City Call*, July 13, 1979, box 5; "Religious Writing Workshop Scheduled, Dean's Newsletter," May 1979, box 5; "Religious Writers' Workshop Slated," *Washington Afro-American*, June 30, 1979, box 5; "Religion Writers' Workshop Slated at Howard June 16–20," *New Washington Sub*, June 15, 1979, box 5; "Religious Writers, Editors Gather at Howard University," *Washington Afro-American*, July 26, 1980, box 5; "Howard Holds Black Religion Writers Workshop," *Still Here*, September 1981, box 5, all in JSTP; *Student Reference Manual and Directory of Classes, Second Semester*, January 1, 1986—May 9, 1986, 66; "Courses," *Howard University Bulletin*, 1981/1982, 237, Howard University Archives, Washington, D.C.

15. Hardy, *James Baldwin's God*, 16.

16. Cone, *Black Theology of Liberation*, 1–20; Cheryl J. Sanders, *Saints in Exile*, 118–20; Paris, *Black Pentecostalism*, 70–71; David D. Daniels III, "'Doing All the Good That We Can,'" 164–82.

17. Paris, *Black Pentecostalism*, 69; Butler, *Women in the Church of God and Christ*, 75–95; Frederick, *Between Sundays*, 139, 178; Hardy, "Church Mothers and Pentecostals in the Modern Age."

18. James S. Tinney, "Is Christianity Eldridge's Lie to Avoid Jail?," *Baltimore Afro-American*, April 9, 1977, 7, box 4, JSTP; "HU Professor Chosen for Talks with PLO," *Baltimore Afro-American*, January 19, 1980, box 4, JSTP; Estrelda Y. Alexander and Amos Young, "Introduction: Black Tongues of Fire: Afro-Pentecostalism's Shifting Strategies and Changing Discourses," in Young and Alexander, *Afro-Pentecostalism*, 1–18.

19. James Tinney, "Black Gays March Down Georgia Avenue," *Washington Blade*, October 27, 1979, box 3, JSTP.

20. Ibid.

21. Janis Johnson, "Pentecostalism on Campus," *Washington Post*, May 27, 1977, box 6; Wanda P. Seay, "Gay Students Organize at Howard," *Washington Blade*, November 8, 1979, box 6; James S. Tinney, "No Change of Heart," *Washington Blade*, January 6, 1983, box 3, all in JSTP.

22. Jil Clark, "First Black University Recognizes Gay Group," *Gay Community News*, April 11, 1981, box 4; James S. Tinney, "Gay Student Group Chartered at Howard," *Washington Afro-American*, April 4, 1981, box 4; "Pentecostal Stand on Gay Rights Causes Furor among Churches Nationwide," 3, box 4, all in JSTP.

23. Clark, "First Black University Recognizes Gay Group"; Tinney, "Gay Student Group Chartered at Howard," box 4; "Pentecostal Stand on Gay Rights Causes Furor among Churches Nationwide," 3, all in JSTP.

24. Mary Luins Small to James S. Tinney, April 5, 1979; Mary Luins Small to James S. Tinney, April 17, 1979; Mary Luins Small to Lyndrey A. Niles, April 18, 1979; Mary Luins Small to James S. Tinney, February 4, 1980, all in box 2, JSTP.

25. Mary Luins Small to Lionel C. Barrow, January 23, 1980; Lawrence N. Kaggwa to James Tinney, "Violation of University Policies," September 26, 1983, both in box 2, JSTP.

26. Jason Miccolo Johnson to James Tinney, October 27, 1981, box 3, JSTP; Mary Lincer, "Black, Gay, and Pentecostal: Howard's James Tinney Will Probably Never Pass," B1, B19.

27. Lionel C. Barrow to James Tinney, December 3, 1981, box 4; Lionel C. Barrow to James Tinney, May 3, 1982, box 4; "From the Dean's Newsletter," April 1980, box 4; "From the Dean's Newsletter," February 1979, box 4; "From the Dean's Newsletter," December 1978, box 4; "From the Dean's Newsletter," December 1981, box 4; also see "From 'Right On' the Campus," May 12, 1976, box 4; "From 'Right On' the Campus," March 19, 1979, box 4; "From 'The Capstone,'" box 4; and Charles L. Sanders to J. G. Gathings, January 25, 1982, box 1, all in JSTP.

28. James S. Tinney, "The Separation of 'Being' and 'Doing': The Last Evangelical Refuge against Homosexuality," July 12, 1980, 1–15 box 4, JSTP.

29. Ibid., 9.

30. Ibid., 13–14.

31. "'Evangelicalism': Workshop Topic," *Washington Afro-American*, December 13, 1980, box 4: "Tinney to Lecture Thursday," *Messenger*, May 12, 1981, box 4; "Seminar on 'Born-Again Politics' Set at Shiloh," *Washington Afro-American*, October 18, 1980, box 4; "Pentecostal Professor Addresses National Organization for Women," n.d., box 5; "Three Local Black Gays," *Washington Blade*, April 16, 1982, box 4, all in JSTP.

32. James S. Tinney, "A Pentecostal Statement on Gay Rights," April 28, 1980, 1–2, box 3, JSTP.

33. James S. Tinney, "I Love My Black Brothers," n.d., box 3; "Black Gay Bible Study Group Started in Chicago," *Newsletter of the Pentecostal Coalition for Human Rights*, vol. 1, no. 1 (1981), box 4, both in JSTP.

34. Taylor, *Black Religious Intellectuals*, 150–97; James Tinney, "Problem Areas in Inter-racial Relations in the Lesbian/Gay Community," June 27, 1981, 2–5, box 4, JSTP.

35. Tinney, "Problem Areas in Inter-racial Relations in the Lesbian/Gay Community," 4–5.

36. "Black Pentecostals Lead at Oral Roberts University Meeting," *Oklahoma Bee*, December 5, 1980, box 6; Father Bob Nugent, "Gay Christians Meet in Washington, D.C.," *Advocate*, June 24, 1982, box 5; Vita, n.d., box 4; Juanita Hayes, "15-Course Institute at Shiloh Baptist," November 15, 1980, box 5, all in JSTP.

37. "Pentecostal Stand on Gay Rights Causes Furor among Churches Nationwide"; "Ohio University Choir Members Shut-Down Speaker, Then Walk-Out of Chapel during Sermon on Gay Rights," n.d., box 3; "Dr. Arthur Brazier, Chicago Minister of Woodlawn Fame Resigns from Board of Pentecostal Journal in Dispute over Gay Rights," n.d., box 5; "Chicago Cleric Objects to Pro-Gay Pentecostal Stand," *Chicago Gay Life*, June 19, 1981, box 5, all in JSTP.

38. Brad Green, "Gay Revival Leads to Excommunication," *Washington Blade*, September 10, 1982, p. 3, box 5; "Tinney Excommunicated for Leadership in Homosexual Concerns, Post Reports," *Pentecostal Evangel*, December 5, 1982, box 5; "Pentecostal Church Ousts Leader," *Weekly News*, September 29, 1982, box 6, all in JSTP; "Dr. Tinney Expelled," *Dignity, Inc. Newsletter*, vol. 14, no. 1 (1982), 1.

39. "Dr. Tinney Expelled," *Dignity, Inc. Newsletter*, vol. 14, no. 1 (1982), 1; "Dr. James S. Tinney Excommunicated on Threshold of City-Wide Lesbian/Gay Revival," memo, n.d., box 4, JSTP.

40. "Faith Temple: A 'Third World' Lesbian/Gay Christian Church," n.d.; "Demonstration by Black Lesbian/Gay Christians in Front of Church That Excommunicated Dr. James S. Tinney," n.d., both in box 4, JSTP.

41. "17 Protestors Picket Bishop's Church in Opposition to Expulsion of Dr. Tinney," n.d., box 4; "Banned Gays are Protested," *Washington Blade*, September 24, 1982, box 3, both in JSTP.

42. "Gay Theologian Ousted from Society for Pentecostal Studies," n.d., box 4, JSTP.

43. "Church That Ousted Tinney Calls on His Services Again," n.d., box 3, JSTP; Kenney L. Woodard with David Gates, "Homosexuals in Churches," *Newsweek*, October 11, 1982, 113.

44. Lawrence N. Kaggwa to James Tinney, August 5, 1983; James S. Tinney to Lawrence Kaggwa, August 12, 1983; James S. Tinney to Lawrence Kaggwa, August 12, 1983; James S. Tinney to Lawrence Kaggwa, September 28, 1983, all in box 3, JSTP.

45. "Absence from Campus Form," September 29, 1983; Lawrence N. Kaggwa to James S. Tinney, October 3, 1983; James S. Tinney to Lawrence N. Kaggwa, October 3, 1983, all in box 3, JSTP.

46. "Absence from Campus Form," September 29, 1983; Lawrence N. Kaggwa to James S. Tinney, October 3, 1983; James S. Tinney to Lawrence N. Kaggwa, October 3, 1983; James Tinney to Ray Boone, October 3, 1983; Lawrence N. Kaggwa to James Tinney, October 5, 1983; "Dr. James S. Tinney Addresses Yale Divinity School," n.d., all in box 3, JSTP.

47. "Law Offices of Susan Silber," October 13, 1983; Lionel C. Barrow to James S. Tinney, November 1, 1984, both in box 3, JSTP.

48. "Tinney Wins Award," *Washington Blade*, June 29, 1984, box 3, JSTP.

49. Tinney, "William J. Seymour."

50. Tinney, "Lesbian and Gay Christians Demand Access to Black Church."

51. James S. Tinney, "Toward a Theology of Gay Liberation," newspaper clipping, n.d, box 3, JSTP.

52. James S. Tinney, "'What Doth Hinder Me?': The Conversion of a Black Homosexual as Recorded by St. Luke," November 15, 1981, box 3, JSTP; James S. Tinney, "Formulating Christian Ethics for Lesbians and Gay Men," box 3, JSTP; Tinney, "Toward Gay Christian Ethics."

Chapter Eight

1. Self, *All in the Family*; Rodgers, *Age of Fracture*; Wilentz, *Age of Reagan*; Cohen, *Boundaries of Blackness,* 219; Brier, *Infectious Ideas,* 75–77.

2. "Bayard Rustin," *Au Courant*, March 13, 1986, BWMT Ephemera Collection, WW.

3. See the following in the *Philadelphia Gay News*: "Black Men Needed," April 8–14, 1988; "City Gives PATF Funds for Up to Five Houses," June 6–12, 1986; "385 AIDS Cases Reported in Phila.," December 19–25, 1986; "Blacks & AIDS: Special Outreach Is Necessary," September 5–11, 1986; "Survey Documents Anti-gay Violence and Discrimination," January 3–9, 1986.

4. See the following in *Philadelphia Gay News*: "Black Leadership Council Collects Food for Respite," November 14–18, 1988; "New Minority . . . Honored All," October 10–15, 1986; "Tyrone Smith Resigns," January 15–21, 1988; Cei Bell, "Racism Charges at Phila. AIDS Task Force Unfounded," April 4–10, 1987.

5. See the following in the *Philadelphia Gay News*: Ted Johnson, "Promoting Minorities," April 10–16, 1987; "Firing Provokes Racism Protest," March 6–12, 1987; "IMPACT Functioning Well within AIDS Task Force," January 9–15, 1987; "Task Force Committed to Black Outreach, Says Ifft," April 11–17, 1986; "Blacks & AIDS: National Action Is Needed—Now," February 7–13, 1986; "The Realism of Racism," November 7–13, 1986.

6. See the following in the *Philadelphia Gay News*: James Charles Roberts, "Blacks & AIDS: Leaders Formulate a National Strategy for Outreach," July 25–31, 1986; "Gay Racism Probed," November 7–13, 1986; "Only Homophobia is Truly Color Blind," October 7–13, 1988; "About Sexual Health Issues," October 7–13, 1988; "City Gives PATF Funds for Up to Five Houses"; "Mayor Issues Ban on AIDS Discrimination," April 18–24, 1986.

7. James Charles Roberts, "Invisible Blacks: How Discrimination Affects Blacks with AIDS"; James Charles Roberts, "Blacks & AIDS: Special Outreach Is Necessary," both in *Philadelphia Gay News*, August 22–28, 1986.

8. Roberts, "Blacks & AIDS," *Philadelphia Gay News*, August 22–28, 1986.

9. "Adodi Philadelphia," n.d., File Blacks, Tommi Avicolli Ephemera; "Adodi Fills Void for Black Men," *Philadelphia Gay News*, April 10–16, 1987; "Gay Racism Probed," *Philadelphia Gay News*, November 7–13, 1986; "Black Nationalism Needed," *Philadelphia Gay News*, June 20–26, 1986; "Being Diagnosed with AIDS, New Journal Helps Fill Gap for Black Gays," *Philadelphia Gay News*, October 3–9, 1986.

10. "New Minority . . . Honored all."

11. Joseph F. Beam, *Philadelphia Gay News*, August 12, 1984, file 13, box 7; Joseph F. Beam, "Between the Covers," file 1, box 1, both in JFBP.

12. *BWMT Newsletter*, February 1982, MACT—Ephemera, 1981–1985, WW.

13. Ibid.; BWMT Quarterly by Mike Smith, October 31, 1981, MACT—Ephemera Collection, WW.

14. Michael J. Smith, *Colorful People and Places (A Resource Guide for Third World Lesbians and Gay Men . . . and for White People Who Share Their Interests)* (San Francisco: Quarterly, 1983), 91–92, MACT Ephemera; BWMT-Philadelphia Newsletter, February 1982, MACT, 1981–1985, MACT—Ephemera; *BWMT Newsletter*, September 1981, MACT, 1981–1985, all in WW.

15. *BWMT Newsletter*, August 1981, MACT—Ephemera Collection, WW.

16. BWMT Quarterly by Mike Smith, October 31, 1981; *BWMT Newsletter*, February 1982, MACT, 1981–1985, MACT—Ephemera Collection, WW.

17. BWMT Quarterly by Mike Smith, October 31, 1981.

18. *Gay Community News*, February 27, 1982; *BWMT Newsletter*, January 1983, MACT—Ephemera, WW.

19. "Gay Racism Probed," *Philadelphia Gay News*, June 17–23, 1986; "Steering Committee," August 14, 1984, MACT—Ephemera, WW; "The Community Police Relations Committee Wishes to Also Endorse Gay Awareness Week," box 1, folder 4, United Papers, Manuscript Division, Wisconsin Historical Society, Madison, Wisc.; Joseph F. Beam to Rita Addessa, July 15, 1984, file 28, box 5, JFBP.

20. "Racism Charges at Phila. AIDS Task Force Unfounded," *Philadelphia Gay News*, April 4–10, 1987; Brett Masseaux, "The Black Scene," *Philadelphia Gay News*, August 1977.

21. "New Allegro Is Closed Down," *Philadelphia Gay News*, July 15–21, 1988.

22. Audre Lorde to JFB, January 1987, file 2, box 5; Joseph F. Beam to Liz, March 10, 1987, file 7, box 7; flier, April 11, 1986, file 7, box 1; Joseph F. Beam to David Toice, December 9, 1987, file 2, box 7; Carlos Segura to JFB, April 30, 1986, file 6, box 7; JFB to (unknown),

February 26, 1988, file 17, box 7; memo, January 24, 1987, file 5, box 7; "Author Joseph Beam," *Baltimore Gay Paper*, March 1987, box 12, folder 17; John Cunningham to JFB, December 11, 1986, file 3, box 4; Don Belton to John Cunningham, December 15,1986, file 3, box 4; Joseph F. Beam to Pearl, n.d., file 2, box 3; "Author at Brown to Help Fund-Raiser for AIDS Project," *Providence Journal-Bulletin*, March 26, 1987, file 7, box 1, all in JFBP.

23. Joseph F. Beam to Steve, November 15, 1986, file 11, box 5; memo, file 7, box 12; memo, February 20, 1987, file 7, box 7; Chuck Tarver to JFB, n.d., file 4, box 4; "In the Life with Editor Joseph Beam," February 26, 1987, file 17, box 7, all in JFBP; James Charles Roberts, "'In the Life,' Enhanced the Stature of Gay Men of Color—Forever," *Gay Community News*, February 5–11, 1989, 8.

24. Barbara Smith to Joseph F. Beam, July 27, 1987, file 8, box 5; Joseph F. Beam to Isaac Julien, January 30, 1987, file 8, box 5; Joseph F. Beam, "notations on rent," Diary, February 3, 1986, file 2, box 3, all in JFBP.

25. Charles Michael Smith to JFB, April 10, 1987, file 26, box 11; JFB to Charles Michael Smith, December 13, 1986, file 26, box 11; Charles Michael Smith to Joseph F. Beam, December 10, 1986, file 26, box 11; Reginald Shepherd to Joseph F. Beam, November 5, 1987, file 25, box 11; Barbara Smith to Joseph F. Beam, May 28, 1988, file 8, box 5; Barbara Smith to JFB, November 22, 1988, file 8, box 5, all in JFBP.

26. Dorothy Beam to Rita Addessa, March 11, 1989, box 1, file 3, series 7, Philadelphia Lesbian and Gay Task Force Papers, Special Collections Research Center, Temple University Library, Philadelphia; Jacqueline Trescott, "Anthology of a Mother's Grief," *Washington Post*, August 17, 1991, 48–49, file 7, box 1, JFBP.

27. Medical Examiner's report on Joseph Beam, "Investigative Log," 6253-88, December 28, 1988, Office of the Medical Examiner, Philadelphia, Pa.

28. B. Smith, "'We Must Always Bury Our Dead Twice,'" 79–80.

29. Frank Broderick, "'He Refused to Wear the Chains of Racism': An Appreciation of Joseph Beam's Expressions of Black Gay Pride," *Au Courant*, February 13, 1989, 1, 14, file 1, box 2, JFBP; "Founding Editor of Black/Out Dies," *Richmond Pride*, January 1989, 4, file 3, box 2, JFBP; S. Smith, *To Serve the Living*.

30. "Joseph Fairchild Beam, 1954–1988," *Black Lesbian and Gay Centre Newsheet*, London, file 3, box 2, JFBP; Andrew Stoner, memorial from Franklin College, *Franklin*, file 3, box 2, JFBP.

31. *Au Courant*, February 13, 1989, file 3, box 2, JFBP; "Risin' to the Love We All Need: A Tribute to Joseph Beam," *Gay Community News*, February 5–11, 1989, file 3, box 2, JFBP; Tommi Avicolli, "Joe Beam Dies," *Philadelphia Gay News*, December 30–January 5, 1989, file 1, box 2, JFBP; *Washington Blade*, January 6, 1989, file 1, box 2, JFBP; Broderick, "He Refused to Wear the Chains of Racism"; "Joseph Fairchild Beam, 1954–1988," *Black Lesbian and Gay Centre Newsheet*, London, January/February 1989, file 1, box 2, JFBP. Philip Brian Harper points out that *Jet* ran an obituary for Sylvester and Max Robinson, but I did not locate one for Beam. Harper, *Are We Not Men?*, 15; James Roberts, "Goodbye, Joe," *Philadelphia Gay News*, January 6–12, 1989, 9, 14; H. T. Seneca, "Day Oh," *Gay Community News*, February 12–18, 1989, 6; Thomas Grimes, "Like a Beam of Light, Poem for Joe Beam," *Gay Community News*, February 12–18, 1989, 6.

32. Craig Harris, "Dream Sharer," *Black/Out*, Summer 1989, 26–28; Kate Rushin, "Speaking for Ourselves, in Memory of Joe Beam," file "Black History," box 1, Philadelphia Lesbian and Gay Task Force Papers.

33. "Temple Sets Up Scholarship in Name of Joseph Beam," *Philadelphia Inquirer*, January 21, 1992, file 7, box 1, JFBP; Andrew Stoner, *Franklin*, file 2, box 2, JFBP.

34. Essex Hemphill, "When My Brother Fell," in Hemphill, *Ceremonies*, 31–33.

35. Trescott, "Anthology of a Mother's Grief"; Broderick, "He Refused to Wear the Chains of Racism"; *Black Lesbian and Gay Center Newsheet*, January/February 1989, file 1, box 2, JFBP.

36. *Au Courant*, January 10, 1992, file 9, box 1; doris davenport to JFB, n.d., file 12, box 4; doris davenport to JFB, July 11, 1986, file 12, box 4; JFB to doris davenport, July 5, 1985, file 12, box 4; doris davenport to JFB, June 26, 1986, file 12, box 4, all in JFBP.

37. Audre Lorde, "Dear Joe," *Black/Out*, Summer 1989, 23, 26–27.

38. Roberts, "Goodbye, Joe," 9, 14.

Epilogue

1. "Young, Gay, Black, and HIV-Positive," *Advocate*, March 13, 2001; "Black Plague," *Advocate*, December 10, 1996; Paris Barclay, "What Would Audre Do?," *Advocate*, May 25, 2004; Johnson, "Effects of Male Incarceration Dynamics"; McCoy, "Ain't I a Man"; Stevenson, "Psychology of Sexual Racism and AIDS."

2. "Catch AIDS from Deep Kiss? Chances Remote Experts Say," *Jet*, July 22, 1991.

3. See the following in *Jet*: "Women with AIDS Die Faster Than Men," January 16, 1995; Scotty Ballard, "Why AIDS Is Rising among Black Women," July 21, 2001, 32; "Oral Sex Can Spread AIDS, Study Reveals," March 6, 2000, 22; "Most Gay Black Men with HIV Unaware They Have the Virus, Study Finds," August 5, 2002; "AIDS on Rise among Black Men and Women, Center for Disease Control Report Reveals," March 4, 1996, 7; "Black Caucus Leads Drive to Declare AIDS Crisis among Blacks a Public Health Emergency," August 17, 1998; "Cases of AIDS in Older Women on the Rise," August 19, 1997; "While Number of AIDS Deaths Decreases, Blacks Account for the Largest Proportion of Cases," August 11, 1997; "AIDS Should Be Treated as a Race Issue: Report," February 1, 1993.

4. See the following in *Jet*: "AIDS Activists Speak on Impact of Magic's Recent HIV Disclosure," November 25, 1991; "Magic Brings Sullivan's Vital AIDS Message Home to Blacks across the U.S.," November 25, 1991; "Magic Johnson Retires Again to Devote Time to Family and AIDS Crusade," November 16, 1992; "Magic, Malone Straighten Record on Retirement," February 15, 1993; "Magic's Life in 4-Hour ABC Miniseries," April 19, 1993; "Magic Johnson: Living 10 Years with AIDS Virus," January 7, 2002; Miki Turner, "Nothing but Magic," July 23, 2012; "Magic Johnson Hosts 20th Annual 'A Midsummer Night's Magic' Gala," August 1, 2005.

5. See the following in *Jet*: "Arthur Ashe Vows to Go Forward Despite His AIDS Disclosure," April 27, 1992; Robert E. Johnson, "Arthur Ashe's New Book, 'Days of Grace,' Tells of His Three Burdens: Race, AIDS, and Davis Cup," July 26, 1993, 34; "Arthur Ashe, Activist Tennis Legend, Succumbs to AID/Pneumonia," February 22, 1993.

6. See the following in *Jet*: "Miami Man Raises His Siblings after Mother Dies of AIDS," June 6, 2006; Clarence Waldron, "A Year Later: Flow of Generosity Helps Son Raise Family after Mother Dies of AIDS in Miami," July 9, 2007; "Study Concludes Women Less Likely to Pass AIDS Virus to Men," May 4, 1992.

7. See the following in *Jet*: Rae Lewis-Thornton, "How to Live with AIDS: A Personal Story by Rae Lewis-Thornton," February 14, 2000; "Speaking Out about AIDS," August 2, 2010; "Rae Lewis-Thornton," March 15, 2010; "Faith under Fire," August 14, 2006.

8. See the following in *Jet*: "What to Do When Your Partner Comes Out of the Closet," February 23, 1998, 59; "Seattle Mayor Norman Rice Lashes Out against Rumors of

Homosexual Affair," June 3, 1996, 32; "Max Robinson Revealed How He Got AIDS on Death Bed," January 3, 198.

9. "Major Events in Black Gay History since Stonewall," *BLK*, June 1989, 12.

10. Kathleen Rose Winter, "Remembering Our Past: James Baldwin and Lorraine Hansberry," *Blacklines*, February 1996, 20–21; "Rustin Honored in Atlanta," *Blacklines*, February 1996, 10; "Bayard Rustin Awards Feb. 24," *Blacklines*, February 1996, 10; "This Black Gay Man Organized a March on Washington So That No American Would Ever Again Be Denied the Right to Vote," *Blacklines*, November 1998, 2; "The Black Divide," *Advocate*, April 27, 2004.

11. "Black Lesbian and Gay Activists Lead Martin Luther King Day Event in Atlanta," *Blacklines*, March 1997, 22; "Black Gays Challenge Christian Coalition to Take Steps for Justice," *Blacklines*, March 1997, 22; "Morehouse Student Assaulted after 'Looking at' Another Student in Shower," *Blacklines*, December 2002, 19; "New Rules, Old Institutions," *Advocate*, August 2011.

12. Don Lemon, "A Sense of Otherness That Binds Us," *Advocate*, August 2013; Darrell Moore, "A Search for Sanctuaries," *Advocate*, August 2013.

13. Marlon Bailey, "Performance as Intravention: Ballroom Culture and the Politics of HIV/AIDS in Detroit," *Souls: A Critical Journal of Black Politics, Culture, and Society* 11 (July–September 2009): 253–74; Matthew Breen, "Laverne Cox: The Making of an Icon," *Advocate*, August/September 2014; Kortney Ziegler, "The Peculiarity of Black Trans Privilege," *Advocate*, August/September 2014; Irene Monroe, "A Garden of Homophobia," *Advocate*, December 9, 1997; Karen Iris, "Still So Sweet," *Advocate*, November 25, 2003; Raymond Gerard, "Billy Belts It Out," *Advocate*, February 15, 2005.

14. "Rev. Carl Bean," *BLK*, July 1989, 9–17; "Bean, McCoy Form New Black Gay Congregation," *BLK*, May 1990, 27.

15. Morgan Kroll, "The 'Ex-Lesbian' Magazine," *Advocate*, March 13, 2007; Jasmyne Cannick, "Pulpit Bullies," *Advocate*, March 15, 2005.

16. Laura Putre, "Amazing Grace and Resolve," *Advocate*, February 19, 2002; "Battling Black Gay Apathy in Church," *Advocate*, July 6, 2004.

17. "Blackout on Proposition 8," *Advocate*, December 16, 2008; "Battling Black Gay Apathy in Church"; Rod McCullom, "Blackout on Proposition," *Advocate*, December 16, 2008; Michael Joseph Gross, "Pride and Prejudice," *Advocate*, December 16, 2008; "Black, White, and Wed," *Advocate*, May 2010.

18. John Gallagher, "Blacks and Gays: The Unexpected Divide," *Advocate*, December 9, 1997; "Minority Report," *Advocate*, September 23, 2008; Bryan Ochalla, "Bridging the Divide," *Advocate*, April 8, 2008; Christopher Lisotta, "Deadly Homophobia," *Advocate*, October 10, 2006.

19. Jasmyne Cannick, "The Politics of Race," *Advocate*, March 11, 2008.

20. "Maryland's Black Gay Hope," *Advocate*, March 14, 2006.

21. "Black Gay vs. Gay Black," *BLK*, June 1990, 25–30; William G. Hawkeswood, "Dear Editor," *BLK*, July 1990, 8.

22. "Don Belton Speaks Our Names," *Blacklines*, May 1996, 21; Charlotte Abbott, "Southern Comfort," *Advocate*, November 18, 2008.

23. "Programs, Stipend for Writers of Color Created," *BLK*, December 1989, 23; "Barbara Smith: A Political Revolutionary Whose Choice of Weapons Is the Written Word," *BLK*, June 1990, 17–23.

24. Christopher Lisotta, "Reaching Out to the Down-Low," *Advocate*, August 17, 2004; Gregg Shapiro, "King of Queens: Kevin Aviance," *Blacklines*, September 2002, 24–25; Steven A. Williams, "Troopin' on the Low," *Blacklines*, December 2001, 14; Keith Boykin, "Not Just a Black Thing," *Advocate*, January 18, 2005.

25. Rhonda Mundhenk, "E. Lynn Harris: No Passing Phase," *Blacklines*, April 1996, 24.

26. Frankie Edozien, "Fighting AIDS Face to Face," *Advocate*, July 8, 2003.

27. "'Tongues Untied' Goes National, but 17 Top PBS Stations Refuse to Air It," *BLK*, August 1991, 22–24; "Riggs Film to Screen," *BLK*, March 1990, 31.

28. "Marlon Riggs Untied," *BLK*, April 1999, 19; David Ehrenestein, "Brothers to the Max," *Advocate*, October 26, 2004.

29. Michelle Garcia, "The Return of Marlon Riggs," *Advocate*, March 25, 2008.

30. "Marlon Riggs Untied," 10.

Bibliography

Primary Sources

MANUSCRIPT COLLECTIONS

Boston, Mass.
  John F. Kennedy Presidential Library and Museum
  Northeastern University, Archives and Special Collections
    William J. Canfield Papers
Frederick, Md.
  University Publications of America
    Bayard Rustin Papers, Microfilm Edition
Los Angeles, Calif.
  Williams Institute
Madison, Wisc.
  Manuscript Division, Wisconsin Historical Society
    The United Papers
  Wisconsin Center for Film and Theater Research
    Shirley Clarke Papers
Milwaukee, Wisc.
  Archives Department, University of Wisconsin–Milwaukee
    Gay People's Union Records
    Eldon Murray Papers
  Salvatorians: Society of the Divine Savior
    Salvatorian Archives
    Brother Grant-Michael Fitzgerald File
New York, N.Y.
  Manuscript Division, Schomburg Center for Research in Black Culture
    Joseph Fairchild Beam Papers
    Lorraine Hansberry Papers
Notre Dame, Ind.
  Archives Department, Hesburgh Library, University of Notre Dame
    National Federation of Priests' Councils Records
Philadelphia, Pa.
  Special Collections Research Center, Temple University Library
    Philadelphia Lesbian and Gay Task Force Records
    Urban Archives

John J. Wilcox Library, William Way Community Century
Tommi Avicolli Ephemera Collection
BWMT Ephemera Collection
Gay Activists Alliance Ephemera Collection
Philadelphia Gay Liberation Ephemera Collection
Privately held (in author's possession)
Jefferson Keith Papers
Washington, D.C.
Howard University Archives
Howard University Bulletin
Library of Congress
Daniel Patrick Moynihan Papers
Moorland-Spingarn Library, Howard University
James S. Tinney Papers
Special Collections Research Center, Gelman Library, George Washington University
Walter E. Fauntroy Papers

GOVERNMENT DOCUMENTS

Federal Bureau of Investigation, U.S. Department of Justice, Washington, D.C.
James Baldwin File
Lorraine Hansberry File
Bayard Rustin File
Office of the Medical Examiner, Philadelphia, Pa.
Medical Examiner's Report on Joseph Beam, "Investigative Log," 6253-88, December 28, 1988

INTERVIEWS

Avella, Steven. Interview with author. Private correspondence in author's possession.
Beam, Dorothy. Email interview with author, September 2007. Private correspondence in author's possession.
D'Emilio, John. Email interview with author, November 25, 2008. Private correspondence in author's possession.
Gresham, Joi. Email interview with author, June 28, 2013. Private correspondence in author's possession.
Hernance, Ed. Interview with author, Philadelphia, Pa., August 2007. Private correspondence in author's possession.
Huffman, Mike. Email interview with author, June 2, 2008. Private correspondence in author's possession.
Molenar, John. Email interview with author, January 30, 2010.
Oehlke, Lynn. Email interview with author, January 27, 2010.

NEWSPAPERS AND PERIODICALS

Advocate

Afro-American

Atlanta Daily World

Au Courant

Baltimore Afro-American
Baltimore Sun
Black Lesbian and Gay Centre Newsletter
Blacklines
Black/Out
Black Panther
Black Scholar
Boston Daily Record
Boston Globe
BWMT Newsletter Philadelphia
Campus Forum
Cavalier
Chicago Daily Tribune
Chicago Defender
Chicago Gay Life
Chicago Sun-Times
Christian Century
Christianity Today
Chronicle of Higher Education
Cinema
Cleveland Call and Post
Commonweal
Coronet
Crisis
Daily Boston Globe
Dignity, Inc. Newsletter
Ebony
Fag Rag
Franklin
Freedomways
Gay
Gay Community News
GPU News
Harper'sJazz Monthly
Jet
Kansas City Call
Kansas Star
Ladder
Liberator
London Festival Choice

Los Angeles Sentinel
Los Angeles Times
Louisville Defender
Mademoiselle
Maryland Monitor
Messenger
Militant
New Films
New Pittsburgh Courier
New Republic
Newsweek
New York Amsterdam News
New Yorker
New York Herald Tribune
New York Journal American
New York Post
New York Times
Oklahoma Bee
One
Our World
Pentecostal Evangel
Philadelphia Gay News
Philadelphia Inquirer
Philadelphia Weekly Gayzette
Pittsburgh Courier
Richmond Pride
San Francisco Chronicle
Saturday Review
Social Problems
The Sun
Time
Times Literary Supplement
Times Picayune
Toronto Film Society
Village Voice
Wall Street Journal
Washington Afro-American
Washington Blade
Washington Post
Weekly News

PUBLISHED WORKS

Bar Room Bail. Canal Street Station, N.Y.: Star Distributors, 1986.
Black Sadist, Male Photo Illustrated. New York: Star Distributors, 1979.

Bradbury, Andrew. "Race and Sex." *One*, October 1964, 16–21.

Clark, Kenneth. *Dark Ghetto*. New York: Harper and Row, 1965.

Cleaver, Eldridge. *Soul on Ice*. New York: McGraw-Hill, 1968.

Dodson, Victor. *Black and Gay*. North Hollywood, Calif.: Barclay House, 1969.

Frazier, E. Franklin. *Black Bourgeoisie: The Rise of a New Middle Class*. New York: Free Press, 1957.

———. *The Negro Family in the United States*. Chicago: University of Chicago Press, 1939.

Garfield, Dick. *Dark Brothers*. San Diego, Calif.: Trojan Classics, 1971.

George, Franz. *Black in White*. San Diego, Calif.: Greenleaf Classics, 1977.

Georgen, David. *The Sexual Celibate*. New York: Seabury Press, 1974.

Grier, Barbara, and Gene Damon. *Lesbiana: Book Reviews from the "Ladder," 1966–1972*. New York: NAIAD Press, 1976.

Hackel, Frances, and John Cunningham. *A Way of Love, a Way of Life: Portraits of Gay Men and Lesbians*. New York: Lothrop, Lee, and Shepard Books, 1979.

Hall, Joel. "Growing Up Black and Gay." In *The Gay Liberation Book*, edited by Len Richmond and Gary Noguera, 51–56. San Francisco: Ramparts, 1973.

Harlow, Sherwood. *Soul Brothers*. Pasadena, Calif.: F. S. Publishing, n.d.

Hernton, Calvin C. *Coming Together: Black Power, White Hatred, and Sexual Hang-ups*. New York: Random House, 1971.

———. *Sex and Racism in America*. New York: Anchor Books, 1965, 1992.

Kardiner, Abram, and Lionel Ovesey. *The Mark of Oppression: A Psychosocial Study of the American Negro*. New York: Norton, 1951.

Kinsey, Alfred C., Wardell B. Pomeroy, Clyde E. Martin, and Paul Gebhard. *Sexual Behavior in the Human Female*. Philadelphia: W. B. Saunders, 1953.

———. *Sexual Behavior in the Human Male*. Philadelphia: W. B. Saunders, 1948.

Kirby, Joseph. *Black Meat*. San Diego, Calif.: Surrey House, 1974.

Lambert, Wm. J., III. *Master Black*. San Diego, Calif.: Greenleaf Classics, 1971.

McBride, Scott. *The Pride and the Power*. Santee, Calif.: Blueboy Library, 1977.

Martin, Del, and Phyllis Lyon. *Lesbian/Woman*. San Francisco: Glide Publications, 1972.

Moody, Howard. "Rationing Our Rights." *Christianity and Crisis*, July 8, 1974.

Nestle, Joan. *A Restricted Country*. Ithaca, N.Y.: Firebrand Books, 1987.

Pittenger, Norman. "Homosexuality and the Christian Tradition." *Christianity and Crisis*, August 5, 1974.

Plowman, Edward E. "Black Revival." *Christianity Today*, April 25, 1975.

Rainwater, Lee, and William L. Yancey. *The Moynihan Report and the Politics of Controversy*. Cambridge, Mass.: MIT Press, 1967.

Seale, Bobby. *A Lonely Rage*. New York: New York Times Books, 1978.

Staples, Robert. *The Black Family: Essays and Studies*. Belmont, Calif.: Wadsworth Publishing, 1971.

———. "Black Sexuality." In *Sexuality and Human Values*, edited by Mary Calderone, 62–71. New York: Associated Press, 1974.

———. "Human Sexuality: The Minority Perspective." *Journal of Social Issues*, Spring 1978, 71–74.

———. "Male-Female Variations: Functions of Biology or Culture." *Journal of Sex Research* 9 (February 1973): 1–21.

———. "Masculinity and Race: The Dual Dilemma of Black Men." *Journal of Social Issues* 34, no. 1 (1978): 169–83.

———. "The Myth of Black Matriarchy." *Black Scholar* 1 (January–February 1970): 8–9, 11–12.

———. "The Myth of the Impotent Black Male." *Black Scholar* 2 (June 1971): 2–9.

———. "Race, Liberalism-Conservativism and Premarital Sexual Permissiveness." *Journal of Marriage and the Family* 40 (November 1978): 733–42.

———. "The Sexuality of Black Women." *Sexual Behavior* (June 1972): 2–18.

Straub, Peter. "Happy Ends." *New Statesman*, June 28, 1974, 930.

Swan, L. Alex. "A Methodological Critique of the Moynihan Report." *Black Scholar* 5 (June 1974): 18–24.

Swim Team Stud. New York: Star Distributors, Canal St. Station, 1986.

Tinney, James S. "Black Catholics: Is There a Future?" *Christianity Today*, September 27, 1974, 44–45.

———. "Friendship Is a Way of Life: Black Churches Today." *Christianity Today*, April 25, 1975, 38–42.

———. "Lesbian and Gay Christians Demand Access to Black Church." *National Leader* 1, no. 4 (May 24, 1982): 25.

———. "Toward Gay Christian Ethics." *Bridges: The EOM Newsletter*, May 1985, 2–3.

———. "William J. Seymour: Father of Modern-Day Pentecostalism." *Journal of the ITC* 4 (Fall 1976): 34–44.

Washington, Joseph R. "The Black Religious Crisis." *Christian Century*, May 1, 1974, 472–75.

Whitney, James. *The Endless Spiral*. Chatsworth, Calif.: 1974.

Secondary Sources

Adams, Stephen. "Giovanni's Room: The Homosexual as Hero." In *James Baldwin: Modern Critical Views*, edited by Harold Bloom, 133. New York: Chelsea House, 1986.

Allyn, David. "Private Acts/Public Policy: Alfred Kinsey, the American Law Institute, and the Privatization of Sexuality." *Journal of American Studies* 3 (December 1996): 405–28.

Anderson, Michael. "Lorraine Hansberry's *Freedom Family*." *American Communist History* 7 (December 2008): 259–69.

Armstrong, Elizabeth. *Forging Gay Identities: Organizing Sexuality in San Francisco 1950–1994*. Chicago: University of Chicago Press, 2002.

Avella, Steven, and Daniel T. Pekarske. *The Moment of Grace: One Hundred Years of Salvatorian Life and Ministry in the United States*. Pt. 2, *1947–1992*. Society of the Divine Savior: Milwaukee, Wisc., 1994.

Avicolli, Tommi. *Smash the Church, Smash the State! The Early Years of Gay Liberation*. San Francisco: City Lights Books, 2009.

Baldwin, James. *The Fire Next Time*. New York: Vintage, 1993.

———. "Lorraine Hansberry at the Summit." In *James Baldwin: The Cross of Redemption*, edited by Randall Kenan, 134–39. New York: Vintage, 2011.

Baldwin, James, Colina MacInnes, and James Mossman. "Race, Hate, Sex & Color." *Encounter*, July 1965, 55–60.

Baraka, Amiri. "Jimmy!" In *James Baldwin: The Legacy*, edited by Quincy Troupe. New York: Touchstone Books, 1989.

Beam, Joseph, ed. *In the Life: A Black Gay Anthology*. New York: Alyson, 1986.

Beemyn, Brett. *Creating a Place for Ourselves: Lesbian, Gay, and Bisexual Community Histories*. New York: Routledge, 1997.

Benhabib, Seyla. *The Claims of Culture: Equality and Diversity in the Global Era*. Princeton, N.J.: Princeton University Press, 2002.

Bergman, David. "The Cultural Work of Sixties Gay Pulp Fiction." In *The Queer Sixties*, edited by Patricia Juliana Smith, 26–41. New York: Routledge, 1999.

Bernardi, Daniel. "Interracial Joysticks: Pornography's Web of Racist Attractions." In *Pornography: Film and Culture*, edited by Peter Lehman. New Brunswick, N.J.: Rutgers University Press, 2006.

Bérubé, Allan. *Coming Out under Fire: The History of Gay Men and Women in World War II*. New York: Free Press, 1990.

Biondi, Martha. *The Black Revolution on Campus*. Berkeley: University of California Press, 2012.

Birchard, Roy. "Metropolitan Community Church: Its Development and Significance." *Foundations*, April–June 1977, 127–32.

Bloom, Joshua, and Waldo E. Martin Jr. *Black against Empire: The History and Politics of the Black Panther Party*. Berkeley: University of California Press, 2013.

Bobia, Rosa. *The Critical Reception of James Baldwin in France*. New York: Peter Lang, 1998.

Bowles, John P. "'Acting Like a Man': Adrian Piper's Mythic Being and Black Feminism in the 1970s." *Signs* 32 (Fall 2007): 634.

Boyd, Herb. "Malcolm and Manning." *Black Scholar* 22 (April 1992): 11–13.

Boyd, Nan Alamilla. *Wide-Open Town: A History of Queer San Francisco to 1965*. Berkeley: University of California Press, 2003.

Boykin, Keith. *Sex, Lies, and Denial in Black America*. New York: Carroll and Graff, 2005.

Bravmann, Scott. *Queer Fictions of the Past: History, Culture, Difference*. New York: Cambridge, 1997.

Brier, Jennifer. *Infectious Ideas: U.S. Political Responses to the AIDS Crisis*. Chapel Hill: University of North Carolina Press, 2009.

Briggs, Laura. *Reproducing Empire: Race, Sex, Science, and U.S. Imperialism in Puerto Rico*. Berkeley: University of California, 2002.

Brinkley, Sidney. "With Friends Like These. . . ." *Blacklight* 5, no. 1 (1984).

Bronski, Michael. *Pulp Friction: Uncovering the Golden Age of Gay Male Pulps*. New York: St. Martin's Griffin, 2003.

Butler, Anthea D. *Women in the Church of God in Christ: Making a Sanctified World*. Chapel Hill: University of North Carolina Press, 2007.

Canaday, Margot. *The Straight State: Sexuality and Citizenship in Twentieth-Century America*. Princeton, N.J.: Princeton University Press, 2009.

Capshew, James H., Matthew W. Adamson, Patricia A. Buchanan, Narisara Murray, and Naoko Wake. "Kinsey's Biographer: A Historiographical Reconnaissance." *Journal of the History of Sexuality* 12 (July 2003): 465–86.

Carbado, Devon W., and Donald Weise, eds. *Time on Two Crosses: The Collected Writings of Bayard Rustin*. San Francisco: Gleis Press, 2003.

Carter, Steven R. *Hansberry's Drama: Commitment amid Complexity*. Urbana-Champaign: University of Illinois Press, 1991.

Cha-Jua, Sundiata Keita. "From Malcolm X to El Haij Malik El-Shabazz: A Life of Revolutionary Transformation; Manning Marable's *Malcolm X: A Life of Reinvention*." *Black Scholar* 41 (Summer 2011): 14–25.

Champagne, John. "Stop Reading Film! Film Studies, Close Analysis, and Gay Porn." *Cinema Journal* 36 (Winter 1997): 76–98.

Chauncey, George. *Gay New York: Gender, Urban Culture, and the Making of the Gay Male World, 1890–1940*. New York: Basic, 1994.

Chiang, Howard Hsueh-Hao. "Effecting Science, Affecting Medicine: Homosexuality, the Kinsey Reports, and the Contested Boundaries of Psychopathology in the United States, 1948–1965." *Journal of the History of the Behavioral Sciences* 44 (Fall 2008): 300–318.

Christa, A. B. *Gay Voices of the Harlem Renaissance*. Bloomington: Indiana University Press, 2003.

Clarke, Cheryl. "The Failure to Transform: Homophobia in the Black Community." In *Home Girls: A Black Feminist Anthology*, edited by Barbara Smith. New York: Kitchen Table Press, 1983.

Cleaver, Eldridge, and Henry Louis Gates. "Eldridge Cleaver on Ice." *The Anniversary Issue: Selections from Transition, 1961–1976* 75–76 (1997): 294–311.

Cobb, William Jelani. "Book Review Forum." *Crisis* 118 (Summer 2011): 25–26.

Cohen, Cathy. *Boundaries of Blackness: AIDS and the Breakdown of Black Politics*. Chicago: University of Chicago Press, 1999.

Cone, James H. *A Black Theology of Liberation*. Maryknoll, N.Y.: Orbis Books, 2010.

Conerly, Greg. "Swishing and Swaggering: Homosexuality in Black Magazines during the 1950s." In *The Greatest Taboo: Homosexuality in Black Communities*, edited by Delroy Constantine-Simms, 385–95. Boston: Alyson, 2001.

Cruse, Harold. *The Crisis of the Black Intellectual*. New York: William and Morrow, 1967.

Curran, Charles. "Homosexuality and Moral Theology: Methodological and Substantive Considerations." *Thomist* 35 (1971): 447–81.

Daniel, Walter C. *Black Journals of the United States*. Westport, Conn.: Greenwood, 1982.

Daniels, David D., III. "'Doing All the Good That We Can': The Political Witness of African American Holiness and Pentecostal Churches in the Post–Civil Rights Era." In *A New Day Begun: African American Churches and Civic Culture in Post–Civil Rights America*, edited by R. Drew Smith. Durham, N.C.: Duke University Press, 2003.

Davies, Carole Boyce. *Left of Karl Marx: The Political Life of a Black Communist*. Urbana: University of Illinois Press, 2007.

D'Emilio, John. "The Homosexual Menace: The Politics of Sexuality in Cold War America." In *Passion and Power: Sexuality in History*, edited by Kathy Peiss and Christina Simmons, 226–40. Philadelphia: Temple University Press, 1989.

———. *Lost Prophet: The Life and Times of Bayard Rustin*. New York: Free Press, 2005.

———. *Sexual Politics, Sexual Communities: The Making of a Homosexual Minority in the United States, 1940–1970*. Chicago: University of Chicago Press, 1998.

———. "The Trajectory of Homophobia and Postwar American Radicalism." *Radical History Review* 62 (Spring 1995): 81–103.

De Veaux, Alexis. *Warrior Poet: A Biography of Audre Lorde*. New York: W. W. Norton, 2004.

Doan, Laura. *Disturbing Practices: History, Sexuality, and Women's Experience of Modern War*. Chicago: University of Chicago Press, 2012.

Doyle, Jennifer. *Sex Objects: Art and the Dialectics of Desire*. Minneapolis: University of Minnesota Press, 2006.

Drucker, Donna J. "Keying Desire: Alfred Kinsey's Use of Punched-Card Machines for Sex Research." *Journal of the History of Sexuality* 22 (January 2013): 105–25.

Duberman, Martin. *Hold Tight Gently: Michael Callen, Essex Hemphill, and the Battlefield of AIDS*. New York: New Press, 2014.

———. *Stonewall*. New York: Dutton, 1993.

Echols, Alice. *Hot Stuff: Disco and the Remaking of American Culture*. New York: Norton, 2010.

Eisenbach, David. *Gay Power: An American Revolution, 1969–1980*. New York: Carroll and Graff, 2006.

Elam, Harry J., Jr. "Cultural Capital and the Presence of Africa: Lorraine Hansberry, August Wilson, and the Power of Black Theater." In *The Cambridge History of African American Literature*, edited by Maryemma Graham and Jerry W. Ward Jr. New York: Cambridge University Press, 2011.

Elgrably, Jordan, and George Plimpton. "The Art of Fiction LXXVIII: James Baldwin." In *Conversations with James Baldwin*, edited by Fred L. Standley and Louis H. Pratt. Jackson: University Press of Mississippi, 1989.

Faderman, Lillian, and Stuart Timmons. *Gay L.A.: A History of Sexual Outlaws, Power Politics, and Lipstick Lesbians*. Berkeley: University of California Press, 2006.

Fairclough, Adam. *To Redeem the Soul of America: The Southern Christian Leadership Conference and Martin Luther King, Jr.* Athens: University of Georgia Press, 1987.

Fanon, Frantz. *Black Skin, White Masks*. New York: Grove Press, 1967.

Feldstein, Ruth. *How It Feels to Be Free: Black Women Entertainers and the Civil Rights Movement*. New York: Oxford, 2013.

Ferguson, Roderick A. *Aberrations in Black: Toward a Queer of Color Critique*. Minneapolis: University of Minnesota Press, 2004.

Fone, Byrne. *Homophobia: A History*. New York: Metropolitan Books, 2000.

Frederick, Marla F. *Between Sundays: Black Women and Everyday Struggles of Faith*. Berkeley: University of California Press, 2003.

"From the Editor." *Black/Out*, Summer 1986, 2.

Gebhard, Paul H., and Alan B. Johnson. *The Kinsey Data: Marginal Tabulations of the Interviews Conducted by the Institute for Sex Research, 1938-1963*. Bloomington: Indiana University Press, 1998.

Gilman, Sander L. *Difference and Pathology: Stereotypes of Sexuality, Race, and Madness*. Ithaca, N.Y.: Cornell University Press, 1985.

Gilroy, Paul. *Postcolonial Melancholia*. New York: Columbia University Press, 2005.

Goffman, Erving. *Asylums: Essays on the Social Situation of Mental Patients and Other Inmates*. 1962; New Brunswick, N.J.: Transaction, 2007.

———. *Encounters: Two Studies in the Sociology of Interaction*. Indianapolis: Bobbs-Merrill, 1961.

Goldstein, Richard. "Go the Way Your Blood Beats: An Interview with James Baldwin." In *James Baldwin: The Legacy*, edited by Quincy Troupe, 173-85 New York: Touchstone Books, 1989.

Gore, Dayo F. *Radicalism at the Crossroads: African American Women Activists in the Cold War*. New York: New York University Press, 2011.

Green, Adam. *Selling the Race: Culture, Community, and Black Chicago, 1940-1955*. Chicago: University of Chicago Press, 2007.

Griffith, R. Marie. "The Religious Encounters of Alfred C. Kinsey." *Journal of American History* 95 (September 2008): 349-77.

Gunn, Drewey Wayne, and Jaime Harker. Introduction to *1960s Gay Pulp Fiction: The Misplaced Heritage*, edited by Drewey Wayne Gunn and Jaime Harker, 1-28. Amherst: University of Massachusetts Press, 2013.

Halperin, David M. *How to Be Gay*. Cambridge, Mass.: Harvard University Press, 2012.

Hamilton, Charles V. *Adam Clayton Powell, Jr.: The Political Biography of an American Dilemma*. New York: Atheneum, 1991.

Hansberry, Lorraine. *The Movement: Documentary of a Struggle for Equality*. New York: Simon and Schuster, 1964.

———. *A Raisin in the Sun*. New York: Vintage, 1994.

———. *A Raisin in the Sun: The Unfilmed Original Screenplay*. New York: Plume, 1992.

———. *To Be Young, Gifted, and Black*. New York: Signet Classics, 2011.

Hardy, Clarence E., III. "Church Mothers and Pentecostals in the Modern Age." In *Afro-Pentecostalism: Black Pentecostal and Charismatic Christianity in History and Culture*, 83-93. New York: New York University Press, 2011.

———. *James Baldwin's God: Sex, Hope, and Crisis in Black Holiness Culture*. Knoxville: University of Tennessee Press, 2003.

Harper, Philip Brian. *Are We Not Men? Masculine Anxiety and the Problem of African American Identity*. New York: Oxford, 1996.

———. "Racism and Homophobia as Reflections of Their Perpetrators." In *Homophobia: How We All Pay the Price*, edited by Warren J. Blumenfield, 64-65. Boston: Beacon Press, 1992.

Harris, Angelique. "'I'm a Militant Queen': Queering Blaxploitation Films." In *Contemporary Black American Cinema: Race, Gender, and Sexuality at the Movies*, edited by Mia Mask, 210-29. New York: Routledge, 2012.

Hartman, Saidiya V. *Scenes of Subjection: Terror, Slavery, and Self-Making in Nineteenth-Century America*. New York: Oxford University Press, 1997.

Haut, Woody. *Pulp Culture: Hardboiled Fiction and the Cold War*. London: Serpent's Tail, 1995.

Hawkeswood, William G. *One of the Children: Gay Black Men in Harlem*. Berkeley: University of California Press, 1996.

Haygood, Will. *King of the Cats: The Life and Times of Adam Clayton Powell, Jr*. New York: Houghton Mifflin, 1993.

Hemphill, Essex. *Brother to Brother: New Writing by Black Gay Men*. Washington, D.C.: Redbone Press, 2007.

———. *Ceremonies: Prose and Poetry*. New York: Plume, 1992.

Hendin, Herbert. *Black Suicide*. New York: Basic, 1969.

Higashida, Cheryl. *Black Internationalist Feminism: Women Writers of the Black Left, 1945–1999*. Urbana: University of Illinois Press, 2013.

———. "To Be(come) Young, Gay, and Black: Lorraine Hansberry's Existentialist Routes to Anti-colonialism." *American Quarterly* 60 (December 2008): 899–924.

Hine, Darlene Clark. "Rape and the Inner Lives of Black Women: Thoughts on the Culture of Dissemblance." In *HineSight: Black Women and the Re-construction of American History*, edited by Darlene Clark Hine, 43–44. Bloomington: Indiana University Press, 1994.

Hoag, Peter. *Same-Sex Affairs: Constructing and Controlling Homosexuality in the Pacific Northwest*. Berkeley: University of California Press, 2003.

Houlbrook, Matt. *Queer London: The Perils and Pleasures in the Sexual Metropolis, 1918–1957*. Chicago: University of Chicago Press, 2005.

Howard, John. *Men Like That: Queer Men of the South*. Chicago: University of Chicago Press, 2005.

Hull, Gloria T., Patricia Bell Scott, and Barbara Smith, eds. *All the Women Are White, All the Blacks Are Men, but Some of Us Are Brave*. New York: Feminist Press, 1982.

Johnson, David K. *The Lavender Scare: The Cold War Persecution of Gays and Lesbians in the Federal Government*. Chicago: University of Chicago Press, 2006.

Johnson, E. Patrick. *Sweet Tea: Black Gay Men of the South*. Chapel Hill: University of North Carolina Press, 2008.

Johnson, Rucker C. "The Effects of Male Incarceration Dynamics on Acquired Immune Deficiency Syndrome Infection Rates among African American Women and Men." *Journal of Law and Economics* 52 (2009): 270.

Jones, Jacqueline. *A Dreadful Deceit: The Myth of Race from the Colonial Era to Obama's America*. New York: Basic, 2013.

Jones, LeRoi. *Selected Plays and Prose of Amiri Baraka / LeRoi Jones*. New York: William Morrow, 1979.

Jones, William P. *The March on Washington: Jobs, Freedom, and the Forgotten History of Civil Rights*. New York: Norton, 2013.

Jordan, Mark D. *The Silence of Sodom: Homosexuality in Modern Catholicism*. Chicago: University of Chicago Press, 2000.

Kahn, Tom, and Bayard Rustin. "The Ambiguous Legacy of Malcolm X." *Dissent* 12 (Spring 1965): 189–92.

Katz, Jonathan Ned. *Gay American History: Lesbians and Gay Men in the U.S.A.* New York: Crowell, 1976.

Keita, Maghan. *Race and the Writing of History: Riddling the Sphinx.* New York: Oxford, 2000.

Kelley, Robin D. G. "The Riddle of the Zoot: Malcolm Little and Black Cultural Politics during World War II." In *Malcolm X: In Our Own Image*, edited by Joe Wood, 155–82. New York: St. Martin's Press, 1992.

Kenan, Randall. *James Baldwin: The Cross of Redemption. Uncollected Writings.* New York: Vintage, 2011.

Kendall, Christopher N. *Gay Male Pornography: An Issue of Sex Discrimination.* Toronto: UBC Press, 2004.

Keppel, Ben. *The Work of Democracy: Ralph Bunche, Kenneth B. Clark, Lorraine Hansberry, and the Cultural Politics of Race.* Cambridge, Mass.: Harvard University Press, 1995.

King, J. L. *On the Down Low: A Journey into the Lives of "Straight" Black Men Who Sleep with Men.* New York: Broadway, 2004.

Kissack, Terrence. "Alfred Kinsey and Homosexuality in the 1950s." *Journal of the History of Sexuality* 9 (October 2000): 474–91.

Kristeva, Julia. *Powers of Horror: An Essay in Abjection.* New York: Columbia, 1982.

Kunzel, Regina. *Criminal Intimacy: Prison and the Uneven History of Modern American Sexuality.* Chicago: University of Chicago Press, 2008.

Leeming, David. *James Baldwin: A Biography.* New York: Alfred Knopf, 1994.

Leslie, Michael. "Slow to Fade? Advertising in *Ebony Magazine*, 1957–1989." *Journalism and Mass Communication Quarterly* 72 (Summer 1995): 426–35.

Lester, Julius. "James Baldwin—Reflections of a Maverick." In *Conversations with James Baldwin*, edited by Fred L. Standley and Louis H. Pratt, 222–31. Jackson: University Press of Mississippi, 1989.

Lewis, Gregory B. "Black-White Differences in Attitudes toward Homosexuality and Gay Rights." *Public Opinion Quarterly* 67 (Spring 2003): 59–78.

Liberman, Robbie. "Measure Them Right: Lorraine Hansberry and the Struggle for Peace." *Science and Society* 75 (April 2011): 205–35.

Lipari, Lisbeth. "The Rhetoric of Intersectionality: Lorraine Hansberry's 1957 Letters to the *Ladder*." In *Queering Public Address: Sexualities in American Historical Discourse*, edited by Charles E. Morris III, 220–48. Columbia: University of South Carolina Press, 2007.

Long, Michael G., ed. *I Must Resist: Bayard Rustin's Life in Letters.* San Francisco: City Lights Books, 2012.

Lubiano, Wahneema. "Black Ladies, Welfare Queens, and State Minstrels: Ideological Wars by Narrative Means." In *Race-ing Justice, En-gendering Power: Essays on Anita Hill, Clarence Thomas, and the Construction of Social Reality*, edited by Toni Morrison, 323–61. New York: Pantheon Books, 1992.

Marable, Manning. *Malcolm X: A Life of Reinvention*. New York: Viking, 2011.

Marcus, Eric. *Making Gay History: The Half-Century Fight for Lesbian and Gay Equal Rights*. New York: HarperCollins, 2002.

Markell Morantz, Regina. "The Scientist as Sex Crusader: Alfred C. Kinsey and American Culture." *American Quarterly* 29 (November 1977): 563–96.

May, Vivian M. "Ambivalent Narratives, Fragmented Selves: Performative Identities and the Mutability of Roles in James Baldwin's *Go Tell It on the Mountain*." In *New Essays on "Go Tell It on the Mountain,"* edited by Trudier Harris, 97–126. New York: Cambridge, 1996.

McBride, Dwight. *Why I Hate Ambercrombie & Fitch*. New York: New York University Press, 2005.

McCall, Leslie. "The Complexity of Intersectionality." *Signs* 30 (Spring 2005): 1771–1800.

McClintock, Anne. "Maid to Order: Commercial S/M and Gender Power." In *Dirty Looks: Women, Pornography, Power*, edited by Pamela Church Gibson and Roma Gibson, 207–31. London: BFI Publishing, 1994.

McCoy, Renee. "Ain't I a Man: Gender Meanings among Black Men Who Have Sex with Men." *Souls* 11 (July–September 2009): 338.

McCune, Jeffrey Q., Jr. *Sexual Discretion: Black Masculinity and the Politics of Passing*. Chicago: University of Chicago Press, 2014.

McDowell, Deborah E. "Reading Family Matters." In *Changing Our Own Words: Essays and Criticism, Theory, and Writing by Black Women*, edited by Cheryl A. Wall, 75–97. New Brunswick, N.J.: Rutgers University Press, 1989.

McDuffie, Erik S. *Sojourning Freedom: Black Women, American Communism, and the Making of Black Left Feminism*. Durham, N.C.: Duke University Press, 2011.

McGreevey, John. *Catholicism and American Freedom: A History*. New York: Norton, 2003.

McIntosh, Mary. "The Homosexual Role." *Social Problems* 16 (Autumn 1968): 182–92.

Medovoi, Leerom. "A Yippie-Panther Pipe Dream: Rethinking Sex, Race, and the Sexual Revolution." In *Swinging Singles: Representing Sexuality in the 1960s*, edited by Hilary Radner and Moya Luckett, 133–78. Minneapolis: University of Minnesota Press, 1999.

Meeker, Martin. *Contacts Desired: Gay and Lesbian Communications and Community, 1940s–1970s*. Chicago: University of Chicago Press, 2006.

Meyerowitz, Joanne. "'How Common Culture Shapes the Separate Lives': Sexuality, Race, and the Mid-Twentieth-Century Social Constructionist Thought." *Journal of American History* 96 (March 2010): 1083–84.

———. *How Sex Changed: A History of Transsexuality in the United States*. Cambridge, Mass.: Harvard University Press, 2002.

———. "Women, Cheesecake and Borderline Material: Responses to Girlie Pictures in the Mid–Twentieth Century United States." *Journal of Women's History* 8 (1996): 9–35.

Mitchell, Michele. *Righteous Propagation: African Americans and the Politics of Racial Destiny after Reconstruction*. Chapel Hill: University of North Carolina Press, 2004.

Molesworth, Charles. *And Bid Him Sing: A Biography of Countee Cullen*. Chicago: University of Chicago Press, 2012.

Moon, Michael. "Outlaw Sex and the Search for America: Representing Male Prostitution and Perverse Desire in Sixties Films (*Hustler* and *Midnight Cowboy*)." *Quarterly Review of Film and Video* 15 (1993–95): 27–40.

Morgan, Tracy D. "Pages of Whiteness: Race, Physique Magazines, and the Emergence of Public Gay Culture." In *Queer Studies: A Lesbian, Gay, Bisexual, and Transgender Anthology,* edited by Brett Beemyn and Mickey Eliason, 280–97. New York: New York University Press, 1996.

Morris, Charles E., III. *Queering Public Address: Sexualities in American Historical Discourse.* Columbia: University of South Carolina Press, 2007.

Mumford, Kevin J. *Interzones: Black/White Vice Districts in Chicago and New York in the Early Twentieth Century.* New York: Columbia University Press, 1997.

———. "The Trouble with Gay Rights: Race and the Politics of Sexual Orientation in Philadelphia, 1969–1982." *Journal of American History* 93 (June 2011): 45–72.

Munoz, Jose. "The Auto-ethnographic Performance: Reading Richard Fung's Queer Hybridity." In *Queer Screen: A Screen Reader,* edited by Jackie Stacey and Sarah Street, 83–99. New York: Routledge, 2007.

Nash, Jennifer C. *The Black Body in Ecstasy: Reading Race, Reading Pornography.* Durham, N.C.: Duke University Press, 2014.

Nemiroff, Robert. *To Be Young, Gifted, and Black: Lorraine Hansberry in Her Own Words.* Englewood Cliffs, N.J.: Prentice-Hall, 1969.

Ngo, Fiona I. B. *Imperial Blues: Geographies of Race and Sex in Jazz Age New York.* Durham, N.C.: Duke University Press, 2014.

Ongiri, Amy Abugo. *Spectacular Blackness: The Cultural Politics of the Black Power Movement and the Search for a Black Aesthetic.* Charlottesville: University of Virginia Press, 2010.

O'Reilly, Kenneth. *Racial Matters: The FBI's Secret File on Black America, 1960–1972.* New York: Free Press, 1989.

Paris, Arthur E. *Black Pentecostalism: Southern Religion in an Urban World.* Amherst: University of Massachusetts Press, 1982.

Pearl, Monica B. *AIDS Literature and Gay Identity: The Literature of Loss.* New York: Routledge, 2012.

Perry, Bruce. *Malcolm: The Life of a Man Who Changed Black America.* New York: Barrytown/Station Hill, 1991.

Petigny, Alan. *The Permissive Society: America, 1941–1965.* New York: Cambridge University Press, 2009.

Pharr, Suzanne. *Homophobia: A Weapon of Sexism.* Inverness, Calif.: Chardon Press, 1988.

Phillips, Kimberley L. *War! What Is It Good For?: Black Freedom Struggles and the U.S. Military from World War II to Iraq.* Chapel Hill: University of North Carolina Press, 2012.

Plant, Rebecca Jo. *Mom: The Transformation of Motherhood in Modern America.* Chicago: University of Chicago Press, 2010.

Porter, Horace A. "James Baldwin and the Problem of Vocation." Ph.D. diss., Yale University, 1981.

———. *Stealing the Fire: The Art and Protest of James Baldwin*. Middleton, Conn.: Wesleyan University Press, 1989.

Rabinovitz, Lauren. *Points of Resistance: Women, Power, and Politics in the Avant-garde Cinema, 1943–1971*. Urbana: University of Illinois Press, 1991.

Radner, Hilary, and Moya Luckett. *Swinging Singles: Representing Sexuality in the 1960s*. Minneapolis: University of Minnesota Press, 1999.

Ralph, Michael. "Manning Marable and the Value of Leadership." *Souls: A Critical Journal of Black Politics, Culture, and Society* 13 (November 2011): 402–8.

Reider, Jonathan. *The Word of the Lord Is upon Me: The Righteous Performance of Martin Luther King, Jr.* Cambridge, Mass.: Harvard University Press, 2008.

Retzloff, Tim. "'Seer or Queer?': Postwar Fascination with Detroit's Prophet Jones." *GLQ: A Journal of Lesbian and Gay Studies* 8 (2002): 217–96.

Rich, Adrienne. "The Problem with Lorraine Hansberry." *Freedomways* 19 (1979): 247–53.

Rodgers, Daniel. *Age of Fracture*. Cambridge, Mass.: Harvard University Press, 2012.

Ross, Marlon B. "Beyond the Closet as Raceless Paradigm." In *Black Queer Studies: A Critical Anthology*, edited by E. Patrick Johnson and Mae Henderson, 161–89. Durham, N.C.: Duke University Press, 2005.

Rupp, Leila. *A Desired Past: A Short History of Same-Sex Love in America*. Chicago: University of Chicago Press, 2002.

Sanders, Cheryl J. *Saints in Exile: The Holiness-Pentecostal Experience in African American Religion and Culture*. New York: Oxford University Press, 1996.

Sarotte, Georges Michel. *Like a Brother, Like a Lover: Male Homosexuality in the American Novel and Theater from Herman Melville to James Baldwin*. New York: Doubleday, 1978.

Schlesinger, Arthur M., Jr. *Robert Kennedy and His Times*. Boston: Houghton Mifflin, 1978.

———. *A Thousand Days: John F. Kennedy in the White House*. New York: Houghton Mifflin, 1965.

Schott, Ann Marie. "'Moonlight and Bosh and Bullshit': Phil Andros's Stud and the Creation of a 'New Gay Ethic.'" In *1960s Gay Pulp Fiction: The Misplaced Heritage*, edited by Drewey Wayne Gunn and Jaime Harker, 143–66. Amherst: University of Massachusetts Press.

Scott, Daryl Michael. *Contempt and Pity: Social Policy and the Image of the Damaged Black Psyche, 1880–1996*. Chapel Hill: University of North Carolina Press, 1997.

Sedgwick, Eve Kosofksy. *Epistemology of the Closet*. Berkeley: University of California Press, 2008.

Seiver, Christopher. *Soul Searching: Black-Themed Cinema from the March on Washington to the Rise of Blaxploitation*. Middletown, Conn.: Wesleyan University Press, 2011.

Self, Robert O. *All in the Family: The Realignment of American Democracy since the 1960s*. New York: Hill and Wang, 2012.

Sides, Josh. *Erotic City: Sexual Revolutions and the Making of Modern San Francisco*. New York: Oxford University Press, 2009.

Simmons, Ron, and Marlon Riggs. "Sexuality, Television, and Death: A Black Gay Dialogue on Malcolm X." In *Malcolm X: In Our Own Image*, edited by Joe Wood, 135–46. New York: St. Martin's Press, 1992.

Sizemore, Barbara A. "Sexism and the Black Male." *Black Scholar* 4 (March–April 1973): 6–11.

Smith, Barbara. "We Must Always Bury Our Dead Twice: A Tribute to James Baldwin." In *The Truth That Never Hurts: Writings on Race, Gender, and Freedom*, 75–80. New Brunswick, N.J.: Rutgers University Press, 1998.

Smith, Suzanne E. *To Serve the Living: Funeral Directors and the American Way of Life*. Cambridge, Mass.: Harvard University Press, 2010.

Smith, Valerie. "Discourses of Family in Black Documentary." In *Struggles for Representation: African-American Documentary Film and Video*, edited by Phyllis R. Klotman and Janet K. Cutler, 250–67. Bloomington: Indiana University Press, 1999.

Spillers, Hortense. "Mama's Baby, Papa's Maybe: An American Grammar Book." *Diacritics* 17 (Summer 1987): 65–81.

Springer, Kimberley. *Living for the Revolution: Black Feminist Organizations, 1968–1980*. Durham, N.C.: Duke University Press, 2005.

Stack, Carol B. *All Our Kin: Strategies for Survival in a Black Community*. New York: Harper and Row, 1974.

Standley, Fred L., and Louis H. Pratt, eds. *Conversations with James Baldwin*. Jackson: University Press of Mississippi, 1989.

Stanford, Adrian. *Black and Queer*. Boston: Good Gay Poets Press, 1977.

Stein, Marc. *City of Sisterly and Brotherly Loves: Lesbian and Gay Philadelphia, 1954–1972*. Philadelphia: Temple University Press, 2004.

———. *Rethinking the Gay and Lesbian Movement*. New York: Routledge, 2012.

———. *Sexual Injustice: Supreme Court Decisions from "Griswold" to "Roe."* Chapel Hill: University of North Carolina Press, 2010.

Stevenson, Howard C., Jr. "The Psychology of Sexual Racism and AIDS: An Ongoing Saga of Distrust and the 'Sexual Other.'" *Journal of Black Studies* 25 (September 1994): 62–80.

Stewart, James H. *American Catholic Leadership: A Decade of Turmoil, 1966–1976*. New York: Mouton, 1978.

Stockton, Kathryn Bond. *The Queer Child, or Growing Sideways in the Twentieth Century*. Durham, N.C.: Duke University Press, 2009.

Strub, Whitney. "Historicizing Pulp: Gay Male Pulp and the Narrativization of Queer Cultural History." In *1960s Gay Pulp Fiction: The Misplaced Heritage*, edited by Drewey Wayne Gunn and Jaime Harker, 43–77. Amherst: University of Massachusetts Press, 2013.

Stryker, Susan, and Jim Van Buskirk. *Gay by the Bay: A History of Queer Culture in the San Francisco Bay Area*. San Francisco: Chronicle Books, 1996.

Summers, Martin. *Manliness and Its Discontents: The Black Middle Class and the Transformation of Masculinity, 1900–1930*. Chapel Hill: University of North Carolina Press, 2004.

Taylor, Clarence. *Black Religious Intellectuals: The Fight for Equality from Jim Crow to the 21st Century*. New York: Routledge, 2002.

Taylor, Edward, David Gillborn, and Gloria Ladson-Billings. *Foundations of Critical Race Theory in Education*. New York: Routledge, 2009.

Thomas, Calvin. *Masculinity, Psychoanalysis, Straight Queer Theory: Essays on Abjection in Literature, Mass Culture, and Film*. New York: Palgrave, 2008.

Thornton, Brian. "The Murder of Emmett Till: Myth, Memory, and National Magazine Response." *Journalism History* 36 (Summer 2010): 96.

Tillery, Tyrone. *Claude McKay: A Black Poet's Struggle for Identity*. Amherst: University of Massachusetts Press, 1992.

Van Den Oever, Roel. *Mama's Boy: Momism and Homophobia in Postwar American Culture*. New York: Palgrave, 2012.

Van Notten, Eleonore. *Wallace Thurman's Harlem Renaissance*. Amsterdam: Rodopi Press, 1994.

Washington, Mary Helen. "Alice Childress, Lorraine Hansberry, and Claudia Jones: Black Women Write the Popular Front." In *Left of the Color Line: Race, Radicalism, and Twentieth-Century Literature of the United States*, edited by Bill V. Mullen and James Smethhurst, 183–204. Chapel Hill: University of North Carolina Press, 2003.

Weatherby, W. J. *James Baldwin: Artist on Fire*. New York: Donald I. Fine, 1989.

Weiss, Jessica. *To Have and to Hold: Marriage, the Baby Boom, and Social Change*. Chicago: University of Chicago Press, 2000.

Welch, Rebecca. "Spokesman of the Oppressed? Lorraine Hansberry at Work: The Challenges of Radical Politics in the Postwar Era." In *The New Black History: Revisiting the Second Reconstruction*, edited by Manning Marable and Elizabeth Hinton, 69–89. New York: Palgrave, 2011.

White, C. Todd. *Pre-Gay L.A.: A Social History of the Movement for Homosexual Rights*. Urbana: University of Illinois Press, 2009.

Wilentz, Sean. *The Age of Reagan: A History, 1974–2008*. New York: Harper Perennial, 2008.

Wilkerson, Margaret. "The Dark Vision of Lorraine Hansberry: Excerpts from a Literary Biography." *Massachusetts Review* 28 (Winter 1987): 644.

Wilkins, Fanon Che. "Beyond Bandung: The Critical Nationalism of Lorraine Hansberry, 1950–1965." *Radical History Review* 95 (Spring 2006): 191–210.

Williams, Linda. *Hard Core: Power, Pleasure, and the Frenzy of the Visible*. Berkeley: University of California Press, 1999.

———, ed. *Porn Studies*. Durham: Duke University Press, 2004.

Williams, Megan E. "'Meet the Real Lena Horne': Representations of Lena Horne in *Ebony* Magazine, 1945–1949." *Journal of American Studies* 43 (May 2009): 11–13.

———. "Skin Flicks on the Racial Border: Pornography, Exploitation, and Interracial Lust." In *Porn Studies*, edited by Linda Williams. Durham: Duke University Press, 2004.

Wilson, James F. *Bulldaggers, Pansies, and Chocolate Babies: Performance, Race, and Sexuality in the Harlem Renaissance*. Ann Arbor: University of Michigan Press, 2010.

Wing, Adrien. *Critical Race Feminism*. New York: NYU Press, 1997.

Wirth, Thomas. *Gay Rebel of the Harlem Renaissance: Selections from the Work of Richard Bruce Nugent.* Durham, N.C.: Duke University Press, 2002.

Wlodarz, Joe. "Beyond the Black Macho: Queer Blaxploitation." *Velvet Light Trap* 53 (Spring 2004): 10–12.

Young, Amos, and Estrelda Y. Alexander. *Afro-Pentecostalism: Black Pentecostal and Charismatic Christianity in History and Culture.* New York: New York University Press, 2011.

Acknowledgments

I was an out black gay man, and a serious student of U.S. history, for twenty years before it occurred to me to write this book. In graduate school, I lived in San Francisco and every week visited A Different Light bookstore in the Castro District to browse the nonfiction section specializing in diversity or multicultural titles. I would skim Joseph Beam's anthology *In the Life: A Black Gay Anthology*, and later I purchased his posthumously published second volume, *Brother to Brother: New Writings by Black Gay Men*. I went on to complete my doctorate and wrote books and articles, essays and reviews, but not until 2005 did I recognize that these men—and indeed myself—had a history that I should look into.

It was around this time that the historian Marc Stein invited me to write an entry on Beam for an LGBT encyclopedia. While negotiating a research trip on the urban crisis in New Jersey, I made a detour to the Schomburg Center for Research in Black Culture in Harlem to consult the Joseph Fairchild Beam Papers. A few minutes into reading the first file I began to weep uncontrollably. As it happened, this file contained a birth certificate and several dozen rejection letters. I was aware that Beam had died from complications arising from AIDS, but seeing the quotidian setbacks and losses in the documents moved me in ways that I had not expected. He was to become my next research project.

In 2004 I won a National Endowment for the Humanities Library Fellowship at the Schomburg, and the following semester I returned to research and write a biography of Beam. From that modest beginning came years of reading, research, and writing on every subject and figure related to black gay history that I could find, document, and interpret. A decade later, I wish to thank the following institutions, colleagues, and friends for the support and encouragement without which this book would not have been possible.

The resources and librarians at the Schomburg are legendary, and the free xeroxing provided by my fellowship proved to be indispensable. I benefited from workshops with my co-fellows, Dayo Gore, Monica Miller, and LaMonda Stallings-Horton, and with the director of the fellowship program, Colin A. Palmer. Special mention must be made of the archivist, and pioneer in black gay historical preservation, Steven Fullwood. In 2006 I was very fortunate to win the Faculty Scholar Fellowship at the University of Iowa, which gave me multiple semesters of paid leave and research funds. In 2008 I combined this award with a fellowship from the Warren Center for Studies in American History at Harvard, where I was privileged to join a remarkably distinguished class of fellows. Zoë Burkholder, Matthew Countryman, Rachel Devlin, Thomas Guglielmo, Peniel Joseph, and Scott Kurashige and the co-directors, Evelyn Brooks Higginbotham and Kenneth Mack, provided me with a year of wonderful commentary and community.

The first round of research and writing was sustained by members of a supportive scholarly home in the Department of History at the University of Iowa. Their commitment to reading and thinking about history is renowned, and in particular I am grateful for the collegiality and advice of Linda Kerber, Jennifer Sessions, and Shelton Stromquist and, outside the department, for Jennifer Glass, Horace Porter, and Adrien Wing. In my new home in the Department of History at the University of Illinois at Urbana–Champaign, I found another community of careful readers. At the History Workshop, Theresa Barnes, Antoinette Burton, Ken Cuno, Nils Jacobsen, Diane Koenker, Kathleen Oberdeck, and Mark Steinberg offered important feedback and much-needed encouragement. A major turning point for the manuscript was made possible by the generosity of Antoinette Burton when she offered to host a potluck workshop. Along with Antoinette, Ikuko Asaka, James Barrett, Tamara Chaplin, Augusto Espiritu, Marc Hertzman, Leslie Reagan, and David Roediger generously agreed to comment on the entire manuscript. Before and since then, Dave has read and reread, serving as a valued critic, mentor, and friend; about his advice and ethical commitments I cannot say enough, so I will leave it at that. My friend Korey Garibaldi invited me to present a chapter for the History Workshop at the University of Chicago, where I fielded probing questions and gained excellent advice.

I was tremendously fortunate to have recruited outstanding research assistants: Stephanie Seawall tracked down an extraordinary number of sources, and Mary Waters and John Costello tirelessly helped me to correct the manuscript. After I completed incorporating my colleagues' suggestions into the final draft, I knew immediately that I would submit it for consideration in the John Hope Franklin Series in African American History and Culture at the University of North Carolina Press and sent an inquiry to senior editor Chuck Grench. To my surprise, he responded with line-by-line queries and comments on my manuscript before even reaching out to possible readers. The reports proved invaluable, and I wish to thank Waldo Martin and the anonymous reader for their time and critical acumen; the comments pushed me to clarify and elaborate in all the right places.

In addition to the readers whom I mentioned above, I want to recognize how much I appreciate my friendships. Thanks for decades of support and comfort go to Gert Hekma, Martha Hodes, and Chris Waters. I also wish to thank my new Chicago friends who have given me the space to brag and complain about my book, especially John D'Emilio, Billy Gonzalez, Fred Hoxie, and Martin Manalanson. My mother, Karen Mumford Moser, passed away before this book was published, but I am certain she would have been pleased for me.

Index

Numbers in *italic* refer to illustrations.

Racism: in Baldwin, 11, 23, 25; and Black and
    White Men Together, 175; erotica and, 74;
    masculinity and, 11; Moynihan Report
    and, 52; prison and, 94; reverse, 177
Raisin in the Sun, A (Hansberry),
    11, *15*, 16, 17
Randolph, A. Philip, 31, 32, 37
Ransom, Dan, 178
Rawlins, Clifford, 174
Redding, J. Saunders, 149
Religion. *See* Catholicism; Pentecostals;
    United Fellowship Church
Respectability, 17, 42, 60, 99, 191
Restricted Country, A (Nestle), 22
Reuther, Walter, 34
Rich, Adrienne, 22
Riggs, Marlon, 81, 198-200
Ritz (bar), 178-79
Roberts, James, 173, 174, 186
Roberts, Oral, 150
Robeson, Paul, 14, 21
Robinson, Billy "Hands," 91-92
Robinson, Cleveland, *33*
Robinson, Max, 188-89
Ross, Marlon, 6
Ruhe, Sylvia, 190
RuPaul's Drag Race
    (television program), 192
Russell, Thaddeus, 41
Rustin, Bayard, 1, *33*, *176*; AIDS and, 171,
    189; award named after, 190; Baldwin
    and, 32-34; Beam and, 141; black power
    and, 82-83, 88, 100; Clarke, Shirley, and,
    64-65; Cleaver and, 87, 88; Communist
    Party and, 31-32, 35-36; FBI and, 35-36;
    Kennedy, Robert, and, 11-13; Law
    Enforcement Institute and, 35; Malcolm
    X and, 81-82; March on Washington
    and, 30; Powell, Adam Clayton, and, 31;
    Sixteenth Street Church bombing and,
    32-34; Thurmond and, 31

Safe sex, 134
Saint, Assotto, 184
Same-sex marriage, 193-94, 195
Scorpio Rising (film), 65
Scudder Homes, 25

Seale, Bobby, 83, 132, 138
Sedgwick, Eve, 6
Segal, Mark, 177
Segregation, of armed services, 40-41
Self-esteem, 195-96
"Separation of 'Being' and 'Doing':
    The Last Evangelical Refuge against
    Homosexuality" (Tinney), 160
Sex and Racism in America (Hernton), 74
Sexology, 48-51, 55
Sexual Behavior in the Human Female
    (Kinsey), 48-49
Sexual Behavior in the Human Male
    (Kinsey), 48-49
Sexual invert, 39
Sexual revolution, 52-53
Seymour, William J., 153, 169
Shaft (film), 71
Shively, Charles, 96-97, 215 (n. 31)
Sign in Sidney Brustein's Window, The
    (Hansberry), 17
Silber, Susan, 168
Simmons, Ron, 80, 132
Sixteenth Street Baptist Church bombing,
    32-34
Smith, Barbara, 22, 125, 141, 182-83, 184, 197
Smith, Craig, 215 (n. 31)
Smith, Jerome, 12, 20, 203 (n. 7)
Smith, Max, 134, 139
Smith, Mike, 139-40, 175
Smith, Willi, 189
Society for the Study of Black Religion, 164
Soul on Ice (Cleaver), 59, 83, 84-85, 86-87,
    88, 149
Southeastern Wisconsin Homes, 109-10
*Speak My Name: Black Men on
    Masculinity and the American Dream*
    (anthology), 196
Spelman College, 190
Stack, Carol, 54
Stanford, Adrian, 97
Staples, Robert, 54-55, 132
Stein, Marc, 2, 90
Stevens, Wallace, 64
Stimak, Louis, 112
Stonewall, 88-89, 189
Stonewall (Duberman), 89